Recipes From The Best of Bri

The Rest
The *of* Best
• *and more* •

Over 100 New Recipes

Written and Published By:
The Best of Bridge Publishing Ltd.

The Rest of The Best and More

Recipes from The Best of Bridge Series

FIRST PRINTING — August 2004

Copyright © 2004
by the Best of Bridge Publishing Ltd.
FAX: 403-252-0206
E-MAIL: order@bestofbridge.com
WEBSITE: www.bestofbridge.com

Library and Archives Canada Cataloguing in Publication
Main entry under title:

The rest of the best and more/Karen Brimacombe . . . [et al.]

Includes index.
ISBN 0-9690425-9-0

1. Cookery   I. Brimacombe, Karen
TX715.6.R478 2004   641.5   C2004-904399-4

Cover design by:
KARO
Calgary, Alberta

Photography by:
Lisa Preston
Bilodeau Preston Photography
Calgary, Alberta

Printed and Produced in Canada by:
Centax Books, a Division of PrintWest Communications Ltd.
1150 Eighth Avenue, Regina, Saskatchewan,
Canada S4R 1C9
www.centaxbooks.com   centax@printwest.com

DEDICATION

TO ALL OF THE FRIENDS AND MARKETING MANAGERS WE'VE NEVER MET:

HOW MANY TIMES HAVE WE HEARD, "THE BEST OF BRIDGE COOKBOOKS ARE THE ONLY COOKBOOKS I USE." "YOUR BOOKS ARE MY BIBLE." YOU SEND SUCH GOOD LETTERS - AND RECIPES. YOU REPORT ON THE PROLIFERATION OF BEST OF BRIDGE COOKBOOKS IN YOUR CORNER OF THE WORLD - AND WE KNOW IT WAS YOU AND YOUR ENTHUSIASM. YOU ARE ALL OUR MARKETING MANAGERS - AND FRIENDS THAT WE HAVEN'T MET - YET!

PLEASE - KEEP TAPPING US ON THE SHOULDER, WRITING LETTERS AND SHARING YOUR NEWS. YOUR FRIENDSHIP IS ONE OF THE BEST PARTS OF THIS 30-YEAR ENDEAVOR. HERE'S TO ANOTHER BESTSELLER - YOU'VE DONE IT AGAIN!

KAREN BRIMACOMBE   HELEN MILES

MARY HALPEN   VAL ROBINSON

LINDA JACOBSON   JOAN WILSON

FOREWARNING

BACK IN 1998 WHEN WE PUBLISHED "THE BEST OF THE BEST AND MORE", WE WERE ABSOLUTELY AMAZED AND DELIGHTED WITH THE RESPONSE. NOT ONLY DID NEW COOKS APPRECIATE THIS INTRODUCTION TO THE SIX-BOOK BEST OF BRIDGE SERIES, BUT OUR LOYAL FANS OF MANY YEARS EMBRACED THE CONVENIENCE OF ONE BOOK OF FAVORITES - AND MORE GREAT RECIPES TO BOOT.

THEN CAME THE MAIL: "WHERE IS 'YUMMY CHICKEN' AND WHAT ABOUT 'SEAFOOD LASAGNE'? WHY DID YOU LEAVE OUT 'CAJUN BREAD PUDDING' AND WHAT HAPPENED TO 'FRENCH LEMON PIE'?" IT'S 2004. AFTER SIX YEARS AND ANOTHER BOOK, "A YEAR OF THE BEST" (2001), WE'VE HAD AN EPIPHANY. "LET'S DO ANOTHER BOOK WITH ALL THE REST OF OUR FAVORITES, INCLUDE MORE OF THE EXCITING NEW RECIPES WE'VE GATHERED AND CALL IT "THE REST OF THE BEST AND MORE - VOLUME 2" - ALL THE GREAT BEST OF BRIDGE RECIPES IN JUST TWO BOOKS - IT'S ALL YOU'LL EVER NEED!"

SO - WE'VE TASTED, TESTED, REVISED SOME OF THE "OLDIES" AND LEARNED A LOT ABOUT NEW FOODS AND FLAVORS.

WE HOPE YOU'LL HAVE AS MUCH FUN IN YOUR KITCHEN AS WE'VE HAD IN OURS. THE "LADIES OF THE BRIDGE" STILL PROMISE YOU "SIMPLE RECIPES WITH GOURMET RESULTS". YOU ARE GOING TO LOVE THIS BOOK!

TABLE OF CONTENTS

FRONT COVER RECIPE

BAKED POTATO AND LEEK SOUP WITH CHEDDAR AND BACON (PAGE 128)

MUFFINS AND BREADS

Berry Best Muffins
A Pail Full of Muffins
Cranberry Muffins
Welsh Cakes
Lemon Loaf
How Cheesy Do You Want It?
Pita Crisps
Parmesan Crisps

LUNCH AND BRUNCH

Breakfast Fruit Kabobs
Midnight French Toast
Night-Before Eggs Benedict
Puffy Hot Pepper Jack Cheese Omelet
Chili Cheddar Frittata
Crab or Chicken Crêpes
Spinach & Camembert Strudel
Cotswold Cheese Flan
Quiche Lorraine
Vegetarian Fiesta Casserole
Vegetarian Texas Tacos
Chilies Rellenos with Sage Cheese
Rene's Sandwich Loaf
Roast Beef Sandwiches with Brie and Caramelized
Onions

BERRY BEST MUFFINS

RAID THE BERRY PATCH! FROZEN BERRIES WORK TOO.

TOPPING

½ CUP GOLDEN BROWN SUGAR, FIRMLY PACKED	125 mL
⅓ CUP FLOUR	75 mL
1½ TSP. GRATED LEMON ZEST	7 mL
½ CUP PECANS OR WALNUTS, TOASTED & CHOPPED	125 mL
2 TBSP. BUTTER, SOFTENED	30 mL

MUFFINS

1½ CUPS FLOUR	375 mL
¾ CUP SUGAR	175 mL
2 TSP. BAKING POWDER	10 mL
1½ TSP. GRATED LEMON ZEST	7 mL
1 TSP. CINNAMON	5 mL
¼ TSP. SALT	1 mL
½ CUP MILK	125 mL
½ CUP BUTTER, MELTED & COOLED	125 mL
1 LARGE EGG, BEATEN	
1½ CUPS BERRIES (A MIXTURE OF BLACKBERRIES, BLUEBERRIES & RASPBERRIES)	375 mL

PREHEAT OVEN TO 350°F (180°C).

TOPPING: IN A MEDIUM BOWL, MIX TOGETHER BROWN SUGAR, FLOUR AND LEMON ZEST. STIR IN NUTS AND BUTTER. MIXTURE SHOULD BE CRUMBLY.

BERRY BEST MUFFINS

CONTINUED FROM PAGE 8.

MUFFINS: IN A LARGE BOWL, COMBINE FLOUR, SUGAR, BAKING POWDER, LEMON ZEST, CINNAMON AND SALT. MAKE A WELL IN THE CENTER AND ADD MILK, BUTTER AND EGG. MIX UNTIL SMOOTH. CAREFULLY FOLD IN BERRIES. PLACE PAPER LINERS IN MUFFIN CUPS AND FILL EACH 2/3 FULL. TOP EACH MUFFIN WITH 1 TBSP. (15 mL) OF TOPPING MIXTURE. BAKE ON MIDDLE RACK FOR 20-25 MINUTES, UNTIL A TOOTHPICK INSERTED IN THE MIDDLE COMES OUT CLEAN. PLACE ON A RACK AND COOL 5 MINUTES. REMOVE MUFFINS FROM TINS AND SERVE WARM. MAKES 12 MEDIUM MUFFINS. (PICTURED ON PAGE 17.)

CONSCIOUSNESS: THAT ANNOYING
TIME BETWEEN NAPS.

A PAIL FULL OF MUFFINS

A CLASSIC! THE BATTER KEEPS IN THE REFRIGERATOR FOR UP TO 6 WEEKS.

2 CUPS BOILING WATER	500 mL
2 CUPS 100% BRAN	500 mL
3 CUPS SUGAR	750 mL
1 CUP BUTTER	250 mL
4 EGGS	
1 QT. BUTTERMILK (PLAIN YOGURT IS A GOOD SUBSTITUTE)	1 L
5 CUPS FLOUR	1.25 L
3 TBSP. BAKING SODA	45 mL
1 TBSP. SALT	15 mL
4 CUPS BRAN FLAKES	1 L
CHOPPED DATES, RAISINS OR BLUEBERRIES (OPTIONAL)	

POUR BOILING WATER OVER BRAN AND LET STAND. CREAM SUGAR AND BUTTER. ADD EGGS TO SUGAR MIXTURE AND BEAT WELL. ADD BUTTERMILK AND BRAN MIXTURE. SIFT FLOUR, SODA, SALT AND ADD TO BRAN FLAKES. FOLD DRY INGREDIENTS INTO LIQUID MIXTURE SLOWLY UNTIL MIXED. STORE IN AIRTIGHT CONTAINER IN REFRIGERATOR, AT LEAST 24 HOURS. BEFORE BAKING, ADD DATES, RAISINS OR BLUEBERRIES. BAKE AS FEW OR AS MANY MUFFINS AS YOU WANT. SPOON INTO GREASED MUFFIN TINS. BAKE ON MIDDLE RACK AT 400°F (200°C) FOR 15-20 MINUTES. MAKES 6 DOZEN MUFFINS.

CRANBERRY MUFFINS

KEEP ORANGES IN THE FRIDGE AND CRANBERRIES IN THE FREEZER - YOU'RE ALWAYS PREPARED.

2 CUPS CRANBERRIES, FRESH OR FROZEN, COARSELY CHOPPED	500 mL
⅓ CUP SUGAR	75 mL
1 TBSP. GRATED ORANGE ZEST	15 mL
½ CUP ORANGE JUICE	125 mL
2 CUPS FLOUR	500 mL
1 TSP. BAKING POWDER	5 mL
½ TSP. BAKING SODA	2 mL
½ TSP. SALT	2 mL
½ CUP BUTTER	125 mL
1 CUP SUGAR	250 mL
1 EGG	

PREHEAT OVEN TO 375°F (190°C). LIGHTLY GREASE MUFFIN TINS. COMBINE CRANBERRIES, ⅓ CUP (75 mL) SUGAR, ORANGE ZEST AND ORANGE JUICE. SET ASIDE. MIX DRY INGREDIENTS TOGETHER. SET ASIDE. CREAM BUTTER, 1 CUP (250 mL) SUGAR AND EGG IN LARGE BOWL. ADD CRANBERRY MIXTURE AND DRY INGREDIENTS. MIX UNTIL JUST BLENDED AND SPOON INTO MUFFIN TINS. BAKE ON MIDDLE RACK FOR 20 MINUTES. MAKES 18 MEDIUM MUFFINS.

WELSH CAKES

THIS MAKES ABOUT 20 LITTLE CAKES FOR BRUNCH, BRIDGE OR AFTERNOON TEA!

1½ CUPS FLOUR	375 mL
½ TSP. SALT	2 mL
½ TSP. BAKING POWDER	2 mL
½ CUP SUGAR	125 mL
1 TSP. NUTMEG	5 mL
½ CUP BUTTER	125 mL
1 EGG	
2 TBSP. ORANGE JUICE (OR LESS)	30 mL
½ CUP CURRANTS	125 mL
2 TBSP. BUTTER (MORE IF NEEDED)	30 mL

SIFT DRY INGREDIENTS TOGETHER. CUT IN BUTTER UNTIL CRUMBLY. ADD EGG AND MIX. ADD ENOUGH ORANGE JUICE TO BIND DOUGH TOGETHER. ADD CURRANTS AND MIX WELL. ROLL ON A FLOURED SURFACE TO ½" (1.3 cm) THICKNESS AND CUT CAKES WITH A 2" (5 cm) CUTTER. MELT BUTTER IN A FRYING PAN AND COOK CAKES OVER MEDIUM HEAT UNTIL LIGHTLY BROWNED, ABOUT 3-4 MINUTES EACH SIDE.

IF THE BROOM FITS, FLY IT.

LEMON LOAF

SUPERB FLAVOR. FREEZES WELL.

½ CUP BUTTER	125 mL
1 CUP SUGAR	250 mL
2 EGGS, BEATEN	
½ CUP MILK	125 mL
1½ CUPS FLOUR	375 mL
1 TSP. BAKING POWDER	5 mL
1 TSP. SALT	5 mL
GRATED ZEST OF 1 LEMON	
½ CUP CHOPPED WALNUTS (OPTIONAL)	125 mL

DRIZZLE

3 TBSP. LEMON JUICE	45 mL
¼ CUP SUGAR	60 mL

PREHEAT OVEN TO 350°F (180°C). IN A LARGE BOWL, CREAM BUTTER AND SUGAR. ADD BEATEN EGGS AND MILK. ADD DRY INGREDIENTS, LEMON ZEST AND WALNUTS. MIX WELL. PLACE IN A 2 X 5 X 9" (5 X 13 X 23 cm) GREASED LOAF PAN AND BAKE FOR 1 HOUR. REMOVE FROM OVEN AND COOL ON A RACK FOR 5 MINUTES. PRICK CAKE WITH FORK AND POUR DRIZZLE OVER LOAF. LET STAND AT LEAST 1 HOUR BEFORE REMOVING FROM PAN.

HOW CHEESY DO YOU WANT IT!

HOW EASY DO YOU WANT IT??

1 LOAF FROZEN BREAD DOUGH, THAWED UNTIL SLICEABLE (APPROXIMATELY 1 HOUR)	
¼ CUP BUTTER	60 mL
1-2 CUPS GRATED CHEDDAR CHEESE (PARMESAN WORKS TOO)	250-500 mL

CUT LOAF INTO 10-12 PIECES. DIP BOTH SIDES IN BUTTER, THEN CHEESE. ARRANGE IN BUNDT PAN. LET RISE 2-3 HOURS. BAKE 20 MINUTES AT 375°F (190°C). IF MAKING THE NIGHT BEFORE, COVER BUNDT PAN WITH DAMP TEA TOWEL AND BAKE WHEN READY. TO SERVE - PULL APART AND PUT IN A BREAD BASKET.

PITA CRISPS

YOU JUST WHIPPED THESE UP? - CLEVER!

1 PKG. MINI PITAS, SPLIT	
¼ CUP MELTED BUTTER	60 mL
¼ CUP LIQUID HONEY	60 mL
¼ CUP SESAME SEEDS	60 mL

BRUSH PITA HALVES WITH BUTTER AND HONEY. SPRINKLE WITH SESAME SEEDS. BROIL UNTIL CRISP AND GOLDEN. WATCH CAREFULLY! SERVE WITH ASIAN CHICKEN SALAD ON PAGE 112.

PARMESAN CRISPS

GREAT TO SERVE WITH SOUP OR SALAD!

¾ CUP COARSELY SHREDDED FRESH PARMESAN CHEESE	175 mL
1 TSP. FLOUR	5 mL

PREHEAT OVEN TO 350°F (180°C). LINE A COOKIE SHEET WITH PARCHMENT PAPER OR COAT WITH VEGETABLE OIL. IN A SMALL BOWL, STIR CHEESE AND FLOUR TOGETHER. SPOON 1 ROUNDED TEASPOON (7 mL) CHEESE MIXTURE ONTO BAKING SHEET. GENTLY SPREAD MIXTURE TO FORM SMALL CIRCLES, ABOUT 2" (5 cm) IN DIAMETER. FILL SHEET WITH 4 OR 5 CIRCLES, LEAVING AT LEAST 2" (5 cm) BETWEEN EACH ONE. BAKE IN CENTER OF OVEN UNTIL GOLDEN, ABOUT 5-7 MINUTES. COOL CRISPS COMPLETELY ON BAKING SHEET BEFORE REMOVING. REPEAT UNTIL ALL CHEESE MIXTURE IS USED. CRISPS CAN BE MADE UP TO 1 DAY BEFORE SERVING. STORE AT ROOM TEMPERATURE IN AN AIRTIGHT CONTAINER. MAKES 10-12 CRISPS.

MARITAL STATUS: NOT GOOD
WIFE'S NAME: PLAINTIFF.

BREAKFAST FRUIT KABOBS

AN ATTRACTIVE ADDITION TO ANY BRUNCH MENU.

WATERMELON
CANTALOUPE
HONEYDEW
PINEAPPLE
STRAWBERRIES
SEEDLESS GRAPES
KIWI FRUIT
6-8 WOODEN SKEWERS

HONEY-LIME DRIZZLE

½ CUP PLAIN YOGURT	125 mL
1 TSP. HONEY	5 mL
¼ TSP. FRESHLY GRATED NUTMEG	1 mL
2 TSP. LIME JUICE	10 mL
1 LIME, THINLY SLICED	

PREPARE FRUIT IN BALLS OR CHUNKS AND THREAD ON SKEWERS. ARRANGE ON A PLATTER. COMBINE YOGURT, HONEY, NUTMEG AND LIME JUICE. DRIZZLE OVER KABOBS. GARNISH WITH LIME SLICES.

NEVER BUY A CAR YOU CAN'T PUSH.

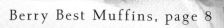
Berry Best Muffins, page 8

Puffy Hot Pepper Jack Cheese Omelet, page 22

MIDNIGHT FRENCH TOAST

WHAT A WAY TO END THE DAY - AND START THE NEXT!!

1 DOZEN EGGS	
½ CUP CREAM	125 mL
½ TSP. VANILLA	2 mL
GRATED ZEST OF 1 ORANGE	
2 TBSP. ORANGE LIQUEUR OR ORANGE JUICE	30 mL
1 LOAF FRENCH BREAD, SLICED 1" (3 cm) THICK	

MIX EGGS, CREAM, VANILLA, ORANGE ZEST AND LIQUEUR IN 9 x 13" (23 x 33 cm) PAN. PLACE SLICED BREAD IN PAN, MAKING SURE SLICES ARE WELL COATED. COVER WITH LID OR PLASTIC WRAP. PLACE IN FRIDGE OVERNIGHT.

NEXT MORNING, PLACE BREAD SLICES ON WELL GREASED COOKIE SHEET. BAKE AT 375°F (190°C) FOR 20-25 MINUTES. SERVE WITH FRUIT OR MAPLE SYRUP. SERVES 6.

WRINKLED WAS NOT ONE OF THE THINGS I WANTED TO BE WHEN I GREW UP.

NIGHT-BEFORE EGGS BENEDICT

PROMISE - THIS WORKS!! THE HOLLANDAISE CAN ALSO BE MADE THE DAY AHEAD.

8 LARGE EGGS
2 SLICES BREAD
8 SLICES BACK BACON, FRIED
4 ENGLISH MUFFINS, SLICED IN HALF

IN A LARGE FRYING PAN, BRING WATER TO A BOIL. REDUCE HEAT TO SIMMER. BREAK 1 EGG AT A TIME INTO A SMALL BOWL, AND THEN SLIDE INTO WATER. REPEAT WITH REMAINING EGGS. COOK UNTIL THE WHITE IS OPAQUE AND JUST SET, ABOUT 2½-3 MINUTES. SPOON EGGS INTO A NON-METALLIC DISH FILLED WITH ICE WATER. COVER AND REFRIGERATE UP TO 24 HOURS. WHEN READY TO SERVE, CAREFULLY REMOVE EGGS FROM WATER AND TRIM EDGES WITH A KNIFE. SLIDE EGGS INTO A PAN OF SIMMERING WATER; WARM 1-2 MINUTES. USING A SLOTTED SPOON, PLACE EGGS ON A SLICE OF BREAD TO DRAIN. (NO - YOU DON'T EAT THE BREAD!)

WHILE EGGS ARE WARMING, TOAST MUFFIN HALVES UNDER THE BROILER. PLACE A SLICE OF BACON ON EACH MUFFIN HALF. PLACE EGGS ON TOP AND SPOON ON HOLLANDAISE SAUCE (PAGE 21).

NIGHT-BEFORE EGGS BENEDICT

CONTINUED FROM PAGE 20.

NEVER-FAIL BLENDER HOLLANDAISE

1 CUP BUTTER	250 mL
4 EGG YOLKS	
1/4 TSP. SALT	1 mL
1/4 TSP. SUGAR	1 mL
1/4 TSP. TABASCO SAUCE	1 mL
1/4 TSP. DRY MUSTARD	1 mL
2 TBSP. FRESH LEMON JUICE	30 mL

HEAT BUTTER TO A FULL BOIL, BEING CAREFUL NOT TO BROWN. COMBINE ALL OTHER INGREDIENTS IN BLENDER. WITH BLENDER TURNED ON HIGH, SLOWLY POUR BUTTER INTO YOLK MIXTURE IN A THIN STREAM UNTIL ALL IS ADDED. MAY BE REFRIGERATED FOR SEVERAL DAYS. WHEN REHEATING, HEAT OVER HOT (NOT BOILING) WATER IN TOP OF DOUBLE BOILER. MAKES ABOUT 1 1/4 CUPS (300 mL) OF SAUCE. SERVES 4.

ETHERNET: A DEVICE USED TO CATCH THE ETHERBUNNY.

PUFFY HOT PEPPER
JACK CHEESE OMELET

PUFFY AS A SOUFFLÉ - "AS GOOD AS IT GETS"
JACK!

4 LARGE EGGS, SEPARATED	
SALT & PEPPER TO TASTE	
PINCH GROUND NUTMEG	
1/3 CUP SOUR CREAM	75 mL
1 TBSP. BUTTER	15 mL
1/2-3/4 CUP SHREDDED HOT PEPPER	125-175 mL
JACK CHEESE	

PREHEAT OVEN TO 350°F (180°C). IN A MEDIUM BOWL, BEAT EGG WHITES WITH SALT AT HIGH SPEED UNTIL STIFF, MOIST PEAKS FORM; SET ASIDE. IN ANOTHER BOWL, BEAT EGG YOLKS WITH PEPPER AND NUTMEG UNTIL VERY THICK AND LEMON COLORED. WHISK IN SOUR CREAM. POUR YOLK MIXTURE OVER BEATEN WHITES AND GENTLY FOLD TOGETHER. MELT BUTTER IN A 10" (25 cm) OVENPROOF FRYING PAN OVER MEDIUM HEAT. TILT TO COVER BOTTOM OF PAN. POUR IN EGG MIXTURE. COOK WITHOUT STIRRING UNTIL OMELET IS PUFFY AND LIGHTLY BROWNED ON BOTTOM (2-3 MINUTES). LIFT EDGE CAREFULLY TO CHECK COLOR. TRANSFER PAN TO OVEN; BAKE UNTIL OMELET TOP IS PALE GOLDEN BROWN (6-8 MINUTES) AND KNIFE INSERTED IN CENTER COMES OUT CLEAN. SPRINKLE EVENLY WITH CHEESE; THEN, USE A SPATULA TO LOOSEN EDGE. CAREFULLY TIP OMELET OUT OF PAN,

PUFFY HOT PEPPER JACK CHEESE OMELET

CONTINUED FROM PAGE 22.

ALLOWING TOP EDGE TO FOLD OVER. SLIDE OMELET ONTO A WARM PLATTER AND SERVE IMMEDIATELY. SERVES 2. (PICTURED ON PAGE 18.)

VARIATION: ADD SAUTÉED MUSHROOMS AND BELL PEPPERS BEFORE FOLDING OMELET IN HALF.

CHILI CHEDDAR FRITTATA

THE AROMA WILL GET EVERYONE OUT OF BED!

½ LB. SHARP WHITE CHEDDAR, SHREDDED	250	g
4 OZ. CAN MILD CHILIES OR JALAPEÑOS, DRAINED, RESERVE LIQUID	115	g
⅓ CUP OIL-PACKED, SUNDRIED TOMATOES, CHOPPED	75	mL
LOTS OF FRESH BASIL		
9 EGGS, WELL BEATEN		

SPRAY A 9" (23 cm) GLASS BAKING DISH. SPRINKLE IN CHEESE, CHILIES, SUNDRIED TOMATOES AND BASIL. BEAT EGGS WITH RESERVED CHILI LIQUID AND POUR OVER ALL. BAKE AT 350°F (180°C) FOR 30 MINUTES. SERVES 6. THIS DOUBLES WELL.

CRAB OR CHICKEN CRÊPES

CRÊPES MAY BE MADE AHEAD OF TIME AND STORED FROZEN BETWEEN LAYERS OF WAXED PAPER.

CRÊPE BATTER

1 CUP COLD WATER	250 mL
1 CUP COLD MILK	250 mL
4 EGGS	
½ TSP. SALT	2 mL
2 CUPS FLOUR	500 mL
2 TBSP. BUTTER	30 mL

WHIRL CRÊPE INGREDIENTS IN BLENDER FOR 2 MINUTES. REFRIGERATE 2 HOURS. USING 6" (15 cm) CRÊPE PAN OR SMALL NONSTICK FRYING PAN, MELT A LITTLE BUTTER AND POUR ABOUT ¼ CUP (60 mL) BATTER INTO PAN, TIPPING UNTIL BATTER COVERS THE BOTTOM. COOK AND TURN UNTIL CRÊPE IS GOLDEN ON BOTH SIDES. TRANSFER TO PLATE. REPEAT METHOD UNTIL ALL BATTER IS USED.

FILLING

¼ CUP CHOPPED GREEN ONION	60 mL
1 TBSP. BUTTER	15 mL
½ CUP SHERRY	125 mL
3 CUPS CRAB OR COOKED DICED CHICKEN	750 mL
SALT & FRESHLY GROUND PEPPER TO TASTE	

CRAB OR CHICKEN CRÊPES

CONTINUED FROM PAGE 24.

SWISS CHEESE SAUCE

¼ CUP BUTTER	60 mL
⅓ CUP FLOUR	75 mL
2 CUPS MILK, HEATED	500 mL
SALT & FRESHLY GROUND PEPPER TO TASTE	
2 EGG YOLKS	
½ CUP WHIPPING CREAM	125 mL
¾ CUP GRATED SWISS CHEESE	175 mL

TO MAKE FILLING: SAUTÉ ONION IN BUTTER; ADD SHERRY AND MIX IN CRAB, SALT AND PEPPER. SET ASIDE.

TO MAKE SAUCE: IN A SAUCEPAN, MELT BUTTER AND ADD FLOUR. BLEND. GRADUALLY ADD MILK, SALT AND PEPPER, STIRRING CONSTANTLY. BOIL FOR 1 MINUTE THEN REMOVE FROM HEAT. BEAT YOLKS AND CREAM TOGETHER. ADD EGG MIXTURE TO SAUCEPAN, STIRRING CONSTANTLY. FOLD IN CHEESE (SAUCE SHOULD BE THICK). SET ⅓ OF THE SAUCE ASIDE. POUR REMAINING SAUCE INTO THE FILLING. FILL AND ROLL CRÊPES AND PLACE IN A SHALLOW 9 X 13" (23 X 33 cm) BAKING DISH. DRIZZLE WITH RESERVED SAUCE. HEAT IN WARM OVEN UNTIL SERVING TIME.

NOTE: THIN SAUCE WITH CREAM IF NECESSARY.

SPINACH AND CAMEMBERT STRUDEL

THIS IS A HIT AT BRUNCH OR LUNCH - THE FLAVORS ARE OUTSTANDING. CAN BE PREPARED AND FROZEN AHEAD OF TIME.

10 OZ. BAG FRESH SPINACH, COOKED & CHOPPED	284 mL
2 TSP. BUTTER	10 mL
½ SMALL ONION, THINLY SLICED	
½ CUP RICOTTA CHEESE	125 mL
3 OZ. CAMEMBERT CHEESE, RIND DISCARDED, CUT INTO SMALL PIECES	85 g
¼ CUP GRATED PARMESAN CHEESE	60 mL
3 TBSP. PINE NUTS, TOASTED	45 mL
¼ TSP. SALT	1 mL
PINCH FRESHLY GROUND PEPPER	
PINCH NUTMEG.	
6 SHEETS PHYLLO	
⅓ CUP MELTED BUTTER	75 mL

COOK SPINACH IN A LITTLE WATER; DRAIN; SQUEEZE OUT ALL LIQUID AND CHOP. IN SMALL FRYING PAN HEAT BUTTER AND SAUTÉ ONION UNTIL SOFT. IN A BOWL, COMBINE SPINACH, ONION, RICOTTA, CAMEMBERT, PARMESAN, PINE NUTS, SALT, PEPPER AND NUTMEG.

PREHEAT OVEN TO 375°F (190°C).

LAY 1 SHEET OF PHYLLO ON COUNTER, LONGEST SIDE FACING YOU. BRUSH WITH MELTED BUTTER. REPEAT UNTIL YOU HAVE 6 SHEETS ON TOP OF

SPINACH AND CAMEMBERT STRUDEL

CONTINUED FROM PAGE 26.

ONE ANOTHER. SPOON ON SPINACH MIXTURE 3" (8 cm) WIDE AND 2" (5 cm) FROM THE BOTTOM. LEAVE ABOUT 1" (2.5 cm) AT EACH SHORT END. FOLD PHYLLO OVER MIXTURE AND CONTINUE TO ROLL. BRUSH BUTTER ON EDGE TO SEAL. PLACE PARCHMENT PAPER ON A COOKIE SHEET. BRUSH REMAINING BUTTER OVER TOP AND SIDES OF STRUDEL AND LIFT ONTO COOKIE SHEET. USING A SHARP KNIFE, SCORE DIAGONALLY (NOT TOO DEEP), ABOUT 2" (5 cm) APART. BAKE 35-40 MINUTES. IF FREEZING, WRAP TIGHTLY IN PLASTIC WRAP. TO BAKE FROZEN, ADD 10 MORE MINUTES TO BAKING TIME. LET STAND FOR 10-15 MINUTES. WHEN READY TO SERVE, SLICE AT SCORED INTERVALS. SERVES 6.

AMAZING!! YOU HANG SOMETHING IN YOUR CLOSET FOR AWHILE AND IT SHRINKS TWO SIZES.

COTSWOLD CHEESE FLAN

THIS RECIPE IS FROM THE COTSWOLD REGION OF ENGLAND WHERE THEY MAKE A NIPPY CHEESE SIMILAR TO CHEDDAR. GOOD SERVED HOT OR AT ROOM TEMPERATURE. TIP - IF YOU'RE IN A HURRY, USE A FROZEN PIE CRUST!

SHORTCRUST PASTRY

½ CUP BUTTER, ICE COLD	125 mL
¼ CUP VEGETABLE SHORTENING, ICE COLD	60 mL
1½ CUPS FLOUR	375 mL
1 EGG YOLK	
¼ CUP ICE WATER	60 mL

CHEDDAR FILLING

1 TBSP. BUTTER	15 mL
1 LARGE ONION, THINLY SLICED	
¾ CUP GRATED SHARP CHEDDAR CHEESE	175 mL
3 TBSP. CHOPPED CHIVES	45 mL
1 WHOLE EGG PLUS 1 EGG YOLK	
¼ CUP CREAM OR MILK	60 mL
1 TSP. SALT	5 mL
½ TSP. PEPPER	2 mL
6 OZS. LARGE FRESH MUSHROOMS	170 g

PREHEAT OVEN TO 400°F (200°C). CUT BUTTER AND SHORTENING INTO FLOUR WITH PASTRY CUTTER UNTIL MIXTURE IS CRUMBLY. ADD EGG YOLK AND SPRINKLE WITH WATER. COMBINE TO MAKE A SOFT DOUGH. ROLL OUT DOUGH ON A LIGHTLY FLOURED SURFACE. LINE A 9" (23 cm) PIE PLATE OR QUICHE PAN WITH DOUGH AND

COTSWOLD CHEESE FLAN

CONTINUED FROM PAGE 28.

PRICK WITH A FORK. BAKE UNTIL CRUST IS JUST SET, ABOUT 15 MINUTES. MELT BUTTER IN A LARGE FRYING PAN OVER MEDIUM-LOW HEAT AND SAUTÉ ONION UNTIL GOLDEN. COMBINE GRATED CHEESE, CHIVES, EGG AND YOLK, CREAM, SALT AND PEPPER IN A MIXING BOWL. REMOVE MUSHROOM STEMS AND PLACE WHOLE MUSHROOM CAPS, STEM SIDE UP, IN THE PREPARED CRUST.

DISTRIBUTE SAUTÉED ONIONS OVER MUSHROOMS. POUR CHEESE MIXTURE OVER ALL. RETURN TO OVEN FOR 15-20 MINUTES, OR UNTIL FILLING IS SET AND BROWN. LET COOL 10 MINUTES BEFORE CUTTING. BRUNCH FOR 8.

HELP WANTED: TELEPATH.
YOU KNOW WHERE TO APPLY.

QUICHE LORRAINE

YOU DON'T HAVE TO BE A PASTRY CHEF TO MAKE A PERFECT QUICHE.

½-14 OZ. PKG. FROZEN PUFF PASTRY	½ OF 397 g
2 TSP. BUTTER	10 mL
1 LARGE ONION, CHOPPED	
12 SLICES BACON, CHOPPED	
4 EGGS	
2 CUPS WHIPPING CREAM	500 mL
½ TSP. SALT	2 mL
PINCH NUTMEG	OUCH!
PINCH PEPPER	OUCH!
PINCH CAYENNE PEPPER	OUCH!
1 CUP GRATED SWISS CHEESE	250 mL

ROLL OUT PASTRY TO FIT A 9" (23 cm) DEEP PIE PLATE. IN A FRYING PAN, MELT BUTTER AND SAUTÉ ONION UNTIL SOFT. FRY BACON UNTIL CRISP. COMBINE EGGS, CREAM AND SPICES IN A LARGE BOWL AND BEAT UNTIL WELL MIXED. SPRINKLE PIE SHELL WITH ONION, BACON AND CHEESE. CAREFULLY POUR EGG MIXTURE ON TOP. BAKE AT 425°F (220°C) FOR 15 MINUTES. REDUCE HEAT TO 300°F (150°C); BAKE ABOUT 40 MINUTES OR UNTIL KNIFE INSERTED IN CENTER COMES OUT CLEAN. SERVES 6-8.

VEGETARIAN FIESTA CASSEROLE

GREAT FOR BRUNCH OR DINNER.

1 TBSP. VEGETABLE OIL	15 mL
1 MEDIUM ONION, DICED	
2 LARGE EGGS, BEATEN	
1 CUP RICOTTA OR COTTAGE CHEESE	250 mL
2-4 OZ. CANS DICED GREEN CHILIES, DRAINED	2-115 g
2 TBSP. CHOPPED FRESH CILANTRO	30 mL
½ TSP. GROUND CUMIN	2 mL
¼ TSP. SALT	1 mL
FRESHLY GROUND PEPPER TO TASTE	
8 CORN TORTILLAS, IN ½" (1.3 cm) STRIPS	
14 OZ. CAN REFRIED BEANS	398 mL
3 MEDIUM TOMATOES, CHOPPED	
2 CUPS GRATED MONTEREY JACK	500 mL
2 CUPS GRATED CHEDDAR CHEESE	500 mL

TOPPINGS

CHOPPED PITTED BLACK OLIVES
SLICED GREEN ONIONS
LIGHT SOUR CREAM

PREHEAT OVEN TO 350°F (180°C). HEAT OIL AND SAUTÉ ONION UNTIL SOFT. IN A MEDIUM BOWL, COMBINE ONION, EGGS, RICOTTA CHEESE, CHILIES, CILANTRO, CUMIN, SALT AND PEPPER.

SPRAY A 9 x 13" (23 x 33 cm) BAKING DISH. LAYER HALF THE TORTILLA STRIPS, RICOTTA MIXTURE, BEANS, TOMATOES AND CHEESES. REPEAT LAYERS. BAKE, UNCOVERED, UNTIL BUBBLY, 30-40 MINUTES. LET STAND 10 MINUTES BEFORE SERVING. PASS THE TOPPINGS.

VEGETARIAN TEXAS TACOS

1 TBSP. VEGETABLE OIL	15 mL
1 MEDIUM ONION, MINCED	
3 GARLIC CLOVES, MINCED	
4 TSP. GROUND CUMIN	20 mL
4 TSP. CHILI POWDER	20 mL
2-19 OZ. CANS BLACK OR PINTO	2-540 mL
BEANS, DRAINED, RINSED	
¾ CUP MEDIUM SALSA	175 mL
½ CUP FROZEN KERNEL CORN	125 mL
SALT & PEPPER TO TASTE	
½-1 TSP. CRUSHED RED PEPPER	2-5 mL
¾ CUP GRATED MONTEREY JACK CHEESE	175 mL
¼ CUP GRATED CHEDDAR CHEESE	60 mL
ABOUT 10 FLOUR TORTILLAS	410 g
TOPPINGS (USE 3 OR MORE PLUS SALSA)	

TOPPINGS

1 MEDIUM DICED ZUCCHINI
SHREDDED LETTUCE
2 SMALL AVOCADOS, DICED & TOSSED WITH
    A SPLASH OF LIME JUICE
GRATED CHEDDAR CHEESE
CHOPPED ONION
DICED RED OR YELLOW PEPPER
DICED FRESH TOMATOES
SALSA

PREHEAT OVEN TO 350°F (180°C). HEAT OIL IN A LARGE FRYING PAN OVER MEDIUM HEAT. ADD ONION AND GARLIC AND COOK, STIRRING OCCASIONALLY, UNTIL ONION IS TRANSLUCENT, ABOUT 5 MINUTES.

VEGETARIAN TEXAS TACOS

CONTINUED FROM PAGE 32.

ADD CUMIN AND CHILI POWDER AND STIR UNTIL THEY ARE AROMATIC, ABOUT 1-2 MINUTES LONGER. ADD BEANS AND SALSA AND MASH WITH A POTATO MASHER TO A CONSISTENCY THAT IS TO YOUR LIKING. ADD CORN AND SEASON WITH SALT, PEPPER AND CRUSHED RED PEPPER.

PUT MIXTURE IN A CASSEROLE AND SPRINKLE CHEESES ON TOP. BAKE FOR 15-20 MINUTES OR UNTIL CHEESE MELTS. WARM TORTILLAS IN OVEN AND LET YOUR FAMILY DO THEIR OWN WRAPPING AND TOPPING. PASS THE SALSA. (PICTURED ON PAGE 35.)

I DECIDED TO TAKE AN AEROBICS CLASS. I BENT, TWISTED, GYRATED AND JUMPED UP AND DOWN FOR AN HOUR. BUT, BY THE TIME I GOT MY LEOTARD ON, THE CLASS WAS OVER.

CHILIES RELLENOS
WITH SAGE CHEESE

OLÉ - A MAKE-AHEAD.

SAGE CHEESE

8 OZ. CREAM CHEESE, SOFTENED	250 g
4 OZ. CHÈVRE, (GOAT CHEESE) SOFTENED	125 g
3 TBSP. MINCED GREEN ONIONS	45 mL
2 TBSP. FINELY CHOPPED FRESH SAGE	30 mL
1 EGG	
1 GARLIC CLOVE, MINCED	
SALT & PEPPER TO TASTE	

SOUFFLÉ

2-7 OZ. CANS WHOLE GREEN CHILIES, DRAINED	2-200 g
8 EGGS	
2 CUPS MILK	500 mL
½ CUP FLOUR	125 mL
⅓ CUP GRATED PARMESAN CHEESE	75 mL

TO MAKE SAGE CHEESE: IN A SMALL BOWL, BEAT ALL INGREDIENTS TOGETHER. SET ASIDE.

TO MAKE SOUFFLÉ: HALVE CHILIES LENGTHWISE; PAT DRY. SPREAD 1-2 TBSP. (15-30 mL) SAGE CHEESE ON CUT-SIDE OF CHILIES. TOP WITH REMAINING CHILI HALVES. ARRANGE IN A SINGLE LAYER IN A GREASED 9 x 13" (23 x 33 cm) BAKING DISH. REFRIGERATE OVERNIGHT IF MAKING AHEAD. PREHEAT OVEN TO 375°F (190°C). COMBINE EGGS, MILK, FLOUR AND PARMESAN; BEAT UNTIL SMOOTH. POUR OVER CHILIES. BAKE FOR 45 MINUTES, OR UNTIL LIGHT BROWN. SERVE IMMEDIATELY WITH SALSA, SAUSAGES, FRUIT AND CORN BREAD. SERVES 8.

Vegetarian Texas Tacos, page 32

Flatbread with Caramelized Onions and Cheese, page 75

RENE'S SANDWICH LOAF

PUTTIN' ON THE RITZ!

8 OZ. PKG. CREAM CHEESE	250	g
1 TBSP. MILK	15	mL
UNSLICED SANDWICH LOAF, SLIGHTLY FROZEN		

HAM FILLING

1 CUP GROUND COOKED HAM	250 mL
2 TBSP. PICKLE RELISH, DRAINED	30 mL
1/2 TSP. HORSERADISH	2 mL
1/3 CUP FINELY CHOPPED CELERY	75 mL
1/4 CUP MAYONNAISE	60 mL

ASPARAGUS TIP FILLING

1 CAN ASPARAGUS TIPS, DRAINED
CHEESE WHIZ

EGG FILLING

4 HARD-BOILED EGGS, CHOPPED	
2 TBSP. FINELY CHOPPED GREEN ONIONS	30 mL
1/2 TSP. PREPARED MUSTARD	5 mL
1/4 CUP MAYONNAISE	50 mL
SALT & PEPPER TO TASTE	

CHOPPED FRESH PARSLEY
PIMIENTO-STUFFED OLIVES

IN A SMALL BOWL, BEAT CREAM CHEESE WITH MILK UNTIL FLUFFY. SET ASIDE. TRIM CRUSTS FROM SANDWICH LOAF AND SLICE BREAD LENGTHWISE IN 4 EQUAL LAYERS. BUTTER EACH SLICE. SPREAD FIRST LAYER WITH HAM FILLING, SECOND LAYER WITH CHEESE WHIZ; TOP WITH ASPARAGUS, AND THIRD LAYER WITH EGG FILLING. FROST TOP SLICE AND SIDES OF LOAF WITH CREAM CHEESE. SPRINKLE WITH PARSLEY AND GARNISH WITH OLIVES. SERVES 8-10.

ROAST BEEF SANDWICHES
WITH BRIE AND CARAMELIZED ONIONS

A BIG HIT !

2/3 CUP SOUR CREAM	150 mL
2-3 TBSP. HORSERADISH, DRAINED	30-45 mL
1/2 TSP. GRATED LEMON ZEST	2 mL
SALT & PEPPER TO TASTE	
3 TBSP. BUTTER	45 mL
1 RED ONION, THINLY SLICED	
4 KAISER ROLLS, CUT IN HALF	
1 LB. MEDIUM-RARE BEEF, THINLY SLICED	500 g
4" (10 cm) ROUND OF BRIE	235 g
1 BUNCH ARUGULA (LETTUCE)	

IN A SMALL BOWL, MIX TOGETHER SOUR CREAM, HORSERADISH, LEMON ZEST, SALT AND PEPPER. IN A HEAVY FRYING PAN, MELT BUTTER OVER LOW HEAT AND STIR IN ONIONS. COOK ABOUT 35 MINUTES, STIRRING OCCASIONALLY, UNTIL CARAMELIZED. REMOVE FROM HEAT AND COOL. SPREAD HORSERADISH MIXTURE ON EACH BUN HALF. LAYER THE ROAST BEEF, BRIE AND ARUGULA. TOP WITH CARAMELIZED ONIONS AND - LUNCH IS READY!

SERVES 4 - YOU MAY WANT TO MAKE MORE!!!

BEVERAGES

Hot Buttered Rum
Hot Rum Canadienne
Lifesaver Punch
Pink Party Punch

OTHER GOOD THINGS

Terrific Turkey Stuffing
Dill Pickles
Processing Pickles
Bread and Butter Pickles
Piccalilli
Crab Apple Chutney
Hot Pepper Orange Chutney
Microwave Peanut Brittle
Peppermint Brittle
Sinfully Rich Low-Fat Fudge Sauce

HOT BUTTERED RUM

STORE IN YOUR FREEZER IN SMALL CONTAINERS. VERY GIFTABLE.

1 LB. BUTTER, ROOM TEMPERATURE	500 g
4 CUPS VANILLA ICE CREAM, SOFTENED	1 L
3½ CUPS ICING (CONFECTIONER'S) SUGAR	875 mL
2 CUPS BROWN SUGAR	500 mL
1½ TSP. CINNAMON	7 mL
½ TSP. ALLSPICE	2 mL

IN A LARGE BOWL, MIX BUTTER AND ICE CREAM TOGETHER. BLEND IN ALL OTHER INGREDIENTS. STORE IN FREEZER.

TO ENJOY ONE SERVING

2 TBSP. HOT RUM BASE	30 mL
1½ OZ. DARK RUM	45 mL
CINNAMON STICK	

IN A LARGE MUG, ADD HOT RUM BASE AND DARK RUM. FILL MUG WITH BOILING WATER AND STIR WITH CINNAMON STICK UNTIL MIXTURE IS BLENDED.

I'D STOP DRINKING BUT I'M NO QUITTER.

HOT RUM CANADIENNE

MARVELOUS AFTER SKIING, AFTER FOOTBALL GAMES, AFTER TOBOGGANING, AFTER ANYTHING!

2 OZ. DARK RUM	60 mL
2 TBSP. MAPLE SYRUP	30 mL
SQUIRT OF LEMON JUICE	
NUTMEG	
CINNAMON (A STICK IS BEST)	
BOILING WATER	
DAB OF BUTTER	

COMBINE FIRST 5 INGREDIENTS, TOP OFF WITH BOILING WATER AND A SMALL DAB OF BUTTER. MAKES 1 STEAMING MUG.

LIFESAVER PUNCH

PERFECT FOR POOL PARTIES. IF YOU ADD VODKA, ADD A LIFEGUARD!

8 OZ. CAN FROZEN STRAWBERRY DACQUIRI MIX	250 mL
12 2/3 OZ. CAN FROZEN PINK LEMONADE	355 mL
4 CUPS SODA WATER (OR GINGER ALE)	1 L
LOTS OF ICE	
FRESH STRAWBERRIES, SLICED	
VODKA, OPTIONAL	

THAW AND COMBINE DACQUIRI MIX AND LEMONADE. ADD SODA WATER AND ICE. FLOAT FRESH STRAWBERRY SLICES ON TOP.

PINK PARTY PUNCH

PERFECT FOR LUNCH WITH LITTLE SQUIRTS.

8 CUPS PINK LEMONADE	2 L
4 CUPS LEMON-LIME SODA OR 7-UP	1 L
2 QTS. RASPBERRY SHERBET	2 L

GARNISH

LEMON OR ORANGE SLICES

MIX PINK LEMONADE AND SODA IN A LARGE BOWL. ADD HALF OF THE SHERBET. STIR TO MAKE A CREAMY, FROTHY MIXTURE. FOR GARNISH, ADD SCOOPS OF REMAINING SHERBET AND LEMON OR ORANGE SLICES. SERVES 20.

INTAXICATION: EUPHORIA AT GETTING A TAX REFUND, WHICH LASTS UNTIL YOU REALIZE IT WAS YOUR MONEY TO START WITH.

TERRIFIC TURKEY STUFFING

FINALLY SOMETHING THAT'S GOOD FOR YOUR CAVITIES!

3 CUPS COOKED WILD RICE	750 mL
2 CUPS FRESH BREAD CRUMBS	500 mL
1 LB. BULK PORK SAUSAGE	500 g
2 STALKS CELERY, FINELY CHOPPED	
1 MEDIUM ONION, FINELY CHOPPED	
SALT & PEPPER, TO TASTE	
1-2 TSP. SAGE	5-10 mL
½ CUP DRIED CRANBERRIES	125 mL

PLACE COOKED RICE AND BREAD CRUMBS IN A LARGE BOWL. FRY SAUSAGE, CELERY AND ONION UNTIL SAUSAGE IS BROWN. DRAIN AND ADD TO RICE MIXTURE. ADD SEASONINGS AND DRIED CRANBERRIES AND TOSS. MIXTURE SHOULD BE MOIST BUT NOT STICKY. ADD MORE BREAD CRUMBS IF NECESSARY. SPOON, BUT DON'T PACK, INTO NECK CAVITY AND BREAST CAVITY OF TURKEY. BE SURE TO REMOVE STUFFING FROM BIRD IMMEDIATELY AFTER REMOVING TURKEY FROM OVEN. KEEP WARM IN A SMALL CASSEROLE.

BEAUTY IS IN THE EYE OF THE BEER HOLDER.

DILL PICKLES

PUCKER UP!

BRINE

1 CUP PICKLING SALT	250 mL
1 QT. VINEGAR (GOOD QUALITY - HEINZ)	1 L
12 CUPS WATER	3 L

PICKLES

22 LBS. PICKLING CUCUMBERS	10 kg
FRESH DILL SPRIGS	
3-4 BULBS GARLIC	
WHOLE PEPPERCORNS	
18-20 GLASS 1-QUART (1 L) JARS	
WITH LIDS	

TO MAKE BRINE: IN A LARGE CANNER OR BROTH POT, COMBINE AND BRING PICKLING SALT, VINEGAR AND WATER TO A BOIL. SET ASIDE.

TO MAKE PICKLES: WASH CUCUMBERS AND PLACE IN STERILIZED JARS. TO EACH JAR ADD 1-2 SPRIGS OF FRESH DILL, 1-2 PEELED GARLIC CLOVES AND A FEW PEPPERCORNS. LADLE HOT BRINE INTO EACH JAR UP TO $\frac{1}{2}$" (1.3 cm) FROM THE TOP AND PUT LIDS ON IMMEDIATELY (DON'T TIGHTEN COMPLETELY). TO PROCESS SEE OPPOSITE PAGE. ALLOW AT LEAST A WEEK TO LET THE FLAVORS COMMINGLE.

PROCESSING PICKLES

TO PROCESS: PLACE FILLED JARS IN A DEEP POT OR CANNER WITH A WIRE RACK IN THE BOTTOM. MAKE SURE THE JARS ARE NOT TOUCHING. POUR IN HOT WATER TO ABOUT 1" (2.5 cm) OVER TOP OF JARS. BRING TO A BOIL AND PROCESS FOR 20 MINUTES. REMOVE JARS AND SET ASIDE. LIDS SHOULD POP AND HAVE A SMALL DIP IN THE MIDDLE AS THEY COOL. LIDS MAY NOW BE TIGHTENED. ALWAYS STORE IN A COOL PLACE. HAPPY CANNING!

A GOOD FRIEND WILL COME AND BAIL YOU OUT OF JAIL, BUT - A TRUE FRIEND WILL BE SITTING NEXT TO YOU SAYING "DAMN ... THAT WAS FUN!"

BREAD AND BUTTER PICKLES

HOMEMADE ARE THE BEST!!

10 CUPS PICKLING CUCUMBERS, UNPEELED, THINLY SLICED	2.5 L
2 GREEN PEPPERS, DICED	
2 CLOVES GARLIC, MINCED	
3 LARGE ONIONS, THINLY SLICED	
1/3 CUP PICKLING SALT	75 mL
12 CUPS OF ICE CUBES	3 L
3 CUPS WHITE VINEGAR	750 mL
4 CUPS SUGAR	1 L
1½ TSP. TURMERIC	7 mL
1½ TSP. CELERY SEED	7 mL
1½ TSP. MUSTARD SEED	7 mL

COMBINE CUCUMBERS, PEPPERS, GARLIC AND ONIONS IN CANNER OR LARGE POT. MIX IN SALT AND ICE CUBES. LET STAND IN A COOL PLACE FOR AT LEAST 4 HOURS. DRAIN AND DISCARD ANY LEFTOVER ICE. SET VEGETABLES ASIDE. IN A LARGE POT COMBINE VINEGAR, SUGAR, TURMERIC, CELERY SEED AND MUSTARD SEED. BRING TO A BOIL AND COOK FOR 3-5 MINUTES. MIX IN VEGETABLES AND BRING TO A BOIL AGAIN. REMOVE FROM HEAT, SPOON INTO STERILIZED JARS AND PUT LIDS ON IMMEDIATELY (DON'T TIGHTEN COMPLETELY) AND PROCESS, PAGE 45. MAKES 10, 8-OZ. (250 mL) JARS.

PICCALILLI

*PICK THIS ONE - IT'S EASIER THAN TRYING TO
PICK ANYTHING ELSE - A ROSE, A MAN, A
DRESS . . .*

10-12 MEDIUM GREEN TOMATOES	
6 MEDIUM GREEN PEPPERS	
6 MEDIUM RED PEPPERS	
4 MEDIUM ONIONS	
6 CUPS VINEGAR	1.5 L
3½ CUPS SUGAR	825 mL
¼ CUP MUSTARD SEED	60 mL
¼ CUP SALT	60 mL
1 TBSP. CELERY SEED	15 mL
2 TSP. ALLSPICE	10 mL
1 TSP. CINNAMON	5 mL

GRIND OR FINELY CHOP ALL VEGETABLES AND
PLACE IN A LARGE DUTCH OVEN. ADD 4 CUPS
(1 L) VINEGAR AND BRING TO A FULL BOIL OVER
HIGH HEAT. REDUCE HEAT AND SIMMER FOR
30 MINUTES, STIRRING OCCASIONALLY. DRAIN AND
RETURN TO POT. ADD 2 CUPS (500 mL) VINEGAR
AND REMAINING INGREDIENTS AND BRING
MIXTURE TO BOIL OVER HIGH HEAT. SIMMER FOR
3 MINUTES. LADLE INTO STERILIZED JARS, PUT
ON LIDS IMMEDIATELY (DON'T TIGHTEN
COMPLETELY) AND PROCESS (SEE PAGE 45). THIS
MAKES 9, 12-OZ. (340 mL) JARS.

CRAB APPLE CHUTNEY

MORE FUN THAN CRAB APPLE JELLY! GREAT SERVED WITH "NOTTA CHEESE BALL" ON PAGE 55.

12 CUPS QUARTERED CRAB APPLES	3	L
8 CUPS SUGAR	2	L
3 LARGE ORANGES, PEELED & CHOPPED		
1 LB. RAISINS	500	g
1 TBSP. CINNAMON	15	mL
1 TBSP. GROUND CLOVES	15	mL
2 CUPS CIDER VINEGAR	500	mL

IN A LARGE POT, MIX INGREDIENTS TOGETHER AND LET STAND OVERNIGHT. NEXT DAY BRING TO A BOIL, REDUCE HEAT AND COOK UNTIL CRAB APPLES ARE SOFT AND MIXTURE IS DARK IN COLOR (APPROXIMATELY ¾-1 HOUR). POUR INTO 8-OZ. (250 mL) STERILIZED JARS, PUT LIDS ON IMMEDIATELY (DON'T TIGHTEN COMPLETELY) AND PROCESS (PAGE 45). MAKES ABOUT 12 JARS. RECIPE CAN BE DOUBLED.

LAST NIGHT I LAY IN BED LOOKING UP AT THE STARS IN THE SKY AND I THOUGHT TO MYSELF, WHERE THE HECK IS THE CEILING?

HOT PEPPER ORANGE CHUTNEY

A SPICY CHUTNEY FOR HAM OR PORK OR SERVE AS AN APPETIZER WITH CREAM CHEESE AND CRACKERS.

8 LARGE ORANGES	
3 CUPS CHOPPED RED PEPPER	750 mL
½ CUP CHOPPED JALAPEÑO PEPPERS	125 mL
1 CUP CHOPPED ONION	250 mL
1 CUP RAISINS	250 mL
1 CUP MIXED GLACÉ PEEL	250 mL
1½ CUPS WHITE WINE VINEGAR	375 mL
2 CUPS BROWN SUGAR	500 mL
¼ TSP. CAYENNE PEPPER	1 mL
1 TSP. CINNAMON	5 mL
½ TSP. NUTMEG	2 mL

PEEL ALL BUT 3 ORANGES. SLICE THE 3 UNPEELED ORANGES THINLY AND CUT EACH SLICE IN HALF. CUT PEELED ORANGES IN ½" (1.3 cm) CHUNKS. PLACE ALL INGREDIENTS IN A LARGE POT OVER MEDIUM-HIGH HEAT AND BRING TO A BOIL. REDUCE HEAT AND SIMMER UNTIL THICKENED. POUR INTO 8-OZ. (250 mL) STERILIZED JARS AND PUT LIDS ON IMMEDIATELY (DON'T TIGHTEN COMPLETELY). PROCESS (SEE PAGE 45). MAKES 12 JARS.

MICROWAVE PEANUT BRITTLE

GIFTABLE AND TRAVELS WELL.

1 CUP SALTED PEANUTS, PECANS OR CASHEWS	250 mL
1 CUP SUGAR	250 mL
½ CUP CORN SYRUP	125 mL
PINCH SALT	
1 TSP. BUTTER	5 mL
1 TSP. VANILLA	5 mL
1 TSP. BAKING SODA	5 mL

STIR FIRST 4 INGREDIENTS TOGETHER IN AN 8 CUP (2 L) MEASURING CUP, OR VERY LARGE "MICROWAVE SAFE" BOWL. COOK ON HIGH 3-4 MINUTES. STIR WELL. COOK 4 MORE MINUTES. STIR IN BUTTER AND VANILLA. COOK 1 MINUTE MORE. ADD BAKING SODA AND GENTLY STIR UNTIL LIGHT AND FOAMY. SPREAD MIXTURE QUICKLY ON LIGHTLY GREASED COOKIE SHEET. COOL FOR ½ HOUR. BREAK INTO PIECES.

A JOURNEY OF A THOUSAND MILES BEGINS WITH A CASH ADVANCE.

PEPPERMINT BRITTLE

WHIP UP A BATCH FOR CHRISTMAS GIFTING. GREAT FOR STOCKING STUFFERS AND FOR KIDS HELPING MOMS COOK!

2 LBS. GOOD-QUALITY WHITE CHOCOLATE	1 kg
1-1½ CUPS CRUSHED CANDY CANES	250-375 mL

LINE A 10 X 15" (25 X 38 cm) EDGED COOKIE SHEET WITH HEAVY-DUTY FOIL. IN A HEAVY SAUCEPAN, MELT CHOCOLATE OVER LOW HEAT - BE VERY CAREFUL NOT TO BURN. ADD CRUSHED CANDY TO CHOCOLATE, POUR ONTO COOKIE SHEET AND CHILL UNTIL SET (ABOUT 1 HOUR). BREAK INTO PIECES BY SLAMMING PAN ON COUNTER (THAT'S FUN!). GOOD COOKING MRS. CLAUS!

WHEN YOU HAVE A HEADACHE - DO WHAT THEY SAY ON THE ASPIRIN BOTTLE: "TAKE 2 ASPIRIN" AND "KEEP AWAY FROM CHILDREN".

SINFULLY RICH LOW-FAT FUDGE SAUCE

SERVE OVER FRUIT, ANGEL FOOD CAKE OR LOW-FAT FROZEN YOGURT. THE BEST!

½ CUP SUGAR	125 mL
¼ CUP COCOA	60 mL
4 TSP. CORNSTARCH	20 mL
½ CUP EVAPORATED SKIM MILK	125 mL
2 TSP. VANILLA	10 mL

IN SMALL SAUCEPAN, COMBINE SUGAR, COCOA AND CORNSTARCH. STIR IN MILK AND WHISK OVER LOW HEAT FOR 3 MINUTES, OR UNTIL MIXTURE BOILS. WHISK 1-2 MINUTES LONGER, UNTIL THICKENED AND SMOOTH. REMOVE FROM HEAT AND STIR IN VANILLA. SERVE WARM OR COLD. REFRIGERATE LEFTOVER SAUCE. MAKES 1 CUP (250 mL).

CELL PHONES ARE SUCH A STATUS SYMBOL. I DON'T HAVE ONE, SO I JUST CARRY AROUND MY GARAGE DOOR OPENER.

APPETIZERS

Grape Tomatoes Au Vodka
Cool Cocktail Grapes
Notta Cheese Ball
Cheese Wheel with Mango Chutney
Ginger Curry Dip with Mango Chutney
Peachy Cheese Dip
Mexican Dip
Cocktail Spread
Potted Pecan Shrimp
Caramelized Onion Dip
White Bean and Artichoke Dip with Pita Chips
Brandied Blue Cheese, Walnut and Pear Crostini
Bomb Shelter Croustades
Seasoned Flatbread
Bruschetta
Cheddar Chutney Tarts
Wonton Crispies
Dilled Cocktail Crackers
Nuts and Bolts
Cheddar-Cayenne Coins
Sesame Coins
Flatbread with Caramelized Onions and Cheese
Jalapeño Poppers
Phyllo Bundles with Two Cheese Fillings
Asian Vegetable Rolls with Dipping Sauce
Wrapped Brie with Caramelized Onions and
Pepper Jelly
Chicken Roca
Chicken Lettuce Wraps
Peanut-Curry Chicken in Wonton Cups
Asparagus Chicken Puffs
Curried Seafood Cocktail Puffs
Smoked Salmon Cheesecake

GRAPE TOMATOES AU VODKA

THIS WOULD GET DR. ATKIN'S VOTE!

1 BASKET OF GRAPE TOMATOES
CITRUS VODKA (LEMON)
COARSE SEA SALT
FANCY TOOTHPICKS

WASH TOMATOES AND PRICK THEM WITH A SMALL SKEWER. PLACE TOMATOES IN A LARGE SEALABLE BAG AND POUR ENOUGH VODKA OVER THEM TO COVER. MARINATE OVERNIGHT IN REFRIGERATOR. TO SERVE, PLACE TOMATOES WITH SOME OF THE MARINADE IN A LARGE STEMMED GLASS. POUR SEA SALT IN A SEPARATE SMALL DISH. SPEAR A TOMATO WITH A TOOTHPICK, DIP IN SEA SALT - ET VOILA! (PICTURED ON PAGE 69.)

COOL COCKTAIL GRAPES

MAKE LOTS - THEY WON'T LAST!!

BLUE CHEESE, SOFTENED
SEEDLESS GRAPES, GREEN OR RED
TOASTED PISTACHIO NUTS, FINELY CHOPPED

FORM SOFTENED CHEESE AROUND EACH GRAPE, THEN ROLL (NOT YOU - THE GRAPES!) IN CRUSHED PISTACHIO NUTS. REFRIGERATE UNTIL SERVING TIME.

THESE CAN BE PREPARED THE NIGHT BEFORE.

NOTTA CHEESE BALL

½ CUP CHOPPED PECANS, TOASTED	125 mL	
8 OZ. PKG. IMPERIAL CHEESE	250	g
(COLD PACK CHEDDAR)		
½ CUP MAYONNAISE	125 mL	
½ CUP CHOPPED RED ONION	125 mL	
3 GARLIC CLOVES, MINCED		
½ TSP. TABASCO	2 mL	
CHUTNEY		

TO TOAST PECANS: PLACE WHOLE NUTS ON A COOKIE SHEET AND BAKE AT 350°F (180°C) FOR 5-7 MINUTES. SET ASIDE, COOL AND CHOP.

IN A MEDIUM BOWL, CREAM CHEESE AND MAYONNAISE UNTIL SMOOTH. MIX IN ONION, GARLIC AND TABASCO. CHOP PECANS AND MIX INTO CHEESE MIXTURE. ON A SERVING PLATE, MAKE A DOUGHNUT SHAPE WITH CHEESE MIXTURE AND POUR SOME CHUTNEY INTO THE CENTER. SERVE WITH CRACKERS. SEE CRAB APPLE CHUTNEY PAGE 48.

AN INVISIBLE MAN MARRIES AN INVISIBLE WOMAN. THE KIDS WERE NOTHING TO LOOK AT EITHER.

CHEESE WHEEL
WITH MANGO CHUTNEY

8 OZ. PKG. CREAM CHEESE, SOFTENED	250	g
4 OZ. SHARP CHEDDAR CHEESE, GRATED	115	g
1/2 TSP. CURRY POWDER	2	mL
1/3 CUP MANGO CHUTNEY OR CRAB APPLE CHUTNEY (PG. 48)	75	mL
1/4 CUP TOASTED SLIVERED ALMONDS (OPTIONAL)	60	mL
3 GRANNY SMITH APPLES		
WATER BISCUITS		

COMBINE CREAM CHEESE, CHEDDAR CHEESE AND CURRY POWDER. BEAT BY HAND UNTIL SMOOTH. SHAPE INTO A 5½" (14 cm) DIAMETER WHEEL ABOUT 1" (2.5 cm) THICK. CHILL UNTIL FIRM (ABOUT 45 MINUTES).

TO SERVE: PLACE CHEESE ON A SERVING DISH AND SPREAD CHUTNEY ON TOP. SPRINKLE WITH TOASTED ALMONDS IF DESIRED. CUT APPLES INTO THIN WEDGES. ARRANGE WEDGES AND WATER BISCUITS AROUND CHEESE.

THE CHEESE WHEEL MAY BE MADE UP TO 2 DAYS IN ADVANCE. COVER AND CHILL UNTIL READY TO SERVE.

GINGER CURRY DIP
WITH MANGO CHUTNEY

8 OZ. PKG. CREAM CHEESE, SOFTENED	250 g
1/2 CUP SOUR CREAM	125 mL
1 CUP MANGO CHUTNEY, DRAINED & CHOPPED	250 mL
1 TSP. CURRY POWDER	5 mL
3 PIECES CANDIED GINGER, FINELY CHOPPED	
1/2 CUP CHOPPED SALTED CASHEWS	125 mL

CREAM INGREDIENTS TOGETHER EXCEPT NUTS. MIX IN NUTS JUST BEFORE SERVING (SAVING SOME TO SPRINKLE ON TOP). TO ENJOY THE BEST FLAVOR, MAKE SEVERAL HOURS AHEAD, COVER AND REFRIGERATE. SERVE AT ROOM TEMPERATURE WITH CRACKERS.

DEAR GOD:

DO YOU REALLY MEAN DO UNTO OTHERS AS THEY DO UNTO YOU, BECAUSE IF YOU DID THEN I'M GOING TO FIX MY BROTHER.

PEACHY CHEESE DIP

8 oz. pkg. cream cheese, softened	250	g
8 oz. pkg. imperial cheese (or cold pack sharp cheddar)	250	g
2 tbsp. sherry	30	mL
1 tsp. curry powder	5	mL
3/4 cup peach jam	175	mL
peach chutney		
chives		

Using a food processor or electric mixer, blend cheeses together. Add sherry, curry and jam, mixing until smooth. Pour into sterilized jars and keep refrigerated. To serve, garnish with chutney and chives and set out with crackers. Makes about 2, 8-oz. (250 mL) jars.

MEXICAN DIP

You have to make this!

1 lb. velveeta cheese, cubed	500	g
8 oz. sharp cheddar cheese, grated	250	mL
3-4 jalapeño peppers, seeds removed, finely chopped		
4 large tomatoes, finely chopped		
1 medium onion, finely chopped		
4 garlic cloves, minced		

MEXICAN DIP

CONTINUED FROM PAGE 58.

PREHEAT OVEN TO 350°F (180°C). FOR EASIER MIXING, SOFTEN CHEESES IN MICROWAVE. COMBINE INGREDIENTS AND SPOON INTO AN OVENPROOF SERVING DISH. BAKE 40 MINUTES, OR UNTIL BUBBLY. SERVE WITH CORN OR TORTILLA CHIPS.

COCKTAIL SPREAD

GUESTS WILL ASK FOR A SPOON. JIMMY DID!

8 OZ. PKG. CREAM CHEESE, SOFTENED	250 mL
½ CUP SOUR CREAM	125 mL
¼ CUP MAYONNAISE	60 mL
3-4 OZ. CANS BROKEN SHRIMP, RINSED & DRAINED OR 1½ CUPS (375 mL) FRESH BABY SHRIMP	3-125 mL
1 CUP SEAFOOD COCKTAIL SAUCE	250 mL
2 CUPS GRATED MOZZARELLA CHEESE	500 mL
3 GREEN ONIONS, CHOPPED	
1 TOMATO, DICED	
1 GREEN PEPPER, CHOPPED	

COMBINE CHEESE, SOUR CREAM AND MAYONNAISE. SPREAD IN A 12" (30 cm) DISH OR PIE PLATE. SCATTER SHRIMP OVER CHEESE. LAYER SEAFOOD SAUCE, THEN MOZZARELLA, GREEN ONIONS, TOMATO AND GREEN PEPPER. COVER UNTIL READY TO SERVE. SERVE WITH CRACKERS.

POTTED PECAN SHRIMP

THIS IS SO EASY - AND SOOO GOOD!

½ CUP PECANS, TOASTED	125 mL
8 OZ. PKG. CREAM CHEESE, SOFTENED	250 g
¼ CUP FINELY CHOPPED CELERY	60 mL
¼ CUP BEER	60 mL
4 TSP. GRATED ONION	20 mL
½ TSP. WORCESTERSHIRE SAUCE	2 mL
¼ TSP. DRY MUSTARD	1 mL
1½ CUPS CHOPPED COOKED FRESH SHRIMP	375 mL

TO TOAST PECANS, BAKE AT 350°F (180°C) FOR 5-7 MINUTES. SET ASIDE, COOL AND CHOP.

IN A MEDIUM BOWL, COMBINE CREAM CHEESE, CELERY, BEER, ONION, WORCESTERSHIRE AND MUSTARD. BLEND WELL. STIR IN SHRIMP AND PECANS. PACK THE MIXTURE INTO A CROCK OR OTHER SERVING CONTAINER. COVER AND REFRIGERATE AT LEAST 1 HOUR. SERVE WITH CRACKERS.

ALWAYS READ STUFF THAT WILL MAKE YOU LOOK GOOD IF YOU DIE IN THE MIDDLE OF IT.

CARAMELIZED ONION DIP

TASTES TERRIFIC ON A HAMBURGER TOO!

¼ CUP VEGETABLE OIL	60 mL
¼ CUP BUTTER	60 mL
1 LARGE YELLOW ONION, HALVED & THINLY SLICED	
¼ TSP. CAYENNE PEPPER	1 mL
1 TSP. SALT	5 mL
½ TSP. GROUND PEPPER	2 mL
4 OZ. PKG. CREAM CHEESE, SOFTENED	115 g
½ CUP SOUR CREAM	125 mL
½ CUP MAYONNAISE	125 mL

HEAT OIL AND BUTTER IN A LARGE FRYING PAN OVER MEDIUM HEAT. ADD ONION, CAYENNE, SALT AND PEPPER AND SAUTÉ FOR 10 MINUTES. REDUCE HEAT TO MEDIUM-LOW AND COOK, STIRRING OCCASIONALLY, FOR 20 MINUTES MORE, UNTIL ONIONS ARE BROWNED AND CARAMELIZED. COOL. BEAT CHEESE, SOUR CREAM AND MAYONNAISE UNTIL SMOOTH. ADD ONIONS AND MIX WELL. SERVE WITH POTATO CHIPS OR CRACKERS.

NEVER BUY A PURSE FROM A MAN WHO IS OUT OF BREATH.

WHITE BEAN AND ARTICHOKE DIP WITH PITA CHIPS

TASTES FINE!! VERY FINE!!

PITA CHIPS

4-8" PITA ROUNDS, SLICED INTO 8 TRIANGLES, SEPARATED INTO 2 PIECES EACH	4-20 cm
3 TBSP. OLIVE OIL	45 mL
CAYENNE PEPPER	
SEA SALT & FRESHLY GROUND PEPPER	

DIP

19 OZ. CAN WHITE KIDNEY BEANS, DRAINED & RINSED	540 mL
2-6 OZ. JARS MARINATED ARTICHOKE HEARTS, DRAINED, RINSED OR 14 OZ. (398 mL) CAN ARTICHOKE HEARTS, DRAINED & CHOPPED	2-170 mL
1 SMALL GARLIC CLOVE, CHOPPED	
2 TBSP. FRESH LEMON JUICE	30 mL
3 TBSP. FRESHLY GRATED PARMESAN CHEESE	45 mL
1 TSP. CHOPPED FRESH ROSEMARY	5 mL
SALT & PEPPER	
CAYENNE	

TO MAKE CHIPS: PUT OVEN RACK TO UPPER-MIDDLE OF OVEN AND HEAT BROILER. TOSS PITA PIECES WITH OIL, PINCH OF CAYENNE AND A GENEROUS AMOUNT OF SALT AND PEPPER. LAY PIECES FLAT ON 2 BAKING SHEETS AND BROIL ON BOTH SIDES UNTIL GOLDEN. WATCH CAREFULLY. REMOVE AND COOL.

WHITE BEAN DIP

CONTINUED FROM PAGE 62.

TO MAKE BEAN DIP: BLEND BEANS, ARTICHOKE HEARTS, GARLIC AND LEMON JUICE IN A FOOD PROCESSOR TO FORM A SMOOTH PASTE. IF NECESSARY, WHILE MACHINE IS RUNNING, DRIZZLE WATER FOR A SMOOTH CONSISTENCY. BLEND IN CHEESE AND ROSEMARY; SEASON WITH SALT AND PEPPER. POUR DIP INTO SERVING BOWL AND SPRINKLE WITH CAYENNE. SERVE WITH PITA CHIPS. MAKES ABOUT 2 CUPS (500 mL).

BRANDIED BLUE CHEESE, WALNUT AND PEAR CROSTINI

4 OZ. BLUE CHEESE, CRUMBLED	125 g
2 TBSP. BUTTER	30 mL
2 TBSP. BRANDY	30 mL
1/4 CUP COARSELY CHOPPED WALNUTS	60 mL
16, 1/2" BAGUETTE SLICES	16, 1.3 cm
1 RIPE PEAR, THINLY SLICED	

SOFTEN CHEESE AND BUTTER. MASH WITH FORK UNTIL SMOOTH. STIR BRANDY AND WALNUTS INTO CHEESE MIXTURE. PLACE BAGUETTE SLICES ON COOKIE SHEET. TOAST 1 SIDE UNDER BROILER. TURN AND PLACE PEAR SLICE ON UNTOASTED SIDE. TOP WITH TEASPOONFUL OF CHEESE MIXTURE. BROIL 4-5" (10-13 cm) FROM HEAT FOR ABOUT 2 MINUTES, OR UNTIL CHEESE IS BUBBLY. SERVES 8.

BOMB SHELTER CROUSTADES

CROUSTADES

24 SLICES WHITE BREAD, THINLY ROLLED	
2 TBSP. BUTTER	30 mL

MUSHROOM FILLING

¼ CUP BUTTER	60 mL
3 TBSP. FINELY CHOPPED, ONION	45 mL
½ LB. FINELY CHOPPED MUSHROOMS	250 g
2 TBSP. FLOUR	30 mL
1 CUP WHIPPING CREAM	250 mL
3 TBSP. DRY WHITE WINE	45 mL
½ TSP. SALT	2 mL
PINCH CAYENNE PEPPER	
1 TBSP. FINELY CHOPPED PARSLEY	15 mL
1½ TBSP. FINELY CHOPPED GREEN ONION	22 mL
3 TBSP. GRATED PARMESAN CHEESE	45 mL

PREHEAT OVEN TO 400°F (200°C).

TO MAKE CROUSTADES: GENEROUSLY BUTTER SMALL TART TINS. CUT A 3" (8 cm) ROUND FROM EACH SLICE OF BREAD. CAREFULLY FIT INTO TART TINS. BAKE FOR 10 MINUTES, OR UNTIL RIMS ARE LIGHTLY BROWNED. REMOVE FROM TINS AND COOL. (MAY BE FROZEN AT THIS POINT.)

TO MAKE FILLING: MELT BUTTER IN A FRYING PAN AND SAUTÉ ONION AND MUSHROOMS. STIR AND COOK UNTIL MOISTURE EVAPORATES. SPRINKLE WITH FLOUR. STIR THOROUGHLY AND ADD CREAM, STIRRING UNTIL IT BOILS. ADD WINE, REDUCE HEAT AND SIMMER A FEW

— BOMB SHELTER CROUSTADES —

CONTINUED FROM PAGE 64.

MINUTES LONGER. REMOVE FROM HEAT, STIR IN
SALT, CAYENNE, PARSLEY AND GREEN ONION.
TRANSFER TO A BOWL. COVER AND REFRIGERATE.

TO SERVE: PREHEAT OVEN TO 350°F (180°C).
SPOON MUSHROOM FILLING INTO CROUSTADES;
LIGHTLY SPRINKLE WITH PARMESAN AND PLACE
ON COOKIE SHEET. HEAT IN OVEN FOR
10 MINUTES, THEN BRIEFLY UNDER THE BROILER.

— SEASONED FLATBREAD —

IS THERE A CARPENTER IN THE HOUSE?

8 OZ. PKG. KAVLI THIN FLATBREAD	250	g
½ CUP BUTTER, SOFTENED	125 mL	
2 LARGE GARLIC CLOVES, MINCED		
⅓ CUP GRATED PARMESAN CHEESE	75 mL	
1 TBSP. FINELY CHOPPED, FRESH PARSLEY	15 mL	

PREHEAT OVEN TO 325°F (160°C). USING A BREAD
KNIFE, SAW STACKED FLATBREAD IN HALVES OR
THIRDS. COMBINE BUTTER, GARLIC, CHEESE AND
PARSLEY; MIX WELL. SPREAD BUTTER MIXTURE
ON FLATBREAD PIECES; PLACE ON A COOKIE
SHEET. BAKE FOR ABOUT 5 MINUTES. LET COOL.
STORE IN COVERED CONTAINER OR FREEZE.

BRUSCHETTA

USE FIRM, RIPE, RED ROMA TOMATOES.

2 LARGE GARLIC CLOVES, CHOPPED
SALT & PEPPER TO TASTE
1/3 CUP OLIVE OIL   75 mL
6-8 ROMA TOMATOES, COARSELY CHOPPED
HANDFUL OF CHOPPED FRESH BASIL
24" BAGUETTE   61 cm
GRATED PROVOLONE, FONTINA OR MOZZARELLA
      CHEESE (OPTIONAL)

IN A SHALLOW BOWL, COMBINE GARLIC, SALT, PEPPER AND A FEW DROPS OF OIL. MASH WITH THE BACK OF A WOODEN SPOON TO MAKE A PASTE. STIR IN OLIVE OIL. ADD TOMATOES AND BASIL. TOSS GENTLY AND SET ASIDE. CUT BREAD IN HALF, LENGTHWISE. BRUSH EACH HALF WITH ADDITIONAL OIL AND PLACE UNDER A PREHEATED BROILER UNTIL GOLDEN BROWN. SPOON TOMATO MIXTURE ONTO EACH HALF AND DRIZZLE WITH REMAINING OIL. (IF DESIRED, SPRINKLE WITH GRATED CHEESE.) BROIL - WATCH CAREFULLY! CUT AND SERVE IMMEDIATELY.

A TRULY HAPPY PERSON IS ONE WHO CAN ENJOY THE SCENERY ON A DETOUR.

CHEDDAR CHUTNEY TARTS

FROM FREEZER TO OVEN FOR RAVE REVIEWS!

8 OZ. PKG. CREAM CHEESE, SOFTENED	250	g
1 CUP GRATED SHARP CHEDDAR CHEESE	250	mL
1 GARLIC CLOVE, MINCED		
1 TSP. CURRY POWDER	5	mL
1/3 CUP MANGO CHUTNEY	75	mL
4 GREEN ONIONS, FINELY CHOPPED		
PINCH CAYENNE PEPPER		
DASH WORCESTERSHIRE SAUCE		
14 OZ. PKG. FROZEN PUFF PASTRY, THAWED	397	g

IN A LARGE BOWL, MIX CREAM CHEESE UNTIL SMOOTH. ADD CHEDDAR, GARLIC AND CURRY; MIX WELL. CHOP LARGE PIECES OF CHUTNEY AND ADD TO CHEESE MIXTURE ALONG WITH REMAINING CHUTNEY, ONIONS, CAYENNE AND WORCESTERSHIRE. MIX WELL. FILLING MAY BE MADE SEVERAL DAYS AHEAD, COVERED AND REFRIGERATED. ON A LIGHTLY FLOURED SURFACE, ROLL HALF THE PASTRY AT A TIME INTO A 12" (30 cm) SQUARE. CUT INTO 2" (5 cm) SQUARES. PRESS INTO SMALL TART TINS AND PRICK WITH A FORK. SPOON 1 TSP. (5 mL) FILLING INTO EACH TART. FREEZE AT THIS STAGE IN AN AIRTIGHT CONTAINER. BAKE IN CENTER OF A 400°F (200°C) OVEN FOR ABOUT 15 MINUTES, OR UNTIL PASTRY IS GOLDEN. SERVE HOT.

WONTON CRISPIES

ADDICTIVE - YOU'LL WANT TO DOUBLE THIS!

¼ CUP BUTTER	60 mL
20 WONTON WRAPPERS	
¼ CUP PARMESAN CHEESE	60 mL

MELT BUTTER AND BRUSH SOME ON AN EDGED BAKING SHEET. CUT EACH WONTON DIAGONALLY TO MAKE TRIANGLES. PLACE CLOSE TOGETHER AND BRUSH TOPS WITH BUTTER. SPRINKLE WITH CHEESE. BAKE AT 375°F (190°C). FOR 5 MINUTES. REPEAT UNTIL ALL ARE BAKED. IF YOU'RE INTO EXPERIMENTING, ADD HERBS OR CHOPPED GREEN ONIONS TO THE CHEESE. MAKES 40.

DILLED COCKTAIL CRACKERS

ALL-TIME FAVORITE - GREAT HOSTESS GIFT.

8 OZ. BOX MINI RITZ ORIGINAL CRACKERS	250 g
OR OYSTER CRACKERS	
1 OZ. PKG. RANCH STYLE SALAD	28 g
DRESSING MIX	
1 TBSP. DILLWEED	15 mL
½ CUP VEGETABLE OIL	125 mL
1 TSP. GARLIC POWDER	5 mL

COMBINE ALL INGREDIENTS IN A PLASTIC CONTAINER. SEAL. SHAKE OFTEN. LET STAND OVERNIGHT OR AT LEAST 6 HOURS.

Grape Tomatoes au Vodka, page 54
Jalapeño Poppers, page 76

Chicken Lettuce Wraps, page 84

NUTS AND BOLTS

FOR THOSE WHO ARE MECHANICALLY DECLINED!
- AND JUST ABOUT ANYONE ELSE!

1 LB. BUTTER	500 g
2 TBSP. WORCESTERSHIRE SAUCE	30 mL
1 TBSP. GARLIC POWDER	15 mL
1½ TSP. ONION SALT	7 mL
1½ TSP. CELERY SALT	7 mL
4 CUPS 'CHEERIOS'	1 L
4 CUPS 'LIFE' CEREAL	1 L
4 CUPS 'SHREDDIES' OR 'WHEAT CHEX'	1 L
2-16 OZ. BOXES PRETZELS	2-454 g
2 CUPS PEANUTS, SALTED (IF YOU INSIST)	500 mL
5½ OZ. BOX 'BUGLES'	150 g
8 OZ. BOX 'CHEESE NIPS' OR 'CHEESE BITES'	250 g

PREHEAT OVEN TO 250°F (120°C). PLACE BUTTER
IN A VERY LARGE ROASTER. PLACE IN OVEN TO
MELT WHILE OVEN IS PREHEATING. REMOVE
ROASTER AND ADD SPICES; STIR. ADD REMAINING
INGREDIENTS, MIXING WELL TO COAT EVENLY
WITH BUTTER MIXTURE. BAKE FOR 1½ HOURS. STIR
AND TURN EVERY ½ HOUR.

MY PHILOSOPHY IS: NO PAIN . . . GOOD.

CHEDDAR-CAYENNE COINS

GREAT FREEZER FARE!

1⅓ CUPS FLOUR	325 mL
1¼ CUPS GRATED SHARP CHEDDAR CHEESE	300 mL
1 TSP. SALT	5 mL
⅛-¼ TSP. CAYENNE PEPPER	0.5-1 mL
½ CUP BUTTER CUT INTO ½" (1.3 cm) PIECES, CHILLED	125 mL
1 LARGE EGG YOLK	
2 TBSP. WATER	30 mL
1⅓ CUPS CHOPPED WALNUTS OR PECANS	325 mL
COARSE SALT FOR SPRINKLING (OPTIONAL)	

IN A LARGE MIXING BOWL COMBINE FLOUR, CHEESE, SALT AND CAYENNE. ADD BUTTER PIECES AND BLEND UNTIL DOUGH RESEMBLES COARSE CRUMBS. STIR EGG YOLK AND WATER TOGETHER AND DRIZZLE OVER DOUGH. MIX UNTIL DOUGH BEGINS TO FORM SMALL MOIST CRUMBS. ADD CHOPPED NUTS AND MIX BRIEFLY, UNTIL CRUMBS BEGIN TO COME TOGETHER. PILE CRUMBS ON AN UNFLOURED WORK SURFACE. WORK CRUMBS WITH YOUR HANDS UNTIL THEY START TO COME TOGETHER AND FORM INTO A 14" (36 cm) LOG 1¼" (3.5 cm) IN DIAMETER. WRAP IN PLASTIC AND REFRIGERATE UNTIL FIRM, ABOUT 4 HOURS.

CHEDDAR-CAYENNE COINS

CONTINUED FROM PAGE 72.

(DOUGH MAY ALSO BE FROZEN FOR UP TO A MONTH AND THAWED FOR AN HOUR AT ROOM TEMPERATURE OR IN REFRIGERATOR OVERNIGHT).

PREHEAT OVEN TO 375°F (190°C). LINE 2 LARGE BAKING SHEETS WITH PARCHMENT. CUT THE LOG INTO 1/4" (6 mm) SLICES. BAKE IN CENTER OF OVEN UNTIL GOLDEN BROWN AROUND THE EDGES, 15-20 MINUTES. SPRINKLE A LITTLE COARSE SALT OVER TOP AS SOON AS THEY COME OUT OF THE OVEN. PLACE ON A RACK TO COOL. STORE IN AN AIRTIGHT CONTAINER. MAKES 4 DOZEN.

KID'S LETTER TO GOD:

DEAR GOD:

THANK YOU FOR THE BABY BROTHER BUT WHAT I ASKED FOR WAS A PUPPY. I NEVER ASKED FOR ANYTHING BEFORE. YOU CAN LOOK THAT UP.

SESAME COINS

1¼ CUPS FLOUR	300 mL
1 TSP. SALT	5 mL
¼ TSP. COARSELY GROUND BLACK PEPPER	1 mL
½ CUP BUTTER, CUT INTO ½" (1.3 cm) PIECES, CHILLED	125 mL
1 LARGE EGG YOLK	
1 TBSP. WATER	15 mL
1 TBSP. DIJON MUSTARD	15 mL
2 TBSP. SESAME SEEDS, TOASTED	30 mL
COARSE SALT FOR SPRINKLING (OPTIONAL)	

IN A MIXING BOWL, COMBINE FLOUR, SALT AND PEPPER UNTIL JUST BLENDED. ADD BUTTER AND MIX UNTIL DOUGH RESEMBLES COARSE CRUMBS. STIR YOLK, WATER AND MUSTARD TOGETHER AND DRIZZLE OVER MIXTURE. MIX UNTIL DOUGH BEGINS TO CLUMP TOGETHER. ADD SESAME SEEDS AND MIX BRIEFLY. PILE ON AN UNFLOURED WORK SURFACE. USING YOUR HANDS, GENTLY WORK TO FORM A 12" (30 cm) LOG 1¼" (3.5 cm) IN DIAMETER. WRAP IN PLASTIC AND REFRIGERATE FOR AT LEAST 4 HOURS. PREHEAT OVEN TO 375°F (190°C). PLACE PARCHMENT PAPER ON 2 LARGE BAKING SHEETS. USING A SHARP KNIFE, SLICE LOG INTO ¼" (6 mm) PIECES AND PLACE ON BAKING SHEETS. BAKE IN CENTER OF OVEN UNTIL EDGES ARE GOLDEN BROWN, ABOUT 15 MINUTES. REMOVE AND SPRINKLE WITH COARSE SALT. COOL ON RACK; STORE IN AIRTIGHT CONTAINER. MAKES 3 DOZEN COINS.

FLATBREAD WITH CARAMELIZED ONIONS AND CHEESE

IT'S DEAD EASY AND ABSOLUTELY DELICIOUS!

3 LARGE ONIONS, CHOPPED	
2 TBSP. OLIVE OIL	30 mL
1 TBSP. BROWN SUGAR	15 mL
2 TSP. BALSAMIC VINEGAR	10 mL
SALT & PEPPER TO TASTE	
14 OZ. PKG. FROZEN PUFF PASTRY	397 g
6 OZ. BRIE (RIND REMOVED), DICED	170 g
6 OZ. MILD BLUE CHEESE, CRUMBLED	170 g
2 TBSP. CHOPPED FRESH PARSLEY	30 mL

HEAT OIL IN LARGE DEEP FRYING PAN ON MEDIUM-HIGH, ADD ONIONS; COOK UNTIL WILTED AND STARTING TO BROWN, ABOUT 10 MINUTES. ADD SUGAR, VINEGAR, SALT AND PEPPER. REDUCE HEAT TO MEDIUM-LOW; COOK FOR 15-25 MINUTES, UNTIL ONIONS ARE CARAMELIZED AND GOLDEN. COOL. PUFF PASTRY PACKAGE HAS 2 POUCHES. PINCH BOTH TOGETHER AND ROLL OUT TO A 12 X 16" (30 X 40 cm) RECTANGLE. PLACE PASTRY ON BAKING SHEET LINED WITH PARCHMENT PAPER. SPREAD ONIONS OVER PASTRY. DOT WITH CHEESE. SPRINKLE WITH PARSLEY AND REFRIGERATE IF NOT BAKING IMMEDIATELY. BAKE IN PREHEATED 400°F (200°C) OVEN FOR 20-25 MINUTES, UNTIL CHEESE IS MELTED AND PASTRY IS CRISP. COOL FOR 5 MINUTES. CUT INTO 20 SQUARES; CUT SQUARES IN HALF DIAGONALLY TO MAKE 40 TRIANGLES. (PICTURED ON PAGE 36.)

JALAPEÑO POPPERS

HOT STUFF FOR THE ADVENTUROUS PALATE.

PARMESAN GARLIC FILLING

2 TSP. VEGETABLE OIL	10 mL
3 TBSP. FINELY MINCED RED ONION	45 mL
3 GARLIC CLOVES, MINCED	
4 OZ. SPREADABLE LIGHT CREAM	115 g
CHEESE	
2 TBSP. FINELY GRATED FRESH	
PARMESAN CHEESE	30 mL
1/8 TSP. SALT	0.5 mL
FRESHLY GROUND BLACK PEPPER TO TASTE	

8 JALAPEÑO PEPPERS	
4 LARGE EGG WHITES	
1 CUP FINE DRY BREAD CRUMBS	250 mL
COOKING SPRAY	
1/2 CUP PREPARED SALSA	125 mL

FILLING: HEAT OIL IN A SMALL FRYING PAN. ADD ONION AND GARLIC AND SAUTÉ UNTIL SOFT, ABOUT 5 MINUTES. DO NOT BROWN. TRANSFER TO A SMALL BOWL AND ADD CREAM CHEESE, PARMESAN, SALT AND PEPPER. STIR TO BLEND. SET ASIDE.

WEARING RUBBER GLOVES, CUT PEPPERS IN HALF, LENGTHWISE. SCRAPE OUT MEMBRANES AND SEEDS. FILL PEPPER HALVES WITH CHEESE FILLING AND SMOOTH SURFACE WITH A SMALL KNIFE. AT THIS POINT, PEPPERS CAN BE COVERED AND REFRIGERATED OVERNIGHT.

JALAPEÑO POPPERS

CONTINUED FROM PAGE 76.

PREHEAT OVEN TO 350°F (180°C). LINE A 12 X 15" (30 X 38 cm) BAKING SHEET WITH PARCHMENT PAPER. WHISK EGG WHITES IN A BOWL UNTIL FROTHY. PLACE BREAD CRUMBS IN A SEPARATE SHALLOW BOWL. DIP PEPPER HALVES, 1 AT A TIME IN EGG WHITES AND THEN DIP INTO BREAD CRUMBS, COATING EVENLY. PLACE PEPPERS CUT SIDE UP ON PREPARED BAKING SHEET. LIGHTLY SPRAY PEPPERS WITH COOKING SPRAY AND BAKE ABOUT 20 MINUTES, OR UNTIL CRISP AND GOLDEN. SPOON SALSA ON TOP AND SERVE PDQ! (PICTURED ON PAGE 69.)

CHILDRENS OBSERVATIONS:
NO MATTER HOW HARD YOU TRY, YOU CAN'T BAPTIZE CATS.
WHEN YOUR MOM IS MAD AT YOUR DAD, DON'T LET HER BRUSH YOUR HAIR.

PHYLLO BUNDLES WITH TWO CHEESE FILLINGS

YOU CAN MAKE THESE ATTRACTIVE BITE-SIZED APPETIZERS THE SAME DAY - OR BETTER YET, DO A MAKE-AHEAD. FREEZE THEM AND BAKE 10 MINUTES BEFORE SERVING.

THE BUNDLES

3 SHEETS PHYLLO PASTRY	
¼ CUP BUTTER	60 mL

TO THAW PASTRY: FOLLOW PACKAGE INSTRUCTIONS.

MELT BUTTER. WORKING ON A FLAT SURFACE, GENEROUSLY BRUSH A SHEET OF PHYLLO WITH BUTTER. TOP WITH SECOND AND THIRD SHEETS, BRUSHING EACH WITH BUTTER. CUT PHYLLO INTO 20, 3" (8 cm) SQUARES. PLACE A DOLLOP OF FILLING IN THE CENTER OF EACH SQUARE. PULL UP THE EDGES, PINCH TOGETHER AND PLACE ON PARCHMENT-PAPER-LINED COOKIE SHEET. IF REFRIGERATING, COVER WITH A DAMP, CLEAN CLOTH OR PLASTIC WRAP. IF FREEZING, COVER WITH PLASTIC WRAP AND SEAL. PREHEAT OVEN TO 400°F (200°C). BAKE REFRIGERATED BUNDLES FOR 8 MINUTES, FROZEN BUNDLES FOR 10 MINUTES, OR UNTIL GOLDEN. SERVE WARM.

CONTINUED FROM PAGE 78.

BLUE CHEESE, WALNUT AND ROASTED RED PEPPER FILLING

1 CUP CHOPPED TOASTED WALNUTS	250 mL
8 OZ. BLUE CHEESE, CRUMBLED	250 mL
½ CUP CHOPPED BOTTLED ROASTED RED PEPPERS	125 mL

MIX INGREDIENTS TOGETHER AND REFRIGERATE UNTIL NEEDED. MAKES ENOUGH FILLING FOR 20 BUNDLES.

CHÈVRE WITH CRANBERRY AND ORHNGE ZEST

8 OZ. CHÈVRE (GOAT CHEESE)	250 g
½ CUP DRIED CRANBERRIES	125 mL
2 TSP. GRATED ORANGE ZEST	10 mL
2 TSP. CHOPPED FRESH CHIVES	10 mL

MIX INGREDIENTS TOGETHER AND REFRIGERATE UNTIL NEEDED. MAKES ENOUGH FILLING FOR 20 BUNDLES.

WHAT'S ANOTHER WORD FOR THESAURUS?

ASIAN VEGETABLE ROLLS WITH DIPPING SAUCE

GREAT CRUNCH! TANGY SAUCE! MAKE AHEAD; FREEZE AND COOK THE DAY OF YOUR PARTY.

2 TBSP. SOY SAUCE	30 mL
1 TSP. CORNSTARCH	5 mL
1 TSP. SUGAR	5 mL
½ TSP. SESAME OIL	2 mL
¼ TSP. PEPPER	1 mL
1 TBSP. BUTTER	15 mL
2 TSP. FRESHLY GRATED GINGER ROOT	10 mL
1½ CUPS CHOPPED FRESH SHIITAKE OR CREMINI MUSHROOMS	375 mL
1 CUP SHREDDED CARROT	250 mL
½ CUP THINLY SLICED GREEN ONION	125 mL
¼ CUP CHOPPED CILANTRO	60 mL
4 CUPS FINELY SHREDDED SUEY CHOY (OR NAPA CABBAGE), WHITE CORE REMOVED	1 L
⅓ CUP COARSELY CHOPPED SALTED PEANUTS	75 mL
6-8 SHEETS PHYLLO PASTRY, THAWED	
⅓ CUP MELTED BUTTER	75 mL

DIPPING SAUCE

JUICE OF 2 LIMES (3 TBSP./45 mL)	
3 TBSP. RICE VINEGAR	45 mL
3 TBSP. SESAME OIL	45 mL
1 TBSP. LIQUID HONEY	15 mL
1 TBSP. GRATED GINGER ROOT	15 mL
2 GARLIC CLOVES, MINCED	
¾ CUP HOISIN SAUCE	175 mL
1 TBSP. CHOPPED CILANTRO	15 mL

ASIAN VEGETABLE ROLLS

CONTINUED FROM PAGE 80.

STIR SOY, CORNSTARCH, SUGAR, SESAME OIL AND PEPPER TOGETHER IN A BOWL. SET ASIDE.

IN A LARGE FRYING PAN, MELT BUTTER; STIR-FRY GINGER ABOUT 15 SECONDS. ADD MUSHROOMS, CARROT, ONION AND CILANTRO; STIR-FRY 2 MINUTES. STIR SOY MIXTURE AND ADD TO VEGETABLES. SAUCE WILL THICKEN IMMEDIATELY. STIR CABBAGE AND PEANUTS INTO VEGETABLES AND REMOVE FROM HEAT. SET ASIDE.

LAY 1 SHEET OF PHYLLO VERTICALLY ON COUNTER; BRUSH BOTTOM HALF WITH BUTTER. FOLD TOP HALF DOWN; PRESS DOWN SO IT STICKS TOGETHER. SPOON VEGETABLE MIXTURE ACROSS SHORT END OF PHYLLO, FORMING A 1½" (4 cm) ROLL. ROLL PHYLLO TIGHTLY AROUND MIXTURE, FOLDING IN SIDES AS YOU GO. SEAL WITH MELTED BUTTER. PLACE ON A COOKIE SHEET, SEALED SIDE DOWN. BRUSH TOP LIGHTLY WITH BUTTER AND SCORE ON DIAGONAL (NOT TOO DEEP) ABOUT 1" (2.5 cm) APART. CONTINUE WITH REMAINING SHEETS AND FILLING. WRAP EACH ROLL IN PLASTIC WRAP AND FREEZE ON A COOKIE SHEET. KEEPS UP TO 2 WEEKS. BAKE AT 375°F (190°C) FOR 15 MINUTES. COOL SLIGHTLY AND CUT AT SCORED INTERVALS. TRIM BROWN ENDS. MAKES 3 DOZEN. COMBINE DIPPING SAUCE INGREDIENTS. REFRIGERATE UNTIL NEEDED.

WRAPPED BRIE WITH CARAMELIZED ONIONS AND PEPPER JELLY

DISAPPEARS IMMEDIATELY!

1 TBSP. BUTTER	15 mL
½ SWEET ONION, THINLY SLICED	
SALT & PEPPER TO TASTE	
¼ CUP SHERRY	60 mL
2 TBSP. CHOPPED PECANS	30 mL
2 SHEETS PHYLLO PASTRY	
2 TBSP. BUTTER, MELTED	30 mL
7 OZ. ROUND OF BRIE	190 g
3 TBSP. RED OR GREEN PEPPER JELLY	45 mL

PREHEAT OVEN TO 350°F (180°C). MELT BUTTER IN FRYING PAN OVER MEDIUM HEAT. ADD ONIONS, SALT AND PEPPER; COOK UNTIL ONIONS ARE GOLDEN. ADD SHERRY, BRING TO A BOIL, REDUCE HEAT AND SIMMER UNTIL LIQUID IS EVAPORATED. COOL. STIR IN PECANS. BRUSH EACH PHYLLO SHEET WITH MELTED BUTTER, FOLD IN HALF AND PLACE ONE ON TOP OF THE OTHER. PLACE ON BAKING SHEET, SET BRIE IN CENTER AND TOP WITH PEPPER JELLY. GATHER PHYLLO UP AROUND SIDES OF BRIE TO CREATE A RAISED, RUFFLED EDGE. SPOON ONIONS INTO MIDDLE, AND BRUSH SIDES OF PHYLLO WITH REMAINING MELTED BUTTER. BAKE FOR 15 MINUTES. SERVE WARM WITH WATER BISCUITS. SERVES 8.

THE PEOPLE FROM SOUTH BEACH WOULD APPROVE . . . SO WOULD THE REST OF THE BEACHES!

MUSTARD DIPPING SAUCE

1 CUP WHIPPING CREAM	250 mL
1 TBSP. DIJON MUSTARD	15 mL
1 TBSP. GRAINY DIJON MUSTARD	15 mL
1 TSP. HONEY	5 mL

3 CHICKEN BREAST HALVES	
¾ CUP DIJON MUSTARD	175 mL
1½ CUPS GROUND PECANS	375 mL

SMALL WOODEN SKEWERS, SOAKED IN
    WATER FOR ½ HOUR

TO MAKE THE SAUCE: IN A SMALL HEAVY POT, BRING CREAM TO A BOIL. LOWER HEAT TO SIMMER AND REDUCE CREAM TO HALF, ABOUT 15-20 MINUTES. WHISK MUSTARDS AND HONEY INTO CREAM. STORE IN REFRIGERATOR.

PREHEAT OVEN TO 350°F (180°C). CUT CHICKEN IN STRIPS ½" (1.3 cm) WIDE BY 4" (10 cm) LONG. THREAD CHICKEN ONTO WOODEN SKEWERS. BRUSH WITH MUSTARD AND ROLL IN GROUND NUTS UNTIL COMPLETELY COVERED. PLACE SKEWERS ON A COOKIE SHEET COVERED WITH PARCHMENT PAPER AND BAKE ABOUT 10 MINUTES. TO SERVE, LET GUESTS SPOON ON A LITTLE MUSTARD DIPPING SAUCE.

CHICKEN LETTUCE WRAPS

SAUCE

¾ CUP HOISIN SAUCE	175 mL
1½ TSP. RICE VINEGAR	7 mL
1 TBSP. LIQUID HONEY	15 mL
2 TBSP. WATER	30 mL
1 TBSP. FRESH LIME JUICE	15 mL
2 TSP. SESAME OIL	10 mL
1 LARGE GARLIC CLOVE, MINCED	
1 TSP. FRESHLY GRATED GINGER	5 mL

WRAPS

2 BONELESS CHICKEN BREASTS	
⅓ CUP GRATED CARROT	75 mL
2 GREEN ONIONS, DIAGONALLY SLICED	
1 CUP DRY STEAM-FRIED NOODLES	250 mL
½ CUP UNSALTED PEANUTS, CHOPPED	125 mL

1 HEAD ICEBURG LETTUCE, SEPARATED
    INTO WHOLE LEAVES, CORE REMOVED

IN A SMALL SAUCEPAN, OVER MEDIUM-LOW HEAT, BLEND SAUCE INGREDIENTS. SET ASIDE TO COOL. POACH CHICKEN IN A SMALL AMOUNT OF WATER UNTIL NO LONGER PINK. COOL. CUT EACH BREAST IN HALF HORIZONTALLY AND THEN DICE TO ABOUT ¼" (6 mm). IN MEDIUM BOWL, TOSS CHICKEN, CARROTS AND ONION WITH ENOUGH SAUCE TO COAT. LET STAND FOR 15 MINUTES. ADD NOODLES AND PEANUTS, GENTLY TOSS WITH MORE SAUCE TO COAT.

TO SERVE: SET OUT LETTUCE AND CHICKEN MIXTURE. LET GUESTS WRAP THEIR OWN. SERVE EXTRA SAUCE ON THE SIDE. (PICTURED ON PAGE 70.)

PEANUT-CURRY CHICKEN IN WONTON CUPS

DEE-LISH!!!

12 WONTON WRAPPERS	
OIL	
3 MEDIUM BONELESS, SKINLESS CHICKEN BREASTS	
¼ CUP MANGO CHUTNEY	60 mL
¼ CUP PLUS 2 TBSP. PLAIN YOGURT	90 mL
3 TBSP. CRUNCHY PEANUT BUTTER	45 mL
1 TBSP. FRESH LIME JUICE	15 mL
1 TSP. CURRY PASTE	5 mL
½ TSP. CURRY POWDER	2 mL
CHIVES, CHOPPED	

PREHEAT OVEN TO 325°F (160°C). PLACE WRAPPERS ON CUTTING SURFACE AND BRUSH TOP WITH OIL. CUT INTO 4 SQUARES. USING MINI MUFFIN TINS, PLACE EACH SQUARE, OILED SIDE UP, INTO A MUFFIN CUP, PRESSING INTO PAN TO FORM A CUP. BAKE UNTIL LIGHT BROWN (5-7 MINUTES). COOL AND REMOVE. IN A FRYING PAN, POACH CHICKEN IN WATER WITH A LITTLE SALT UNTIL JUST COOKED THROUGH (DON'T OVERCOOK.!). TRANSFER TO PAPER TOWEL AND COOL. DICE CHICKEN AND SET ASIDE. IN A MEDIUM BOWL, COMBINE CHUTNEY, YOGURT, PEANUT BUTTER, LIME JUICE, CURRY PASTE AND CURRY POWDER. STIR IN CHICKEN AND CHECK SEASONING. PLACE 1 TSP. (5 mL) OF FILLING INTO EACH CUP AND GARNISH WITH CHIVES. MAKES ABOUT 48 HOT AND SPICY BITES.

ASPARAGUS CHICKEN PUFFS

1 LARGE BONELESS CHICKEN BREAST, COOKED & CUBED	
2 TBSP. MAYONNAISE	30 mL
1/2-1 TSP. CURRY POWDER	2-5 mL
SALT & PEPPER TO TASTE	
14 OZ. PKG. PUFF PASTRY	397 g
12 OZ. CAN ASPARAGUS, WELL-DRAINED OR 12 FRESH SMALL ASPARAGUS, BLANCHED	341 mL
1 EGG, BEATEN	
SESAME SEEDS	

IN A FOOD PROCESSOR, PURÉE CHICKEN, MAYONNAISE, CURRY, SALT AND PEPPER UNTIL SMOOTH. ROLL PASTRY INTO RECTANGULAR SHAPE, 10 x 14" (25 x 36 cm). CUT LENGTHWISE INTO 3 EVEN STRIPS. SPREAD CHICKEN MIXTURE ALONG 1 SIDE OF EACH STRIP OF PASTRY. PLACE ASPARAGUS SPEARS LENGTHWISE BESIDE CHICKEN MIXTURE. BRUSH EDGES OF PASTRY WITH EGG. ROLL PASTRY OVER TO CLOSE COMPLETELY. BRUSH TOP WITH EGG, CUT ROLLS DIAGONALLY INTO 1" (2.5 cm) PIECES AND SPRINKLE WITH SESAME SEEDS. PLACE ON GREASED COOKIE SHEET AND BAKE AT 450°F (230°C) FOR 10 MINUTES. LOWER TEMPERATURE TO 350°F (180°C); BAKE FOR ANOTHER 10 MINUTES, OR UNTIL GOLDEN BROWN. MAKES 48 APPETIZERS.

CURRIED SEAFOOD COCKTAIL PUFFS

THESE ELEGANT PUFFS CAN BE MADE AHEAD, FROZEN THEN FILLED AT SERVING TIME.

PUFFS (CHOUX PASTRY)

½ CUP BUTTER	125 mL
1 CUP BOILING WATER	250 mL
1 CUP FLOUR	250 mL
½ TSP. SALT	2 mL
4 EGGS	

SEAFOOD FILLING

7 OZ. CRAB OR SHRIMP	200 g
⅓ CUP MAYONNAISE	75 mL
1 TSP. CURRY POWDER	5 mL
2 TBSP. CHOPPED GREEN ONION	30 mL

PREHEAT OVEN TO 400°F (200°C).

TO MAKE PUFFS: IN A MEDIUM SAUCEPAN, HEAT BUTTER WITH BOILING WATER UNTIL MELTED. TURN HEAT TO LOW, ADD FLOUR AND SALT, STIRRING VIGOROUSLY UNTIL MIXTURE FORMS A SMOOTH BALL. REMOVE FROM HEAT. ADD EGGS 1 AT A TIME, BEATING WELL WITH A SPOON AFTER EACH ADDITION. DROP BY TEASPOONFULS ONTO LIGHTLY GREASED COOKIE SHEET; BAKE 20-25 MINUTES, UNTIL GOLDEN. COOL, CUT IN HALF.

TO MAKE FILLING: MIX FILLING INGREDIENTS TOGETHER. FILL PUFFS, REPLACING TOPS. HEAT BEFORE SERVING. MAKES ABOUT 2 DOZEN.

SMOKED SALMON CHEESECAKE

GREAT FOR A CROWD! THIS FREEZES WELL FOR UP TO 1 MONTH.

BASE

½ CUP FINE, DRY BREAD CRUMBS	125 mL
2 TBSP. BUTTER, MELTED	30 mL
1 TSP. DRIED DILL	5 mL

FILLING

1 TBSP. BUTTER	15 mL
1 SMALL ONION, FINELY CHOPPED	
3-8 OZ. PKGS CREAM CHEESE	3-250 g
3 EGGS	
⅓ CUP LIGHT CREAM	75 mL
½ LB. SMOKED SALMON, CHOPPED	250 g
1 CUP GRATED SWISS CHEESE	250 mL

TO MAKE BASE: COMBINE BREAD CRUMBS, BUTTER AND DILL. PRESS INTO A 9" (23 cm) SPRINGFORM PAN. BAKE AT 350°F (180°C) FOR 5-7 MINUTES, OR UNTIL GOLDEN.

TO MAKE FILLING: MELT BUTTER AND SAUTÉ ONION; COOL. BEAT CREAM CHEESE WITH EGGS AND CREAM. MIX IN SALMON, SWISS CHEESE AND SAUTÉED ONION. POUR FILLING OVER BASE.

BAKE FOR 75 MINUTES AT 350°F (180°C). TURN OVEN OFF AND OPEN DOOR SLIGHTLY. ALLOW PAN TO COOL IN OVEN FOR 1 HOUR. REFRIGERATE AT LEAST 2 HOURS BEFORE REMOVING SIDES AND BOTTOM OF PAN. SERVE AT ROOM TEMPERATURE WITH SMALL BAGELS OR WATER BISCUITS.

SALADS

Grilled Feta with Tomatoes
Layered Mozzarella and Tomato Salad (Caprese)
Watermelon with Feta
Pomegranate & Feta Salad
Spinach Salad with Pears, Brie and Raspberries
Warm Spinach Salad with Apples and Brie
Pear and Stilton Salad
Mixed Greens with Apples and Cider Vinaigrette
Cucumber Fruit Salad
Super Salad
Patrick's Salad
Napa Cabbage Salad
Thai Noodle Salad
Show-Off Tortellini Salad
Asparagus Pasta Salad
Mediterranean Orzo & Vegetable Salad
Chicken Atlanta
Chicken and Mixed Rice Salad
with Orange Vinaigrette
Asian Chicken Salad
Mango and Spicy Shrimp Salad

GRILLED FETA WITH TOMATOES

BUY SOME FRESH TOMATOES AT THE FARMER'S MARKET AND CREATE THIS SUPERB SALAD.

1 LB. MIXTURE OF YELLOW, GREEN & RED TOMATOES	500	g
BUTTER LETTUCE		
1 LB. CHUNK FETA CHEESE	500	g
2 TBSP. EXTRA-VIRGIN OLIVE OIL	30	mL
BUNCH OF FRESH BASIL LEAVES		
¼ CUP EXTRA-VIRGIN OLIVE OIL	60	mL
FRESHLY GROUND PEPPER		

SLICE TOMATOES AND ARRANGE ON SERVING PLATES WITH LETTUCE. CUT FETA INTO 6 EVEN SLICES AND PLACE ON LIGHTLY OILED COOKIE SHEET. DRIZZLE WITH OIL AND HEAT UNDER BROILER UNTIL LIGHTLY BROWNED. PLACE WARM FETA ON TOP OF TOMATOES. CHOP BASIL AND SPRINKLE OVER SALAD. DRIZZLE WITH OIL AND SPRINKLE WITH FRESHLY GROUND PEPPER. SERVES 6.

A NICE BOX OF CHOCOLATES PROVIDES YOUR TOTAL DAILY INTAKE OF CALORIES IN ONE PLACE. ISN'T THAT HANDY?

LAYERED MOZZARELLA AND TOMATO SALAD (CAPRESE)

AN ATTRACTIVE BUFFET PLATTER.

10 ROMA TOMATOES	
2 LBS. BOCCONCINI (FRESH MOZZARELLA)	1 kg
CUT INTO 1/4" (6 mm) SLICES	
1/4 CUP CHOPPED FRESH BASIL	60 mL
1/4 CUP CHOPPED FRESH PARSLEY	60 mL

VINAIGRETTE

3/4 CUP OLIVE OIL	175 mL
1/4 CUP WINE VINEGAR	60 mL
FRESHLY GROUND PEPPER	

ARRANGE SLICED TOMATOES AND CHEESE
ALTERNATELY ON A PLATTER. SPRINKLE WITH
BASIL, PARSLEY AND VINAIGRETTE.

TO MAKE VINAIGRETTE: COMBINE ALL INGREDIENTS.

WATERMELON WITH FETA

QUICK & DELICIOUS

1/2 SMALL RED ONION	
3 CUPS WATERMELON BALLS	750 mL
1/2 CUP CRUMBLED FETA CHEESE	125 mL
BALSAMIC VINEGAR, FOR DRIZZLING	

SLICE ONION INTO THIN RINGS. TO MAKE MELON
BALLS, USE A MELON BALLER; PLACE IN MEDIUM
BOWL. ADD ONION AND FETA CHEESE AND
DRIZZLE WITH BALSAMIC VINEGAR. TOSS GENTLY.
CHILL IN REFRIGERATOR UNTIL READY TO SERVE.

POMEGRANATE AND FETA SALAD

THE POMEGRANATE SEEDS ADD SPARKLE TO THIS SALAD!

1 HEAD ROMAINE LETTUCE, WASHED & TORN
1 BUNCH SPINACH, STEMS REMOVED, WASHED & TORN
SEEDS OF 1 POMEGRANATE OR
     ½ CUP (125 mL) DRIED CRANBERRIES
¼ CUP TOASTED PINE NUTS   60 mL
½ CUP CRUMBLED FETA CHEESE   125 mL

DRESSING

⅓ CUP OLIVE OIL   75 mL
1 TBSP. RED WINE VINEGAR   15 mL
2 TBSP. MAPLE SYRUP   30 mL
1 TSP. DIJON MUSTARD   5 mL
½ TSP. OREGANO   2 mL
SALT & FRESHLY GROUND PEPPER

TOSS LETTUCE AND SPINACH TOGETHER IN A LARGE SALAD BOWL. ADD POMEGRANATE SEEDS, PINE NUTS AND FETA. WHISK DRESSING INGREDIENTS TOGETHER; STORE IN REFRIGERATOR. TOSS WITH SALAD INGREDIENTS JUST BEFORE SERVING. SERVES 6.

I HAVE A DEGREE IN LIBERAL ARTS. DO YOU WANT FRIES WITH THAT?

SPINACH SALAD WITH PEARS, BRIE AND RASPBERRIES

YOUR NEXT FAVORITE SUMMER SALAD.

DRESSING

3 TBSP. RASPBERRY VINEGAR	45 mL
1/3 CUP VEGETABLE OIL	75 mL
1 TBSP. SUGAR	15 mL
1/4 CUP FRESH RASPBERRIES, MASHED	60 mL

SALAD

10 OZ. BAG BABY SPINACH	283 g
2 RIPE PEARS, CORED & THINLY SLICED	
1/2 LB. BRIE CHEESE, ROOM TEMPERATURE, SLICED	250 g

GARNISH

RASPBERRIES
SLIVERED ALMONDS, TOASTED

TO MAKE DRESSING: WHISK INGREDIENTS TOGETHER AND REFRIGERATE UNTIL READY TO SERVE.

WASH SPINACH AND REMOVE ANY LONG STEMS. DIVIDE AMONG 4 PLATES. GARNISH WITH PEARS, CHEESE, RASPBERRIES AND A SPRINKLE OF ALMONDS. DRIZZLE WITH DRESSING. A GREAT ACCOMPANIMENT TO BALSAMIC HONEY TENDERLOIN PAGE 222. SERVES 4.

WARM SPINACH SALAD WITH APPLES AND BRIE

A WINNER!

4 LARGE GRANNY SMITH APPLES	
¼ CUP MAPLE SYRUP	60 mL
8 CUPS WASHED SPINACH LEAVES	2 L
½ LB. BRIE, CUT IN SMALL PIECES	250 g
½ CUP TOASTED PECANS	125 mL

DRESSING

¼ CUP APPLE CIDER OR APPLE JUICE	60 mL
3 TBSP. CIDER VINEGAR	45 mL
1 TSP. DIJON MUSTARD	5 mL
1 GARLIC CLOVE, MINCED	
¼ CUP OLIVE OIL	60 mL
SALT & PEPPER TO TASTE	

PEEL AND CORE APPLES; CUT INTO ½" (1.3 cm) SLICES. ARRANGE ON BAKING SHEET AND BRUSH WITH SYRUP. BROIL UNTIL GOLDEN; TURN, BRUSH SYRUP ON OTHER SIDE AND BROIL. PLACE SPINACH IN A LARGE BOWL. WHISK DRESSING INGREDIENTS TOGETHER IN A SMALL SAUCEPAN AND HEAT UNTIL SIMMERING. POUR OVER SPINACH; TOSS AND ADD CHEESE, APPLES AND NUTS. DEE-LISH!

MY MIND NOT ONLY WANDERS, IT SOMETIMES LEAVES COMPLETELY.

PEAR AND STILTON SALAD

SHOP AHEAD FOR THIS SALAD SO YOU CAN RIPEN THE PEARS!

DRESSING

¼ CUP FRESH LEMON JUICE	60 mL
¼ CUP CANOLA OIL	60 mL
1 TBSP. LIQUID HONEY	15 mL
2 TSP. GRAINY OR DIJON MUSTARD	10 mL

BUTTER LETTUCE	
2 FRESH, RIPE PEARS, CORED & SLICED	
4 OZ. STILTON CHEESE, CRUMBLED, OR	125 g
ASIAGO CHEESE, SHAVED	
¼ CUP FRESH PINE NUTS, TOASTED	60 mL

TO MAKE DRESSING: WHISK INGREDIENTS TOGETHER AND REFRIGERATE UNTIL READY TO SERVE.

PLACE LETTUCE LEAVES ON INDIVIDUAL PLATES. ARRANGE SLICED PEARS ON TOP AND SPRINKLE WITH STILTON AND PINE NUTS.

DRIZZLE DRESSING OVER TOP. A DELICIOUS STARTER SALAD FOR 4.

SEEN UPSIDE DOWN ON A JEEP: IF YOU CAN READ THIS, PLEASE FLIP ME OVER.

MIXED GREENS WITH APPLES AND CIDER VINAIGRETTE

A DELICIOUS SIMPLE SALAD - THIS DRESSING IS ABOUT TO BECOME YOUR NEW HOUSE FAVORITE.

CIDER VINAIGRETTE

¼ CUP APPLE CIDER VINEGAR	60 mL
3 TBSP. MINCED SHALLOTS	45 mL
2 TSP. DIJON MUSTARD	10 mL
2 TSP. HONEY	10 mL
½ CUP LIGHT OLIVE OIL	125 mL

1 CRISP RED-SKINNED APPLE, CORED
     AND THINLY SLICED
MIXED GREENS FOR 6

TO MAKE VINAIGRETTE: WHISK TOGETHER INGREDIENTS AND REFRIGERATE UNTIL READY TO SERVE.

TOSS APPLES AND MIXED GREENS WITH DRESSING, USING JUST ENOUGH TO LIGHTLY COAT GREENS.

THE HARDNESS OF BUTTER IS PROPORTIONAL TO THE SOFTNESS OF THE BREAD.

CUCUMBER FRUIT SALAD

YEAR-ROUND PARTNER FOR CHICKEN OR FISH.

½ CUP SOUR CREAM	125 mL
1 TBSP. SUGAR	15 mL
1 MEDIUM ENGLISH CUCUMBER, PEELED & DICED	
1 GRANNY SMITH APPLE, CHOPPED	
1 CUP SEEDLESS GREEN GRAPES, CUT IN HALF	250 mL
1 CUP SEEDLESS RED GRAPES, CUT IN HALF	250 mL
1 TSP. FRESH PARSLEY, MINCED	5 mL
½ CUP WALNUTS, CHOPPED	125 mL

IN A MEDIUM BOWL, COMBINE SOUR CREAM AND SUGAR. ADD REMAINING INGREDIENTS AND MIX THOROUGHLY. REFRIGERATE.

TYPICAL SYMPTOMS OF STRESS: EATING TOO MUCH, IMPULSE BUYING AND DRIVING TOO FAST. ARE YOU KIDDING? THAT'S MY IDEA OF A PERFECT DAY!

SUPER SALAD

GREAT FOR BUFFETS AND BARBECUES.

1 HEAD ROMAINE LETTUCE	
1 HEAD BUTTER LETTUCE	
1 HEAD ICEBERG LETTUCE	
1/2 CUP GRATED PARMESAN CHEESE	125 mL
2 OZ. BLUE CHEESE, CRUMBLED	55 g
3 AVOCADOS, PEELED & SLICED	
1 LARGE CUCUMBER, PEELED & DICED	
1 1/2 CUPS CHERRY TOMATOES, HALVED	375 mL
6 SLICES OF BACON, COOKED CRISP & CRUMBLED	
1 RED PEPPER, SLICED	
1 GREEN PEPPER, SLICED	
1/2 CUP SLICED RIPE OLIVES	125 mL
8 OZ. BOTTLE ITALIAN DRESSING	250 mL
FRESH PARSLEY, CHOPPED	

WASH, DRY AND TEAR SALAD GREENS INTO A
LARGE SALAD BOWL. SPRINKLE WITH CHEESES.
ARRANGE REMAINING INGREDIENTS ON TOP, TOSS
WITH DRESSING AND SPRINKLE WITH PARSLEY.
SERVES 12-14.

THE BEST WAY TO FORGET ALL YOUR TROUBLES IS TO
WEAR TIGHT SHOES.

PATRICK'S SALAD

GOES WITH EVERYTHING - THANKS PATRICK!

DRESSING

½ CUP OLIVE OIL	125 mL
¼ CUP VINEGAR (RED OR WHITE WINE)	60 mL
JUICE OF HALF A SMALL LIME	
2 TSP. SOY SAUCE	10 mL
PINCH OF CAYENNE PEPPER	
1 LARGE GARLIC CLOVE, MINCED	
SALT & PEPPER TO TASTE	
3 TBSP. CHOPPED FRESH PARSLEY	45 mL
2 TBSP. MINCED RED ONION	30 mL
3-4 TBSP. SUGAR	45-60 mL

SALAD

ROMAINE LETTUCE
1 LARGE RED PEPPER
SNOW PEAS
SLIVERED ALMONDS, TOASTED

TO MAKE DRESSING: COMBINE INGREDIENTS IN A BLENDER AND BLEND WELL. POUR INTO A JAR AND REFRIGERATE.

WASH AND TEAR ROMAINE INTO BITE-SIZED PIECES. CUT RED PEPPER AND PEA PODS INTO LONG STRIPS. ADD TOASTED ALMONDS. TOSS WITH DRESSING JUST BEFORE SERVING.

NAPA CABBAGE SALAD

ALWAYS A HIT AT PICNICS, BUFFETS - AND
THE FAMILY BUN FIGHT!

1 LARGE NAPA CABBAGE (SUEY CHOY), CHOPPED	
2 BUNCHES GREEN ONIONS, CHOPPED	
1 RED BELL PEPPER, SEEDED & DICED	
1/4 CUP BUTTER	60 mL
1 CUP SLIVERED ALMONDS	250 mL
2 PKGS. CHICKEN-FLAVORED ORIENTAL SOUP NOODLES WITH SEASONING MIX	

DRESSING

1 CUP VEGETABLE OIL	250 mL
1/2 CUP RED WINE VINEGAR	125 mL
2 GARLIC CLOVES, MINCED	
2 TSP. SOY SAUCE	10 mL
1/3 CUP SUGAR	75 mL

PLACE CABBAGE, GREEN ONIONS AND RED
PEPPER IN LARGE SALAD BOWL. MELT BUTTER IN
FRYING PAN AND SAUTÉ ALMONDS, BROKEN
NOODLES AND SEASONINGS UNTIL GOLDEN. ADD
TO CABBAGE MIXTURE AND TOSS. SHAKE
DRESSING INGREDIENTS IN A JAR. POUR OVER
SALAD AND TOSS AT LEAST 1/2 HOUR BEFORE
SERVING. YOU WILL HAVE EXTRA DRESSING,
REFRIGERATE AND USE AGAIN. SERVES 10-12.

THAI NOODLE SALAD

SERVE WITH THAI GRILLED CHICKEN PAGE 197.

VINAIGRETTE

1/4 CUP FRESH LIME JUICE	60 mL
3 TBSP. VEGETABLE OIL	45 mL
3 TBSP. SOY SAUCE	45 mL
2 TBSP. BROWN SUGAR	30 mL
1 TBSP. SESAME OIL	15 mL
1 TBSP. MINCED GARLIC	15 mL
1 TBSP. GRATED ORANGE OR LIME ZEST	15 mL
1 TBSP. MINCED JALAPEÑO PEPPER	15 mL
SALT & PEPPER TO TASTE	

1/2 LB. GREEN BEANS OR ASPARAGUS SPEARS, TRIMMED	250	g
8 OZ. CHINESE EGG NOODLES, FRESH OR DRIED	250	g
2 CUPS PEELED, SHREDDED CARROTS	500 mL	
1/2 CUP SLIVERED RED PEPPER	125 mL	
1 CUP THINLY SLICED GREEN ONIONS	250 mL	

TO MAKE VINAIGRETTE: WHISK INGREDIENTS TOGETHER AND SET ASIDE. CUT GREEN BEANS OR ASPARAGUS DIAGONALLY INTO 1/2" (1.3 cm) PIECES. COOK IN BOILING WATER UNTIL TENDER-CRISP. PLUNGE INTO COLD WATER (TO RETAIN COLOR); DRAIN AND SET ASIDE. COOK NOODLES ACCORDING TO PACKAGE DIRECTIONS. DRAIN. TOSS NOODLES WITH VEGETABLES AND VINAIGRETTE. COVER AND REFRIGERATE AT LEAST 2 HOURS OR OVERNIGHT. GARNISH WITH GREEN ONIONS BEFORE SERVING. SERVES 6.

— SHOW-OFF TORTELLINI SALAD —

YOU'LL BE A HIT AT THE NEXT POTLUCK. HOPE THE OTHER PEOPLE BRING THEIR SHARE.

12 OZ. PKG. HERB TORTELLINI WITH CHEESE	340	g
12 OZ. PKG. SPINACH TORTELLINI WITH CHEESE	340	g
2 CUPS BROCCOLI FLORETS	500	mL
14 OZ. CAN ARTICHOKE HEARTS, QUARTERED	398	mL
12 OZ. PITTED BLACK OLIVES, SLICED	341	mL
1 LB. SHRIMP, COOKED & TAILS REMOVED	500	g
16 OZ. BOTTLE GOLDEN CAESAR DRESSING OR SPICY ITALIAN DRESSING	455	mL
2 CUPS HALVED CHERRY TOMATOES	500	mL
1 CUP FRESHLY GRATED PARMESAN CHEESE	250	mL

COOK TORTELLINI ACCORDING TO PACKAGE DIRECTIONS. DRAIN WELL. IN A LARGE BOWL, TOSS TORTELLINI, BROCCOLI, ARTICHOKES, OLIVES AND SHRIMP WITH DRESSING. MARINATE OVERNIGHT IN REFRIGERATOR. PRIOR TO SERVING, TOSS WITH TOMATOES AND PARMESAN CHEESE. SERVES 8.

THE FOUR BASIC FOOD GROUPS: CANNED, FROZEN, CARRY-OUT AND DELIVERED.

Mediterranean Orzo and Vegetable Salad, page 106

Asian Chicken Salad, page 112

ASPARAGUS PASTA SALAD

A TASTY AND ATTRACTIVE LUNCHEON, SPRINGTIME PICNIC OR BUFFET DISH!

DRESSING

1 GARLIC CLOVE, MINCED	
2 ANCHOVY FILLETS, RINSED	
2 TSP. DIJON MUSTARD	10 mL
½ TSP. SALT	2 mL
½ TSP. GROUND PEPPER	2 mL
½ TSP. WORCESTERSHIRE SAUCE	2 mL
1 EGG YOLK	
2 TBSP. FRESH LEMON JUICE	30 mL
1 TBSP. WHITE WINE VINEGAR	15 mL
½ CUP OLIVE OIL	125 mL
¼ CUP GRATED PARMESAN CHEESE	60 mL

SALAD

2 CUPS SMALL PASTA SHELLS, COOKED, DRAINED & COOLED	500 mL
1 LB. ASPARAGUS, CUT INTO 2" (5 cm) PIECES, COOKED TENDER-CRISP & COOLED	500 g
1 MEDIUM RED PEPPER, CHOPPED	
1 CUP SLICED MUSHROOMS	250 mL
1 CUP SLICED GREEN ONION	250 mL
¼ CUP CHOPPED PARSLEY	60 mL
2 TBSP. CHOPPED FRESH BASIL	30 mL
2 TBSP. SLIVERED ALMONDS	30 mL

TO MAKE DRESSING: PLACE ALL INGREDIENTS IN BLENDER AND BLEND WELL. ASSEMBLE SALAD INGREDIENTS IN A LARGE BOWL, TOSS WITH DRESSING AND REFRIGERATE AT LEAST 1 HOUR BEFORE SERVING. SERVES 6.

MEDITERRANEAN ORZO AND VEGETABLE SALAD

THIS IS GREAT WITH GRILLED LAMB OR CHICKEN.

1 CUP UNCOOKED ORZO	250 mL
12 ASPARAGUS SPEARS, CHOPPED IN 1-2" (2.5-5 cm) PIECES	

DRESSING

3 TBSP. WHITE WINE VINEGAR	45 mL
1 TBSP. GRAINY DIJON MUSTARD	15 mL
1 TBSP. MAPLE SYRUP OR HONEY	15 mL
2 TBSP. COARSELY CHOPPED FRESH DILL	30 mL
1 TSP. FINELY CHOPPED CAPERS	5 mL
1 GARLIC CLOVE, PEELED & SLICED	
SALT & PEPPER TO TASTE	
1/3 CUP EXTRA-VIRGIN OLIVE OIL	75 mL

1 CUP HALVED RED CHERRY OR GRAPE TOMATOES	250 mL
1/4 CUP PITTED & COARSELY CHOPPED KALAMATA OLIVES	60 mL
1 TBSP. TOASTED PINE NUTS	15 mL

BRING A MEDIUM-LARGE POT OF SALTED WATER TO A BOIL AND ADD ORZO. COOK ORZO FOR ABOUT 10 MINUTES, UNTIL AL DENTE, ADDING ASPARAGUS TO POT DURING LAST 2 MINUTES. DRAIN ORZO AND ASPARAGUS IN COLANDER, RINSE WITH COLD WATER AND SET ASIDE.

MEDITERRANEAN ORZO AND VEGETABLE SALAD

CONTINUED FROM PAGE 106.

TO MAKE DRESSING: IN BLENDER OR FOOD PROCESSOR, COMBINE VINEGAR, MUSTARD, MAPLE SYRUP, DILL, CHOPPED CAPERS, GARLIC, SALT AND PEPPER. SLOWLY ADD OIL AND CONTINUE TO BLEND UNTIL MIXTURE EMULSIFIES.

PLACE ORZO AND ASPARAGUS IN A LARGE BOWL AND TOSS WITH DRESSING. REFRIGERATE, COVERED, FOR 1 HOUR. REMOVE SALAD FROM REFRIGERATOR 30 MINUTES BEFORE SERVING AND GENTLY TOSS IN TOMATOES, OLIVES AND PINE NUTS. SERVES 4-6. (PICTURED ON PAGE 103.)

HUSBAND: WHAT'S FOR DINNER?

WIFE STANDING IN FRONT OF THE FREEZER: THAT DEPENDS. WILL YOU BE HUNGRY IN 10-12 MINUTES OR 18-20 MINUTES?

CHICKEN ATLANTA

We were gifted with this recipe while on a promotional trip to Atlanta. Mint Juleps, anyone?

ORANGE SOUFFLÉ

2-¼ oz. envelopes (1 Tbsp./15 mL each) gelatin	2-7 g
2 cups sugar	500 mL
Dash of salt	
4 egg yolks	
2½ cups orange juice, divided	625 mL
1½ tsp. grated orange zest	5 mL
1 tsp. grated lemon zest	5 mL
3 Tbsp. lemon juice	45 mL
1 cup halved orange sections	250 mL
2 cups whipping cream, whipped	500 mL

CHICKEN SALAD

1 cup mayonnaise	250 mL
Dash of white vinegar	
½ cup whipping cream, whipped	125 mL
Salt & pepper to taste	
3 cups diced cooked chicken breast or turkey	750 mL
½ cup diced celery	125 mL
½ cup slivered almonds, toasted	125 mL

To make soufflé: Mix gelatin, sugar and salt in a saucepan. Beat together egg yolks and 1 cup (250 mL) of orange juice. Stir into gelatin mixture; cook over medium heat, stirring constantly, until mixture comes to a boil. Remove from heat and stir

CHICKEN ATLANTA

CONTINUED FROM PAGE 108.

IN ORANGE AND LEMON ZEST AND REMAINING JUICES. CHILL, STIRRING OCCASIONALLY, UNTIL MIXTURE MOUNDS WHEN DROPPED FROM A SPOON. STIR IN ORANGE SECTIONS. FOLD IN WHIPPED CREAM AND POUR INTO A 2-QUART (2 L) RING MOLD. COVER AND CHILL OVERNIGHT.

TO MAKE SALAD: COMBINE MAYONNAISE AND VINEGAR. FOLD IN WHIPPED CREAM, SALT AND PEPPER. ADD CHICKEN AND CELERY. REFRIGERATE UNTIL READY TO ASSEMBLE.

TO SERVE: UNMOLD SOUFFLÉ ONTO A GLASS PLATE AND MOUND CHICKEN IN CENTER. GARNISH WITH ALMONDS. SERVES 8.

HUSBAND PACKING LUNCHBOX FOR 6 YEAR OLD: "WHAT ELSE SHOULD I PUT IN?"
WIFE: "WHAT WOULD YOU PUT IN IF I WASN'T HERE?"
HUSBAND: "FIVE DOLLARS."

CHICKEN AND MIXED RICE SALAD WITH ORANGE VINAIGRETTE

SALAD

4 CUPS CHICKEN BROTH	1 L
1 CUP WILD RICE, UNCOOKED	250 mL
1 CUP LONG-GRAIN BROWN RICE, UNCOOKED	250 mL
4 CHICKEN BREAST HALVES, COOKED & CUBED	
1 CUP PECANS, TOASTED	250 mL
3 GREEN ONIONS, SLICED	
½ CUP GOLDEN RAISINS	125 mL
½ CUP CHOPPED CELERY	125 mL
2 TSP. GRATED ORANGE ZEST	10 mL

ORANGE VINAIGRETTE

¼ CUP RICE WINE VINEGAR	60 mL
¼ CUP ORANGE JUICE, FRESHLY SQUEEZED	60 mL
2 TBSP. DIJON MUSTARD	30 mL
2 TBSP. MANGO CHUTNEY	30 mL
½ TSP. SALT	2 mL
¼ TSP. WHITE PEPPER	1 mL
½ CUP CANOLA OR VEGETABLE OIL	125 mL

GARNISH

2 TBSP. FRESH CHIVES, MINCED	30 mL

TO MAKE SALAD: IN A LARGE SAUCEPAN, BRING CHICKEN BROTH TO A BOIL. STIR IN WILD RICE AND SIMMER, COVERED, FOR 10 MINUTES. ADD BROWN RICE; SIMMER MIXTURE, COVERED, FOR 30-35 MINUTES, UNTIL LIQUID IS ABSORBED. REMOVE FROM HEAT, COOL TO ROOM TEMPERATURE.

CHICKEN AND MIXED RICE SALAD WITH ORANGE VINAIGRETTE

CONTINUED FROM PAGE 110.

IN A LARGE BOWL: COMBINE RICE, CHICKEN, PECANS, GREEN ONIONS, RAISINS, CELERY AND ORANGE ZEST.

TO MAKE VINAIGRETTE: IN A SMALL BOWL, COMBINE VINEGAR, ORANGE JUICE, MUSTARD, CHUTNEY, SALT AND PEPPER. ADD OIL IN A SLOW, STEADY STREAM, WHISKING CONSTANTLY, UNTIL SLIGHTLY THICKENED AND THOROUGHLY COMBINED. ADD TO RICE MIXTURE, TOSSING GENTLY TO MIX. SPRINKLE WITH CHIVES AND SERVE AT ROOM TEMPERATURE.

EMPLOYEE: THE AMOUNT OF MY PAYCHECK SEEMS LOWER THAN USUAL.

BOSS: IT'S NOT AS LOW AS IT SEEMS - I'VE JUST STARTED PAYING YOU IN CENTIGRADE.

ASIAN CHICKEN SALAD

IT'S A HOT SUMMER'S NIGHT AND DINNER'S READY!

DRESSING

½ CUP OLIVE OIL	125 mL
2 TBSP. APPLE CIDER VINEGAR	30 mL
2-3 TBSP. SOY SAUCE	30-45 mL
1½ TBSP. DARK SESAME OIL	22 mL
½ TBSP. HONEY	7 mL
1 GARLIC CLOVE, MINCED	
½ TSP. MINCED FRESH GINGER	2 mL
2 TSP. SALT (SEA SALT IF POSSIBLE)	10 mL
GROUND PEPPER TO TASTE	
2 TBSP. SESAME SEEDS, TOASTED	30 mL

SALAD

4 CHICKEN BREAST HALVES	
SALT & PEPPER TO TASTE	
12 ASPARAGUS SPEARS	
1 RED PEPPER, CHOPPED	
2 CUPS SUGAR SNAP PEAS,	500 mL
2 GREEN ONIONS, CUT DIAGONALLY INTO ½" (1.3 cm) PIECES	
1 TBSP. SESAME SEEDS, TOASTED	15 mL

TO MAKE DRESSING: IN A SCREW-TOP JAR, COMBINE ALL INGREDIENTS. SHAKE VIGOROUSLY.

AH, THE PRAIRIES. . . WHERE YOU CAN WATCH YOUR DOG RUN AWAY FOR A WEEK.

ASIAN CHICKEN SALAD

CONTINUED FROM PAGE 112.

TO MAKE SALAD: SALT AND PEPPER CHICKEN AND SAUTÉ UNTIL NO LONGER PINK. (DO NOT OVER COOK.) COOL CHICKEN AND CUT INTO CUBES. BLANCH ASPARAGUS FOR 2 MINUTES AND RUN UNDER COLD WATER. CUT EACH SPEAR DIAGONALLY INTO 1" (2.5 cm) PIECES. IN A LARGE BOWL, COMBINE CHICKEN, ASPARAGUS, RED PEPPERS, PEAS, GREEN ONIONS AND SESAME SEEDS. POUR DRESSING OVER SALAD AND TOSS. SERVE WITH PITA CRISPS ON PAGE 14.

VARIATION: ADD SOME COOKED RICE VERMICELLI. (PICTURED ON PAGE 104.)

TEACHER: GIVE ME A SENTENCE USING THE TERM "CAESARIAN SECTION".

CHILD: THE CAESARIAN SECTION IS A DISTRICT IN ROME.

MANGO AND SPICY SHRIMP SALAD

AN ELEGANT STARTER OR MAIN-COURSE SALAD.

HONEY-CHIVE SALAD DRESSING

1 EGG YOLK	
2 TBSP. WHITE WINE VINEGAR	30 mL
1 TSP. FRESH LEMON JUICE	5 mL
1¼ CUPS CANOLA OIL	300 mL
3 TBSP. SNIPPED FRESH CHIVES	45 mL
1 TBSP. MINCED FRESH PARSLEY	15 mL
1 TBSP. LIQUID HONEY	15 mL
1 GARLIC CLOVE, MINCED	
PINCH OF SALT	

3 MANGOES, PEELED & SLICED	
JUICE OF 1 LIME	
24 LARGE, RAW SHRIMP, PEELED & DEVEINED	
1 TBSP. CAJUN SEASONING	15 mL
1 TBSP. CANOLA OIL	15 mL
1 MEDIUM JICAMA, PEELED & SLICED	
¼ ENGLISH CUCUMBER, PEELED & CUT IN STRIPS	
2 RADISHES, THINLY SLICED	
1 PKG. MIXED LETTUCE	

TO MAKE DRESSING: WHISK EGG YOLK, GRADUALLY ADDING VINEGAR AND LEMON JUICE. WHISK IN OIL. ADD REMAINING INGREDIENTS, SHAKE WELL AND REFRIGERATE. TOSS MANGO WITH LIME JUICE. COAT SHRIMP WITH CAJUN SEASONING AND QUICKLY PAN-FRY IN OIL UNTIL JUST COOKED (PINK). DIVIDE LETTUCE AMONG 6 PLATES. ARRANGE MANGO AND VEGETABLES ON LETTUCE. DRIZZLE WITH HONEY-CHIVE DRESSING AND PLACE SHRIMP ON EACH SALAD. SERVES 6.

SOUPS

Avocado Soup with Tomato-Cucumber Salsa
Pear & Watercress Soup
Forest Mushroom Chowder
Tomato Basil Soup
Cream of Tomato Soup
Cheddar Cheese Soup
Broccoli Soup
Carrot Fennel Soup with Maple Crème Fraîche
Roasted Squash Soup with Apple and Brie
Red Lentil Soup
Garlicky Tortellini, Spinach and Tomato Soup
Baked Potato and Leek Soup with
Cheddar and Bacon
Zuppa Du Jour
Crab and Corn Chowder
Chicken, Apple and Curry Soup
Turkey Soup
Beef and Barley Soup

AVOCADO SOUP WITH TOMATO-CUCUMBER SALSA

An ideal summer soup that doesn't require cooking.

SOUP

2 large ripe avocados	
3 cups chicken broth	750 mL
2 tbsp. plus 1 tsp. fresh lemon juice	35 mL
2 tbsp. finely chopped fresh chives	30 mL
½ tsp. chili powder	2 mL
salt to taste	
¼ cup sour cream	60 mL

To make soup: Peel avocados and cut into large pieces. Place in a food processor or blender with a small amount of broth. Process until smooth. Add remaining broth, lemon juice, chives, chili powder and salt to taste and process until smooth. Cover and refrigerate until chilled, at least 4 hours or overnight.

To serve: Ladle soup into bowls and garnish with a dollop of sour cream and tomato-cucumber salsa (see opposite page). Serves 4.

TOMATO-CUCUMBER SALSA

2 LARGE TOMATOES, PEELED, SEEDED
     & FINELY CHOPPED

½ CUP PEELED, SEEDED & FINELY   125 mL
     CHOPPED ENGLISH CUCUMBER

1 MEDIUM JALAPEÑO CHILI, SEEDED
     & FINELY CHOPPED*

1 TBSP. FINELY CHOPPED FRESH   15 mL
     CILANTRO

1 TBSP. FRESH LEMON JUICE   15 mL

1 MEDIUM GARLIC CLOVE, MINCED

SALT TO TASTE

TO MAKE SALSA: COMBINE INGREDIENTS IN A
MEDIUM BOWL AND MIX WELL. TASTE FOR
SEASONING. COVER AND REFRIGERATE. THIS CAN
BE PREPARED 3 DAYS IN ADVANCE.

*REMEMBER TO WEAR RUBBER GLOVES WHEN
DEALING WITH JALAPEÑO CHILIES.

A LOT OF MONEY IS TAINTED - IT TAINT YOURS AND
IT TAINT MINE.

PEAR AND WATERCRESS SOUP

DELICIOUS HOT OR COLD.

3 TBSP. BUTTER	45 mL
2 MEDIUM POTATOES, PEELED & CUBED	
4 GREEN ONIONS, SLICED	
14 OZ. CAN PEARS, DRAINED &	398 mL
COARSELY CHOPPED, RESERVE JUICE	
2 TSP. GRATED LEMON ZEST	10 mL
½ TSP. DRIED TARRAGON	2 mL
2 CUPS CHICKEN BROTH	500 mL
1 BUNCH WATERCRESS, COARSELY	
CHOPPED, ENDS REMOVED	
½ CUP LIGHT CREAM	125 mL
SALT & FRESHLY GROUND PEPPER	
WATERCRESS OR GREEN ONIONS,	
FINELY SLIVERED FOR GARNISH	

IN A SAUCEPAN OVER MEDIUM HEAT, MELT BUTTER. ADD POTATOES AND COOK 5-8 MINUTES, STIRRING FREQUENTLY. ADD GREEN ONIONS, PEARS, LEMON ZEST AND TARRAGON. STIR, COVER AND SIMMER 3-5 MINUTES. CAREFULLY POUR IN BROTH AND RESERVED PEAR JUICE. BRING SOUP JUST TO A BOIL AND ADD WATERCRESS. COVER AND REDUCE HEAT. SIMMER UNTIL POTATOES ARE TENDER AND WATERCRESS IS SLIGHTLY WILTED. REMOVE SOUP FROM HEAT. PURÉE SOUP IN BLENDER IN SMALL BATCHES. RETURN SOUP TO SAUCEPAN AND SLOWLY STIR IN CREAM. HEAT OVER MEDIUM-LOW HEAT UNTIL WARMED THROUGH. SEASON AND GARNISH. SERVES 4-6.

FOREST MUSHROOM CHOWDER

A soup made with care is a delight to the soul. (So there!)

2 TBSP. VEGETABLE OIL	30 mL
1 GARLIC CLOVE, MINCED	
½ CUP SLICED ONIONS	125 mL
½ CUP DICED CARROTS	125 mL
3 CUPS SLICED WILD MUSHROOMS	750 mL
(CHANTERELLE, MOREL,	
SHIITAKE, OYSTER)	
3 CUPS CHICKEN BROTH	750 mL
2 CUPS WHIPPING CREAM	500 mL
¼ CUP DICED POTATOES	60 mL
¼ CUP FROZEN CORN NIBLETS	60 mL
½ APPLE, PEELED & DICED	
2 BAY LEAVES	
3 TBSP. SHERRY	45 mL
2 TBSP. CHOPPED PARSLEY	30 mL
SALT & FRESHLY GROUND PEPPER	

IN LARGE SAUCEPAN OR DUTCH OVEN, HEAT OIL AND SAUTÉ GARLIC, ONIONS, CARROTS AND MUSHROOMS. DO NOT BROWN.

ADD BROTH AND CREAM TO VEGETABLE MIXTURE. BRING TO A BOIL AND REDUCE HEAT TO SIMMER.

ADD POTATOES, CORN, APPLE, BAY LEAVES, SHERRY AND PARSLEY TO SOUP. SIMMER ABOUT ½ HOUR. REMOVE BAY LEAVES AND SEASON WITH SALT AND PEPPER. SERVES 6.

TOMATO BASIL SOUP

SIMPLE, QUICK, DELICIOUS AND LOADED WITH NUTRITION.

2 TBSP. BUTTER	30 mL
1 CARROT, CHOPPED	
1 LARGE ONION, CHOPPED	
5 LARGE TOMATOES, CHOPPED	
¾ TSP. SUGAR	3 mL
2 CUPS CHICKEN BROTH	500 mL
1 CUP CHOPPED FRESH BASIL	250 mL
SALT & PEPPER TO TASTE	

MELT BUTTER IN A LARGE FRYING PAN AND SAUTÉ CARROT AND ONION. ADD TOMATOES, SUGAR AND BROTH. SIMMER FOR 15 MINUTES. PROCESS BASIL IN FOOD PROCESSOR, ADD BROTH AND PROCESS AGAIN. ADD SALT AND PEPPER AND REHEAT FOR SERVING. SPRINKLE WITH GARLIC CROÛTONS, IF YOU'RE NOT ON THE SOUTH BEACH DIET!

GARLIC CROÛTONS

1 LOAF DAY-OLD SOURDOUGH BREAD	
¼ CUP OLIVE OIL	60 mL
1 TSP. GARLIC POWDER	5 mL
1 TSP. CRUSHED DRIED PARSLEY	5 mL
¾ TSP. PAPRIKA	3 mL
SALT & PEPPER	

CUT BREAD INTO ½" (1.3 cm) CUBES. COMBINE OIL, GARLIC POWDER, PARSLEY, PAPRIKA, SALT AND PEPPER. WORK GARLIC-OIL MIXTURE INTO BREAD. SPREAD CUBES IN SHALLOW PAN AND BAKE AT 325°F (160°C) FOR 25 MINUTES.

CREAM OF TOMATO SOUP

THIS IS SO DARN GOOD, YOU'LL WISH YOU'D DOUBLED THE RECIPE!

2-19 OZ. CANS TOMATOES	2-540 mL
1 LARGE ONION, FINELY CHOPPED	
1 CUP CHOPPED CELERY	250 mL
10 OZ. CAN CHICKEN BROTH	284 mL
½ CUP SPICY CLAMATO JUICE	125 mL
1 TSP. DILL	5 mL
¼ CUP BUTTER	60 mL
½ CUP FLOUR	125 mL
4 CUPS MILK	1 L
1 CUP CHEESE WHIZ	250 mL
CHOPPED PARSLEY FOR GARNISH	

SIMMER TOMATOES, ONION, CELERY, BROTH, CLAMATO JUICE AND DILL UNTIL VEGGIES ARE COOKED, ABOUT 20 MINUTES. PURÉE IN BLENDER IF SMOOTH CONSISTENCY IS DESIRED. IN A MEDIUM-SIZED PAN, MELT BUTTER AND BLEND IN FLOUR TO MAKE A PASTE. ADD MILK SLOWLY, STIRRING CONSTANTLY, TO MAKE A THICK WHITE SAUCE. STIR IN TOMATO SOUP. FOLD IN CHEESE WHIZ AND GARNISH WITH PARSLEY. SERVES 4-6.

IN MY DAY, WE DIDN'T NEED ALL THIS THERAPY. WE HAD A LITTLE THING CALLED THE MARTINI.

CHEDDAR CHEESE SOUP

BEST SERVED THE DAY IT'S MADE.

2 TBSP. BUTTER	30 mL
½ LARGE RED PEPPER, CUT INTO MATCHSTICKS	
½ LARGE YELLOW PEPPER, CUT INTO MATCHSTICKS	
¾ CUP CHOPPED ONION	175 mL
2 GARLIC CLOVES, MINCED	
¼ CUP FLOUR	60 mL
1½ CUPS CHICKEN BROTH	375 mL
1 CUP WHOLE MILK	250 mL
1 CUP WHIPPING CREAM	250 mL
2 CUPS GRATED SHARP WHITE CHEDDAR CHEESE	500 mL
SALT & PEPPER TO TASTE	

IN HEAVY LARGE POT OVER MEDIUM HEAT, MELT BUTTER. ADD PEPPERS, ONION AND GARLIC AND SAUTÉ UNTIL TENDER. ADD FLOUR AND STIR FOR 2 MINUTES. WHISK IN BROTH, THEN MILK AND CREAM. SIMMER UNTIL SLIGHTLY THICKENED, STIRRING CONSTANTLY. GRADUALLY ADD CHEESE ½ CUP (125 mL) AT A TIME, STIRRING AFTER EACH ADDITION UNTIL MELTED AND SMOOTH. ADD SALT AND PEPPER. SERVES 4-6.

TEACHER: HOW CAN YOU DELAY MILK TURNING SOUR?
CHILD: KEEP IT IN THE COW.

BROCCOLI SOUP

OK - IT'S THE MIDDLE OF WINTER AND YOU HAVE NOTHING PLANNED FOR DINNER. TRY THIS!

6 CUPS CHOPPED BROCCOLI FLORETS	1.5 L
1/4 CUP FINELY CHOPPED ONION	60 mL
2 CUPS CHICKEN BROTH	500 mL
2 TBSP. BUTTER	30 mL
1 TBSP. FLOUR	15 mL
1 TSP. SALT	5 mL
PEPPER TO TASTE	
PINCH OF MACE	
2 CUPS HALF & HALF CREAM	500 mL
2 CUPS GRATED CHEDDAR CHEESE (OPTIONAL)	500 mL

IN A LARGE SAUCEPAN, COMBINE BROCCOLI WITH ONION AND BROTH. BRING TO A BOIL, REDUCE HEAT AND SIMMER FOR 10 MINUTES. BLENDERIZE FOR A SMOOTH CONSISTENCY. IN A LARGE SAUCEPAN, MELT BUTTER, ADD FLOUR, SALT, PEPPER AND MACE. SLOWLY ADD CREAM AND STIR UNTIL SMOOTH. ADD BROCCOLI AND CHEESE, IF USING, AND WARM UNTIL CHEESE IS MELTED. SERVES 4-6.

I GAVE HIM THE SKINNIEST YEARS OF MY LIFE.

CARROT FENNEL SOUP WITH MAPLE CRÈME FRAÎCHE

FENNEL - AN INSPIRED CHOICE.

SOUP

3 TBSP. OLIVE OIL	45 mL
1 MEDIUM RED ONION, DICED	
2 SMALL FENNEL BULBS, TRIMMED & CHOPPED	
5 MEDIUM CARROTS, PEELED, CHOPPED	
1/4 CUP CHOPPED FRESH DILL	60 mL
8 CUPS CHICKEN BROTH	2 L
SALT & PEPPER TO TASTE	

MAPLE CRÈME FRAÎCHE

1/3 CUP SOUR CREAM	75 mL
1 TSP. MAPLE SYRUP	5 mL

GARNISH

FRESH DILL SPRIGS

TO MAKE SOUP: HEAT OIL IN A MEDIUM SAUCEPAN, SAUTÉ ONION AND FENNEL FOR 2-3 MINUTES. ADD CARROTS AND SAUTÉ ANOTHER 2-3 MINUTES. ADD DILL AND BROTH; BRING TO A BOIL. SIMMER 10-12 MINUTES, UNTIL CARROTS ARE TENDER. SEASON WITH SALT AND PEPPER. PURÉE SOUP UNTIL SMOOTH, ADDING MORE BROTH IF IT'S TOO THICK.

TO MAKE CRÈME FRAÎCHE WHISK SOUR CREAM AND MAPLE SYRUP TOGETHER IN A SMALL BOWL; SET ASIDE. SERVE SOUP WITH A DOLLOP OF CRÈME FRAÎCHE AND A DILL SPRIG. SERVES 6-8.

ROASTED SQUASH SOUP
WITH APPLE AND BRIE

1 LARGE BUTTERNUT SQUASH	
1 CARROT	
1 MEDIUM ONION	
1 LEEK, WHITE PORTION ONLY	
2 TBSP. BUTTER	30 mL
8 CUPS CHICKEN BROTH	2 L
1 APPLE, PEELED & CHOPPED	
1 BAY LEAF	
1 TSP. SUGAR	5 mL
SALT & FRESHLY GROUND PEPPER	
8 OZ. BRIE CHEESE	250 g
SNIPPED CHIVES	

CUT SQUASH IN HALF LENGTHWISE AND REMOVE SEEDS. PLACE CUT-SIDE DOWN ON PAN AND BAKE AT 350°F (180°C) UNTIL TENDER, ABOUT 45 MINUTES (OR MICROWAVE CUT-SIDE DOWN IN A SMALL AMOUNT OF WATER, COVERED, ABOUT 10 MINUTES). CHOP CARROT, ONION AND LEEK INTO 1" (2.5 cm) PIECES AND PLACE IN A LARGE POT. GENTLY SAUTÉ IN BUTTER. DO NOT BROWN. ADD COOKED SQUASH TO VEGETABLES. ADD BROTH AND BRING TO A BOIL. ADD APPLE, BAY LEAF AND SUGAR. SIMMER, UNCOVERED, FOR 40 MINUTES. REMOVE BAY LEAF AND PURÉE SOUP IN BATCHES. SEASON WITH SALT AND PEPPER TO TASTE. SLICE OFF RIND OF BRIE AND CUT BRIE INTO ½" (1.3 cm) PIECES. PLACE CHEESE IN BOTTOM OF SOUP BOWLS AND FILL WITH HOT SOUP. GARNISH WITH CHIVES. SERVES 6-8.

RED LENTIL SOUP

THIS VARIATION OF LENTIL SOUP IS LIGHT, BRIGHT AND PACKED WITH FRESH VEGETABLES.

1½ TBSP. OLIVE OIL	22 mL
1 LARGE ONION, CHOPPED	
3 GARLIC CLOVES, CHOPPED	
2 LARGE CARROTS, CHOPPED	
½ CUP CHOPPED FRESH OR CANNED TOMATOES	125 mL
1 CELERY STALK, CHOPPED	
1¼ TSP. GROUND CUMIN	6 mL
½ TSP. SALT	2 mL
1 CUP DRIED RED LENTILS	250 mL
4 CUPS WATER	1 L
1½ CUPS CHICKEN BROTH	375 mL
2 TBSP. CHOPPED FRESH PARSLEY	30 mL
SALT & PEPPER TO TASTE	

HEAT OIL IN A 4-5-QUART (4-5 L) HEAVY SAUCEPAN OVER MODERATELY HIGH HEAT. SAUTÉ ONION, STIRRING UNTIL GOLDEN. ADD GARLIC, CARROT, TOMATOES, CELERY, CUMIN AND SALT AND SAUTÉ, STIRRING, FOR ABOUT 2 MINUTES. ADD LENTILS, WATER AND BROTH AND SIMMER, UNCOVERED, STIRRING OCCASIONALLY, UNTIL LENTILS ARE TENDER, ABOUT 20 MINUTES. STIR IN PARSLEY AND SEASON WITH SALT AND PEPPER. MAKES APPROXIMATELY 7 CUPS (1.75 L).

GARLICKY TORTELLINI, SPINACH AND TOMATO SOUP

BADDA BOOM - BADDA BING - IF SOUP IS YOUR THING!

1 TBSP. BUTTER	15 mL
6-8 CLOVES GARLIC, CHOPPED (USE IT ALL - HONEST!)	
4 CUPS CHICKEN BROTH	1 L
6 OZ. CHEESE TORTELLINI	170 g
14 OZ. CAN DICED TOMATOES, WITH LIQUID OR 2½ CUPS (625 mL) SKINNED, CHOPPED FRESH RIPE TOMATOES	398 mL
10 OZ. BAG OF SPINACH, STEMS REMOVED	300 g
8-10 FRESH BASIL LEAVES, COARSELY CHOPPED	
PARMESAN CHEESE, GRATED	

MELT BUTTER IN A LARGE SAUCEPAN OVER MEDIUM-HIGH HEAT. ADD GARLIC AND SAUTÉ ABOUT 2 MINUTES. ADD BROTH AND BRING TO A BOIL. ADD TORTELLINI AND COOK HALFWAY (ABOUT 5 MINUTES IF FROZEN, LESS IF USING FRESH). ADD TOMATOES AND THEIR LIQUID; REDUCE HEAT TO SIMMER AND COOK JUST UNTIL PASTA IS TENDER. STIR IN SPINACH AND BASIL AND COOK UNTIL WILTED, 1-2 MINUTES. TO SERVE, SPRINKLE WITH PARMESAN CHEESE. SERVES 4. (PICTURED ON PAGE 137.)

BAKED POTATO AND LEEK SOUP WITH CHEDDAR AND BACON

A SUPERB DINNER FOR A WINTER'S NIGHT - SERVE WITH SALAD AND CRUSTY ROLLS.

2 MEDIUM BAKER POTATOES	
1/4 CUP BUTTER	60 mL
2 1/2 CUPS SLICED LEEKS (WHITE & LIGHT GREEN PARTS), WELL RINSED	625 mL
2 GARLIC CLOVES, MINCED	
SALT & FRESHLY GROUND PEPPER TO TASTE	
2 CUPS CHICKEN BROTH	500 mL
2 CUPS WATER	500 mL
4 SLICES BACON, CUT INTO 1/2" (1.3 cm) PIECES	
1/2 CUP MILK	125 mL
1/2 CUP SOUR CREAM	125 mL
1 CUP GRATED SHARP CHEDDAR CHEESE	250 mL
2 TBSP. SLICED GREEN ONIONS OR CHIVES	30 mL

WASH POTATOES AND BAKE UNTIL TENDER. SET ASIDE TO COOL. MELT BUTTER IN DUTCH OVEN OVER MEDIUM-LOW HEAT. ADD LEEKS AND GARLIC, SEASON WITH SALT AND PEPPER AND COOK, STIRRING OCCASIONALLY, UNTIL SOFTENED, ABOUT 10 MINUTES. ADD BROTH AND WATER. SIMMER OVER MEDIUM HEAT AND COOK UNTIL LEEKS ARE TENDER, ABOUT 20 MINUTES. COOK BACON UNTIL BROWN AND CRISP. DRAIN ON PAPER TOWEL.

BAKED POTATO AND LEEK SOUP WITH CHEDDAR AND BACON

CONTINUED FROM PAGE 128.

CUT POTATOES IN HALF LENGTHWISE. USE A LARGE SPOON TO SCOOP PULP IN 1 PIECE FROM EACH HALF. CUT PULP INTO ½" (1.3 cm) CUBES AND SET ASIDE. COARSELY CHOP POTATO SKIN AND ENTIRE REMAINING POTATO AND ADD TO POT WITH LEEKS.

IN A BLENDER OR FOOD PROCESSOR, PURÉE IN BATCHES. RETURN PURÉED SOUP TO A CLEAN POT AND REHEAT OVER MEDIUM-LOW. IN A SMALL BOWL, WHISK TOGETHER MILK AND SOUR CREAM UNTIL SMOOTH, THEN WHISK INTO SOUP WITH ½ CUP (125 mL) OF CHEDDAR. STIR IN DICED POTATO.

IF SOUP IS TOO THICK, IT MAY BE THINNED WITH A LITTLE WATER. SEASON TO TASTE AND GARNISH WITH REMAINING CHEDDAR, BACON AND CHIVES. SERVES 4. (PICTURED ON FRONT COVER.)

YOU NEVER FEEL MORE CLEVER THAN WHEN YOU KNOW THE ANSWER AND THE CONTESTANT DOESN'T.

ZUPPA DU JOUR

A COLD WINTER'S NIGHT, HOMEMADE SOUP, A LOAF OF BREAD AND PERHAPS A VIDEO??

6 SLICES BACON, CHOPPED	
2 MEDIUM ONIONS, CHOPPED	
3 STALKS CELERY, CHOPPED	
3-4 GARLIC CLOVES, MINCED	
1/4 TSP. EACH MARJORAM, THYME	1 mL
1/2 TSP. EACH OREGANO, ROSEMARY	2 mL
2 TBSP. CHOPPED FRESH BASIL	30 mL
OR 2 TSP. (10 mL) DRIED	
1/4 CUP CHOPPED FRESH PARSLEY	60 mL
1/2 TSP. HOT RED PEPPER FLAKES	2 mL
5 CUPS CHICKEN BROTH	1.25 L
28-OZ. CAN ITALIAN TOMATOES,	798 mL
CHOPPED	
2/3 CUP BABY SHELL PASTA	150 mL
14-OZ. CAN ARTICHOKE HEARTS	398 mL
(12-14 COUNT), DRAINED & CUT	
INTO WEDGES	
SALT & PEPPER TO TASTE	
GRATED PARMESAN CHEESE TO SPRINKLE	

IN A LARGE HEAVY POT, COOK BACON, ONIONS, CELERY, GARLIC, HERBS AND HOT PEPPER FLAKES, UNTIL ONIONS ARE SOFTENED. STIR IN BROTH AND TOMATOES. BRING TO BOIL. ADD PASTA. REDUCE HEAT AND SIMMER, UNCOVERED, 10 MINUTES, OR UNTIL PASTA IS JUST TENDER. STIR IN ARTICHOKES AND SEASON TO TASTE. SERVE WITH A SPRINKLING OF PARMESAN CHEESE. SERVES 6.

CRAB AND CORN CHOWDER

WHAT COULD BE BETTER THAN CHOWDER, FRENCH BREAD AND WINE AFTER A DAY'S SKIING - OR A DAY OF ANYTHING!

4 SLICES BACON	
¼ CUP BUTTER	60 mL
1 SMALL ONION, CHOPPED	
⅓ CUP FLOUR	75 mL
3 CUPS MILK	750 mL
2 MEDIUM POTATOES, PEELED & DICED & SET IN COLD WATER	
1 SMALL GREEN PEPPER, SEEDED & CHOPPED	
1 STALK CELERY, DICED	
1 BAY LEAF	
1 CUP HALF & HALF CREAM	250 mL
10 OZ. CRABMEAT	305 g
12 OZ. CAN WHOLE KERNEL CORN	341 mL
SALT & PEPPER TO TASTE	
1 TBSP. CHOPPED PARSLEY	15 mL

FRY BACON UNTIL CRISP. COOL AND CRUMBLE. SET ASIDE. IN A LARGE SAUCEPAN, MELT BUTTER AND SAUTÉ ONION UNTIL SOFT. ADD FLOUR, STIR AND COOK GENTLY FOR 1 MINUTE. GRADUALLY ADD MILK, STIRRING CONSTANTLY UNTIL THICKENED. DRAIN POTATOES AND ADD TO SAUCE WITH PEPPER, CELERY, BAY LEAF AND CREAM. SIMMER 35-40 MINUTES. ADD CRAB, CORN AND BACON; HEAT THROUGH. SEASON WITH SALT AND PEPPER. GARNISH EACH BOWL WITH PARSLEY. SERVES 6.

CHICKEN, APPLE AND CURRY SOUP

FEELS LIKE AUTUMN!

2 TBSP. OLIVE OIL	30 mL
2 CUPS CHOPPED CELERY	500 mL
1 CUP CHOPPED CARROTS	250 mL
1/2 CUP CHOPPED ONION	125 mL
4 CUPS CHICKEN BROTH	1 L
1 CUP CHOPPED APPLE	250 mL
1/4 CUP UNCOOKED LONG-GRAIN RICE	60 mL
2 TSP. CURRY POWDER	10 mL
1/8 TSP. DRIED THYME	0.5 mL
1/2 CUP HALF & HALF CREAM	125 mL
2 TBSP. FLOUR	30 mL
1 CUP CHOPPED COOKED CHICKEN	250 mL
SALT & PEPPER TO TASTE	

IN A LARGE SAUCEPAN, HEAT OIL AND COOK CELERY, CARROTS AND ONION FOR 5 MINUTES. CAREFULLY ADD BROTH, APPLE, RICE, CURRY POWDER AND THYME. BRING TO A BOIL; REDUCE HEAT AND SIMMER, COVERED, FOR 15-20 MINUTES, OR UNTIL RICE IS TENDER.

IN A GLASS-MEASURING CUP, BLEND CREAM AND FLOUR. STIR INTO VEGETABLES IN SAUCEPAN. COOK AND STIR UNTIL THICKENED AND BUBBLY. STIR IN CHICKEN, SEASON TO TASTE AND HEAT THROUGH.

TO SERVE: LADLE SOUP INTO BOWLS, GARNISH EACH SERVING WITH AN APPLE SLICE. SERVES 4.

TURKEY SOUP

AHHH - THE AROMA OF SOUP BUBBLING ON THE BACK BURNER - LIFE IS GOOD!

LEFTOVER TURKEY CARCASS (BONES, SKIN, EVERYTHING!)	
8 CUPS WATER	2 L
3 CHICKEN BOUILLON CUBES	
1 TSP. SALT	5 mL
1/4 TSP. POULTRY SEASONING OR SAGE	1 mL
1 BAY LEAF	
1/2 CUP BARLEY	125 mL
2 CUPS CHOPPED CARROTS	500 mL
1 CUP CHOPPED ONION	250 mL
1 CUP CHOPPED CELERY	250 mL
28 OZ. CAN TOMATOES	796 mL
3 CUPS CHOPPED TURKEY	750 mL
1 CUP MACARONI OR NOODLES, UNCOOKED (OPTIONAL)	250 mL
1/4 CUP CHOPPED FRESH PARSLEY	60 mL

IN A LARGE DUTCH OVEN, COMBINE TURKEY CARCASS, WATER, BOUILLON CUBES, SALT, POULTRY SEASONING AND BAY LEAF. BRING TO A BOIL. REDUCE HEAT, COVER AND SIMMER FOR 2 HOURS. STRAIN AND DISCARD BONES. PLACE BROTH IN REFRIGERATOR OVERNIGHT. SKIM FAT OFF SOLIDIFIED BROTH. SIMMER IN DUTCH OVEN WITH REMAINING INGREDIENTS FOR 2-3 HOURS. SERVE WITH FRESH BREAD AND A GREEN SALAD.

BEEF AND BARLEY SOUP

"OH, THE WEATHER OUTSIDE IS FRIGHTFUL."

1½ LBS. BEEF ROUND STEAK, TRIMMED & CUT INTO ½" (1.3 cm) CUBES	750 g
¾ TSP. SALT	3 mL
½ TSP. PEPPER	2 mL
2 TBSP. VEGETABLE OIL, DIVIDED	30 mL
2 CUPS FINELY CHOPPED ONION	500 mL
1 CUP DICED CARROT	250 mL
½ CUP CHOPPED CELERY	125 mL
1 LB. MUSHROOMS, SLICED	500 g
1 TSP. MINCED GARLIC	5 mL
¼ TSP. DRIED THYME	1 mL
2 CUPS BEEF BROTH	500 mL
2 CUPS CHICKEN BROTH	500 mL
2 CUPS WATER	500 mL
½ CUP PEARL BARLEY	125 mL
3 TBSP. CHOPPED FRESH PARSLEY	45 mL

SPRINKLE BEEF WITH SALT AND PEPPER. PLACE 1 TBSP. (15 mL) OIL IN DUTCH OVEN AND BROWN BEEF UNTIL NO LONGER PINK. SET ASIDE. HEAT REMAINING OIL IN SAME POT AND ADD ONION, CARROT AND CELERY. COOK AND STIR UNTIL VEGETABLES ARE SOFTENED, ABOUT 5 MINUTES. STIR IN MUSHROOMS, GARLIC AND THYME, COOK 5 MINUTES MORE. ADD BEEF AND CHICKEN BROTHS WITH WATER, BARLEY AND BEEF; BRING TO A BOIL. REDUCE HEAT; COVER AND SIMMER UNTIL BEEF IS TENDER, ABOUT 1½ HOURS. ADD MORE WATER IF NECESSARY. SPRINKLE WITH PARSLEY JUST BEFORE SERVING. SERVES 8.

PASTA

Orzo With Parmesan and Basil
Pronto Primavera
Fresh Tomato and Cheese Pasta
Marinara Sauce and Rose Sauce
Pasta With Sausage and Mushrooms
Spinach Fettuccine Alfredo with
Chicken and Broccoli
Pad Thai
Roasted Vegetable Manicotti with Cheese Sauce
Crab Manicotti with Parmesan Cheese Sauce
Creamy Ravioli with Spinach
Vegetable Lasagne
Best Seafood Lasagne

— ORZO WITH PARMESAN & BASIL —

THE PASTA THAT LOOKS LIKE RICE - GREAT WITH CHICKEN OR FISH.

3 TBSP. BUTTER	45 mL
1½ CUPS ORZO	375 mL
3 CUPS CHICKEN BROTH	750 mL
½ CUP GRATED PARMESAN CHEESE	125 mL
6 TBSP. CHOPPED FRESH BASIL OR	90 mL
2 TBSP. (30 mL) DRIED	
SALT & PEPPER TO TASTE	

MELT BUTTER IN A FRYING PAN OVER MEDIUM-HIGH HEAT. ADD ORZO AND SAUTÉ FOR 2 MINUTES, UNTIL SLIGHTLY BROWNED. ADD BROTH AND BRING TO A BOIL. REDUCE HEAT, COVER AND SIMMER UNTIL ORZO IS TENDER AND LIQUID IS ABSORBED, ABOUT 20 MINUTES. MIX IN PARMESAN AND BASIL. SEASON WITH SALT AND PEPPER. TRANSFER TO SHALLOW BOWL. SERVES 6.

VARIATION: FOR A CREAMIER PASTA DISH, TRY STIRRING IN 2 TBSP. (30 mL) PLAIN YOGURT THINNED WITH A LITTLE MILK.

A TINY FORTUNE TELLER WHO ESCAPES FROM PRISON IS A SMALL MEDIUM AT LARGE.

Garlicky Tortellini, Spinach and Tomato Soup, page 127

Pad Thai, page 144

PRONTO PRIMAVERA

FAST AND FRESH - NEED WE SAY MORE!

1 CUP BROCCOLI FLORETS	250 mL
1 SMALL ZUCCHINI, SLICED	
1 SMALL RED PEPPER, CUT IN STRIPS	
1/2 CUP SNOW PEAS	125 mL
1/4 CUP BUTTER	60 mL
1 CUP CREAM, WARMED	250 mL
FRESHLY GROUND PEPPER	
1 LB. LINGUINI, COOKED & DRAINED	500 g
1/4 CUP CHOPPED FRESH BASIL	60 mL
GRATED PARMESAN CHEESE	

IN A LARGE FRYING PAN, SAUTÉ BROCCOLI, ZUCCHINI, RED PEPPER AND SNOW PEAS IN BUTTER UNTIL TENDER-CRISP. ADD CREAM AND BLACK PEPPER. COOK UNTIL SLIGHTLY REDUCED. MIX WITH PASTA AND BASIL AND SPRINKLE WITH PARMESAN. SERVE IMMEDIATELY. SERVES 4.

MY WIFE WENT AWAY FOR THE WEEKEND AND LEFT ME TO MY OWN DEVICES - THE CAN OPENER AND THE MICROWAVE.

FRESH TOMATO AND CHEESE PASTA

BOY, THIS IS GOOD!

BOW TIE PASTA FOR 4

2 GARLIC CLOVES, MINCED		
2 CUPS QUARTERED, FRESH ROMA TOMATOES (6)	500 mL	
2 TBSP. OLIVE OIL	30 mL	
½ CUP FRESH BASIL, CHOPPED	125 mL	
½ LB. BRIE CHEESE, REMOVE RIND	250 g	
½ CUP PINE NUTS, TOASTED (OPTIONAL)	125 mL	

FRESHLY GROUND SALT & PEPPER TO TASTE
CHOPPED PARSLEY
PARMESAN CHEESE

COOK PASTA ACCORDING TO PACKAGE DIRECTIONS. SAUTÉ GARLIC AND TOMATOES IN OIL. ADD BASIL AND PINCHED-OFF PIECES OF BRIE. STIR UNTIL BRIE IS PARTIALLY MELTED. ADD PINE NUTS. SPRINKLE WITH SALT AND PEPPER. ADD COOKED PASTA TO PAN AND MIX GENTLY. PLACE IN A PASTA BOWL AND SPRINKLE WITH PARSLEY AND PARMESAN. SERVE WITH A GREEN SALAD AND GARLIC TOAST.

MY IDEA OF CLEANING THE HOUSE IS SWEEPING THE ROOM WITH A GLANCE.

MARINARA AND ROSE SAUCES

A STAPLE FOR ITALIAN CUISINE. DO TRY THE ROSE SAUCE - RICH AND WORTH IT!

3 TBSP. OLIVE OIL	45 mL
1 ONION, DICED	
2 GARLIC CLOVES, CHOPPED	
28 OZ. CAN PLUM TOMATOES	796 mL
½ CUP CHOPPED FRESH BASIL	125 mL
SALT & FRESH BLACK PEPPER	
1 TBSP. CHOPPED FRESH PARSLEY	15 mL

FOR MARINARA SAUCE: IN A LARGE FRYING PAN, HEAT OIL AND ADD ONION. SAUTÉ UNTIL SOFT AND TRANSLUCENT. ADD GARLIC AND COOK FOR 1 MINUTE; REMOVE FROM HEAT. PLACE TOMATOES IN A BLENDER AT THE LOWEST SPEED FOR A FEW SECONDS TO CHOP COARSELY. ADD TOMATOES TO FRYING PAN, STIR AND RETURN TO HEAT. ADD BASIL, SALT AND PEPPER AND SIMMER, COVERED, FOR 30 MINUTES.

FOR ROSE SAUCE: ADD ½ CUP (125 mL) WHIPPING CREAM TO MARINARA SAUCE AND HEAT GENTLY.

HOW'S YOUR DIET GOING?
THE ONLY THING GETTING SLIMMER IS MY CHANCE OF STICKING TO IT.

PASTA WITH SAUSAGE AND MUSHROOMS

FREEZE EXTRA SAUCE - BE PREPARED!

3 TBSP. OLIVE OIL	45 mL
2½ LBS. ITALIAN SWEET (OR SPICY) SAUSAGES, CASING REMOVED & CUT INTO BITE-SIZED PIECES	1.25 kg
1½ LBS. FRESH MUSHROOMS, SLICED	750 g
1 MEDIUM ONION, CHOPPED	
1½ CUPS CHOPPED FRESH BASIL	375 mL
¼ CUP CHOPPED FRESH OREGANO	60 mL
7 GARLIC CLOVES, CHOPPED	
1 CUP DRY WHITE WINE	250 mL
28 OZ. & 19 OZ. CANS DICED TOMATOES	1.3 L
2 TBSP. BUTTER	30 mL
SALT & PEPPER TO TASTE	
BROAD NOODLES, COOKED	
PARMESAN CHEESE TO GARNISH	

IN A LARGE HEAVY POT, HEAT 1 TBSP. (15 mL) OIL; SAUTÉ SAUSAGE UNTIL NO LONGER PINK. TRANSFER TO A LARGE BOWL. ADD REMAINING OIL TO SAUSAGE DRIPPINGS. ADD MUSHROOMS AND ONION; SAUTÉ UNTIL TENDER. STIR IN BASIL, OREGANO AND GARLIC; COOK BRIEFLY. ADD WINE AND COOK UNTIL ALMOST ABSORBED. ADD SAUSAGE AND TOMATOES; SIMMER OVER MEDIUM HEAT UNTIL SAUCE IS THICKENED (ABOUT 25 MINUTES). STIR IN BUTTER, SALT AND PEPPER. TOSS COOKED PASTA WITH SAUCE. SPRINKLE WITH PARMESAN CHEESE.

SPINACH FETTUCCINE ALFREDO WITH CHICKEN AND BROCCOLI

12 oz. SPINACH FETTUCCINE	340	g
2 CUPS BROCCOLI FLORETS	500	mL
2 TSP. OLIVE OIL	10	mL
1 LB. SKINLESS, BONELESS CHICKEN BREASTS, CUT INTO 1" (2.5 cm) PIECES	500	g
3 GARLIC CLOVES, MINCED		
2 TBSP. FLOUR	30	mL
½ TSP. SALT	2	mL
¼ TSP. GROUND BLACK PEPPER	1	mL
1½ CUPS LOW-FAT MILK	375	mL
4 TBSP. GRATED PARMESAN CHEESE	60	mL

COOK PASTA ACCORDING TO PACKAGE DIRECTIONS, ADDING BROCCOLI FOR THE LAST 30 SECONDS. DRAIN AND RETURN PASTA AND BROCCOLI TO POT. HEAT OIL IN A LARGE FRYING PAN OVER MEDIUM-HIGH HEAT. ADD CHICKEN AND GARLIC AND COOK FOR 3-5 MINUTES, UNTIL CHICKEN IS GOLDEN BROWN ON ALL SIDES. ADD FLOUR, SALT AND PEPPER; STIR TO COAT. ADD MILK AND 2 TBSP. (30 mL) CHEESE; BRING TO A BOIL, STIRRING CONSTANTLY. SIMMER FOR 1-2 MINUTES, UNTIL SAUCE THICKENS.

POUR SAUCE OVER FETTUCCINE AND BROCCOLI AND TOSS TO COMBINE. TOP WITH REMAINING PARMESAN WHEN SERVING. SERVES 4.

PAD THAI

THAILAND'S MOST WELL-KNOWN NOODLE DISH - WITH EVERYTHING IN IT!

8 OZ. WIDE RICE STICK NOODLES	250	g
1/2 CUP CHICKEN BROTH	125	mL
1/4 CUP SUGAR	60	mL
1/4 CUP FISH SAUCE	60	mL
3 TBSP. LIME JUICE	45	mL
2 TBSP. KETCHUP	30	mL
1/4 TSP. HOT PEPPER FLAKES	1	mL
4 OZ. BONELESS PORK OR CHICKEN BREASTS	125	g
6 OZ. FIRM TOFU	170	g
1/4 CUP VEGETABLE OIL	60	mL
1 EGG, BEATEN		
3 GARLIC CLOVES, MINCED		
8 OZ. LARGE RAW SHRIMP, PEELED & DEVEINED	250	g
1 RED PEPPER, DICED		
2 CUPS BEAN SPROUTS	500	mL
1/2 CUP COARSELY CHOPPED CILANTRO	125	mL
6 GREEN ONIONS, THINLY SLICED		
1/4 CUP PEANUTS, CHOPPED	60	mL

IN A LARGE BOWL, SOAK NOODLES IN WARM WATER FOR 15 MINUTES, DRAIN AND SET ASIDE. IN A SMALL BOWL, WHISK CHICKEN BROTH, SUGAR, FISH SAUCE, LIME JUICE, KETCHUP AND HOT PEPPER FLAKES; SET ASIDE. CUT PORK ACROSS GRAIN INTO 1/4" (6 mm) STRIPS. CUT TOFU INTO 1/2" (1.3 cm) CUBES; SET ASIDE. IN WOK OR LARGE FRYING PAN, HEAT 1 TSP. (5 mL) OIL OVER MEDIUM HEAT. COOK EGG, STIRRING OCCASIONALLY, UNTIL

PAD THAI

CONTINUED FROM PAGE 144.

SCRAMBLED AND SET. TRANSFER TO A LARGE PLATE. WIPE WOK, ADD 1 TBSP. (15 mL) OIL, INCREASE HEAT TO MEDIUM-HIGH AND STIR-FRY GARLIC, SHRIMP AND PORK UNTIL SHRIMP ARE BRIGHT PINK. ADD TO EGG. HEAT REST OF OIL; STIR IN TOFU AND RED PEPPER. COOK, STIRRING OCCASIONALLY, UNTIL TOFU BEGINS TO BROWN. STIR IN NOODLES FOR 1 MINUTE, OR UNTIL THEY START TO SOFTEN. POUR IN SAUCE; STIR-FRY UNTIL NOODLES ARE TENDER. RETURN EGG MIXTURE TO PAN; ADD BEAN SPROUTS, CILANTRO AND HALF THE GREEN ONIONS. STIR UNTIL HEATED THROUGH. REMOVE TO WARM SERVING PLATTER. GARNISH WITH PEANUTS AND REMAINING GREEN ONIONS. SERVES 4. (PICTURED ON PAGE 138.)

TAKE MY ADVICE - I'M NOT USING IT.

ROASTED VEGETABLE MANICOTTI WITH CHEESE SAUCE

1 ONION	
2 CUPS CHOPPED BROCCOLI	500 mL
2 CUPS CHOPPED CAULIFLOWER	500 mL
2 CUPS CHOPPED CARROT	500 mL
1 RED PEPPER	
3 TBSP. OLIVE OIL	45 mL
1 TBSP. BALSAMIC VINEGAR	15 mL
2 GARLIC CLOVES, MINCED	
3 CUPS SPINACH	750 mL
1 CUP FRESHLY GRATED PARMESAN CHEESE	250 mL
1 CUP RICOTTA CHEESE	250 mL
1 EGG, BEATEN	
2 SLICES BREAD	
½ CUP FRESH PARSLEY	125 mL
½ CUP FRESH BASIL	125 mL
SALT & PEPPER TO TASTE	
16 MANICOTTI SHELLS	
2-14 OZ. CANS TOMATO SAUCE	2-398 mL
CHEESE SAUCE, PAGE 147	
ASIAGO CHEESE, GRATED	

CHOP VEGETABLES INTO 1" (2.5 cm) PIECES. TOSS WITH OIL, VINEGAR AND GARLIC. ROAST AT 350°F (180°C) FOR 40 MINUTES, STIRRING OCCASIONALLY.

MIX SPINACH WITH HOT VEGETABLES AND SET ASIDE TO COOL. PULSE VEGETABLES IN FOOD PROCESSOR TO A COARSE TEXTURE.

MIX TOGETHER PARMESAN, RICOTTA AND EGG. BLEND WITH VEGETABLES. IN FOOD PROCESSOR, WHIRL BREAD, HERBS AND SEASONINGS. ADD TO VEGETABLE MIXTURE.

ROASTED VEGETABLE MANICOTTI

CONTINUED FROM PAGE 146.

COOK MANICOTTI ACCORDING TO PACKAGE DIRECTIONS. DRAIN WELL. FILL WITH VEGETABLE MIXTURE USING SPOON OR VERY SMALL KNIFE. POUR TOMATO SAUCE IN BOTTOM OF 2, 9 X 13" (23 X 33 cm) BAKING DISHES AND ARRANGE STUFFED MANICOTTI IN EACH BAKING DISH. MAKE CHEESE SAUCE, BELOW, AND POUR OVER MANICOTTI. SPRINKLE WITH GRATED ASIAGO. BAKE AT 350°F (180°C) FOR ABOUT 30 MINUTES. SERVES 8-10.

CHEESE SAUCE

3 TBSP. BUTTER	45 mL
3 TBSP. FLOUR	45 mL
3 CUPS MILK	750 mL
2 CUPS GRATED MOZZARELLA OR SWISS CHEESE	500 mL
1 TSP. WORCESTERSHIRE SAUCE	5 mL
DASH HOT PEPPER SAUCE	
SALT & PEPPER TO TASTE	

MELT BUTTER OVER MEDIUM HEAT; BLEND IN FLOUR. COOK FOR 1 MINUTE, STIRRING UNTIL SMOOTH AND BUBBLY. REDUCE HEAT TO MEDIUM-LOW. GRADUALLY ADD MILK, STIRRING UNTIL THICKENED. ADD CHEESE, WORCESTERSHIRE AND PEPPER SAUCE. STIR UNTIL CHEESE MELTS. ADD SALT AND PEPPER.

CRAB MANICOTTI
WITH PARMESAN CHEESE SAUCE

A GREAT MAKE-AHEAD!

14-16 MANICOTTI SHELLS, COOKED		
1/2 LB. FRESH OR FROZEN CRABMEAT, FLAKED (OR MOCK CRABMEAT)	250	g
1 LB. FRESH SPINACH,* WILTED, DRAINED	500	g
1 1/2 CUPS RICOTTA CHEESE	375	mL
1/2 CUP FRESHLY GRATED PARMESAN CHEESE	125	mL
1/2 CUP CHOPPED GREEN ONIONS	125	mL
1 LARGE EGG, BEATEN		
1 TSP. SALT	5	mL
PARMESAN CHEESE SAUCE, PAGE 149		
1/2 CUP GRATED ASIAGO CHEESE	125	mL

PREHEAT OVEN TO 400°F (200°C). COOK MANICOTTI SHELLS AS DIRECTED ON PACKAGE; SET ASIDE. SPRAY A 9 x 13" (23 x 33 cm) BAKING DISH. IN A MEDIUM BOWL, COMBINE CRAB, SPINACH, CHEESES, ONIONS, EGG AND SALT. MIX WELL. USING A SPOON OR YOUR FINGERS, (JULIA CHILD SAYS IT'S OKAY) FILL SHELLS AND PLACE IN DISH. COVER WITH PARMESAN CHEESE SAUCE. SPRINKLE WITH ASIAGO CHEESE; BAKE, UNCOVERED, UNTIL BUBBLY, ABOUT 25 MINUTES. (PICTURED ON PAGE 171.)

*TO WILT SPINACH, PLACE IN A SIEVE; POUR BOILING WATER OVER, THEN POUR ICE-COLD WATER OVER. DRAIN WELL ON PAPER TOWELS.

PARMESAN CHEESE SAUCE

¼ CUP BUTTER	60 mL
¼ CUP FLOUR	60 mL
2½ CUPS MILK	625 mL
1 CUP FRESHLY GRATED PARMESAN CHEESE	250 mL
¼ TSP. SALT	1 mL
PEPPER TO TASTE	
TABASCO TO TASTE	

IN A SAUCEPAN OVER MEDIUM HEAT, MELT BUTTER. ADD FLOUR AND STIR UNTIL BUBBLY. ADD MILK AND STIR UNTIL THICKENED. ADD CHEESE, SALT, PEPPER AND TABASCO. STIR UNTIL CHEESE MELTS.

RESEARCH HAS SHOWN THAT MEN USUALLY SLEEP ON THE RIGHT SIDE OF THE BED. EVEN IN THEIR SLEEP, THEY HAVE TO BE RIGHT.

CREAMY RAVIOLI WITH SPINACH

1 GARLIC CLOVE, MINCED	
2 TSP. OLIVE OIL	10 mL
1/2 CUP CHICKEN BROTH	125 mL
2 CUPS LIGHT CREAM	500 mL
1/4 CUP FRESHLY GRATED PARMESAN CHEESE	60 mL
1 LB. RICOTTA SPINACH RAVIOLI	500 g
2 CUPS CHOPPED FRESH SPINACH	500 mL
8 OZ. CRAB (OPTIONAL)	250 g
2 TBSP. CHOPPED FRESH DILL	30 mL
2 FRESH TOMATOES, CHOPPED	
1/4 CUP FRESHLY GRATED PARMESAN CHEESE	60 mL

OVER MEDIUM HEAT, SAUTÉ GARLIC IN OIL, ADD BROTH AND SIMMER UNTIL REDUCED BY HALF. ADD CREAM AND PARMESAN, STIRRING UNTIL CHEESE HAS MELTED.

COOK RAVIOLI ACCORDING TO PACKAGE DIRECTIONS.

ADD RAVIOLI, SPINACH, CRAB AND DILL TO SAUCE AND HEAT THROUGH.

BLANCH TOMATOES IN BOILING WATER FOR 1 MINUTE, THEN PLUNGE INTO COLD WATER. PEEL OFF SKINS WITH A SHARP KNIFE. CUT IN HALF AND USE A SMALL SPOON TO REMOVE SEEDS. SPRINKLE WITH PARMESAN. SERVES 6.

VEGETABLE LASAGNE

2 TBSP. OLIVE OIL	30 mL
1 MEDIUM ONION, CHOPPED	
1 MEDIUM ZUCCHINI, GRATED	
1 LARGE CARROT, GRATED	
4 CUPS SLICED FRESH MUSHROOMS	1 L
½ TSP. THYME	2 mL
½ TSP. OREGANO	2 mL
½ TSP. BASIL	2 mL
3 CUPS SPAGHETTI SAUCE (HOT & SPICY IS GOOD)	750 mL
9 LASAGNE NOODLES	
2 CUPS RICOTTA CHEESE	500 mL
3-4 CUPS FRESH SPINACH, CHOPPED	750 mL-1 L
3 CUPS GRATED MOZZARELLA CHEESE	750 mL

HEAT OIL IN FRYING PAN; SAUTÉ ONION, ZUCCHINI, CARROT AND MUSHROOMS UNTIL TENDER. ADD THYME, OREGANO AND BASIL. STIR IN SPAGHETTI SAUCE. SIMMER FOR 20 MINUTES. COOK LASAGNE NOODLES ACCORDING TO PACKAGE DIRECTIONS. GREASE A 9 X 13" (23 X 33 cm) CASSEROLE. LAYER WITH ½ OF THE SAUCE, 3 NOODLES, ½ OF THE RICOTTA CHEESE, COVER WITH ALL OF THE SPINACH, THEN ⅓ OF THE MOZZARELLA CHEESE. REPEAT LAYERS, ENDING WITH THE LAST 3 NOODLES AND MOZZARELLA. BAKE AT 350°F (180°C) FOR 40 MINUTES, OR UNTIL BUBBLY. LET SIT FOR AT LEAST 10 MINUTES BEFORE CUTTING. SERVES 8.

BEST SEAFOOD LASAGNE

A TASTY VARIATION OF AN OLD FAVORITE.

8 LASAGNE NOODLES	
2 TBSP. BUTTER	30 mL
1 CUP CHOPPED ONION	250 mL
8 OZ. PKG. CREAM CHEESE, SOFTENED	250 g
1½ CUPS RICOTTA CHEESE	375 mL
1 EGG, BEATEN	
2 TSP. BASIL	10 mL
½ TSP. SALT	2 mL
⅛ TSP. PEPPER	0.5 mL
2-10 OZ. CANS CREAM OF MUSHROOM SOUP	2-284 mL
⅓ CUP DRY WHITE WINE OR DRY VERMOUTH	75 mL
5 OZ. CRABMEAT	140 mL
1 LB. SHRIMP, DEVEINED & COOKED	500 g
¼ CUP GRATED PARMESAN CHEESE	60 mL
½ CUP SHREDDED, SHARP CHEDDAR CHEESE	125 mL

COOK NOODLES. PLACE 4 NOODLES IN A 9 X 13" (23 X 33 cm) BAKING DISH. COOK ONION IN BUTTER. ADD CHEESES, EGG, BASIL, SALT AND PEPPER. SPREAD HALF THE CHEESE MIXTURE OVER NOODLES. COMBINE SOUP AND WINE. STIR IN CRAB AND SHRIMP AND SPREAD HALF OVER CHEESE LAYER. REPEAT ALL LAYERS. SPRINKLE WITH PARMESAN AND CHEDDAR. BAKE, UNCOVERED, AT 350°F (180°C) FOR 45 MINUTES. LET STAND 15 MINUTES BEFORE SERVING. SERVES 8-10. FREEZES WELL.

VEGGIES

Stir-Fried Sugar Snap Peas
Sesame Spinach
Cheese-Fried Zucchini
Dill and Parmesan Tomatoes
Veggie Stacks
Baked Corn Pudding with a Kick
Red Cabbage
Creamed Onions
Caramelized Onion and Potato Flan
Whipped Potato with Celery Root
Potatoes Rosti
Roasted Sweet Potato Wedges
Turnips 'n' Apples
Perfect Parsnips
Oven-Roasted Autumn Vegetables
Lemon Risotto
Mushroom Barley Risotto
Basmati Rice Pilaf
Oven-Baked Wild Rice

STIR-FRIED SUGAR SNAP PEAS

FAST AND DELICIOUS. JUST REMEMBER NOT TO OVERCOOK THEM - THEY STILL NEED TO SNAP.

½ LB. FRESH SUGAR SNAP PEAS	250	g
2 TBSP. VEGETABLE OIL	30	mL
1 TSP. SESAME OIL	5	mL
3 TBSP. PINE NUTS	45	mL
1 TBSP. MINCED FRESH GINGER	15	mL
2 TBSP. DRY SHERRY	30	mL
2 TBSP. SOY SAUCE	30	mL

TO PREPARE PEAS, SNAP OFF STEMS AND PULL STRINGS OFF ALONG SEAMS. HEAT A WOK OR HEAVY FRYING PAN OVER HIGH HEAT. ADD VEGETABLE OIL AND, WHEN HOT, ADD SESAME OIL. STIR-FRY PINE NUTS AND GINGER UNTIL BROWN, BEING CAREFUL NOT TO BURN THEM. ADD SNAP PEAS AND STIR-FRY TO COAT WITH OIL. MIX IN SHERRY AND SOY SAUCE. COVER WOK AND LOWER HEAT TO MEDIUM. COOK FOR ABOUT 2 MINUTES.

I'VE DISCOVERED VICTORIA'S SECRET: NOBODY UNDER 30 CAN FIT INTO THEIR STUFF!

SESAME SPINACH

FINALLY, A SPINACH THAT STAYS BRIGHT GREEN.

10 OZ. PKG. FRESH SPINACH	283	g
2 TBSP. DARK SESAME OIL	30	mL
1/4 TSP. CRUSHED RED PEPPER FLAKES	1	mL
2 GARLIC CLOVES, CHOPPED		
2 TSP. SESAME SEEDS	10	mL
PINCH OF SALT		

RINSE SPINACH WELL. PICK OVER AND DISCARD ANY TOUGH LEAVES AND STEMS. DRY LEAVES WELL.

IN FRYING PAN OVER MEDIUM HEAT, ADD SESAME OIL, CRUSHED RED PEPPER FLAKES, GARLIC AND SESAME SEEDS AND SAUTÉ UNTIL SLIGHTLY BROWNED. ADD SPINACH AND COOK, STIRRING FREQUENTLY. WATCH CAREFULLY AND REMOVE FROM HEAT WHEN JUST WILTED. DRAIN OFF ANY JUICES AND SEASON WITH SALT. (PICTURED ON PAGE 189.)

EVER WONDER ABOUT THOSE PEOPLE WHO SPEND $2.95 ON THOSE LITTLE BOTTLES OF EVIAN WATER? TRY SPELLING IT BACKWARDS.

CHEESE-FRIED ZUCCHINI

MAY ALSO BE SERVED AS AN APPETIZER.

1/4 CUP DRIED BREADCRUMBS	60 mL
2 TBSP. GRATED PARMESAN CHEESE	30 mL
2 TBSP. FLOUR	30 mL
1 TSP. SALT (GARLIC SALT OR ONION SALT IF PREFERRED)	5 mL
2 MEDIUM ZUCCHINI, SLICED LENGTHWISE IN STICKS	
1 EGG, BEATEN	
2-4 TBSP. OLIVE OIL	30-60 mL

COMBINE BREADCRUMBS, CHEESE, FLOUR AND SALT IN A PLASTIC BAG. DIP ZUCCHINI IN EGG, THEN SHAKE IN PLASTIC BAG. USING A LARGE SKILLET, HEAT OIL AND FRY ZUCCHINI UNTIL GOLDEN BROWN AND CRISPY, TURNING OCCASIONALLY. DRAIN ON PAPER TOWEL. SERVE IMMEDIATELY. SERVES 4.

DUCT TAPE IS LIKE THE FORCE. IT HAS A LIGHT SIDE AND A DARK SIDE, AND IT HOLDS THE UNIVERSE TOGETHER.

DILL AND PARMESAN TOMATOES

QUICK AND DELICIOUS - VITAMINS AND COLOR FOR YOUR COMPANY!

3 MEDIUM TOMATOES	
2 TBSP. BUTTER	30 mL
½ CUP BREAD CRUMBS	125 mL
1 TBSP. FRESH CHOPPED DILL	15 mL
OR ½ TSP. (2 mL) DRIED DILL	
SALT & PEPPER TO TASTE	
½ CUP GRATED PARMESAN CHEESE	125 mL

CUT EACH TOMATO INTO 4 SLICES AND PLACE ON A COOKIE SHEET. MELT BUTTER, ADD BREAD CRUMBS, DILL, SALT, PEPPER AND CHEESE. STIR TOGETHER AND SPOON CRUMB MIXTURE ONTO TOMATO SLICES. PLACE IN COLD OVEN UNDER BROILER (NOT TOO CLOSE) AND TURN ON BROILER. BROIL UNTIL CRUST TURNS GOLDEN - ABOUT 5 MINUTES. SERVES 6.

HARLEZ-VOUS FRANCAIS? CAN YOU DRIVE A FRENCH MOTORCYCLE?

VEGGIE STACKS

GREAT WITH ROAST BEEF OR STEAK. ALLOW
1 STACK PER PERSON.

FOR ONE STACK

1/4"	SLICE EGGPLANT OR PORTOBELLO MUSHROOM	6 mm
1/4"	SLICE RED ONION	6 mm
1/4"	SLICE BOCCONCINI CHEESE	6 mm
	FRESH BASIL LEAVES	
1/4"	SLICE FRESH TOMATO	6 mm
	GRATED ASIAGO CHEESE	

ASSEMBLE STACKS BY LAYERING 1 SLICE OF
EGGPLANT, RED ONION, BOCCONCINI, BASIL
LEAVES AND TOMATO. SPRINKLE WITH GRATED
ASIAGO. PLACE STACKS ON A COOKIE SHEET AND
BAKE AT 375°F (190°C) FOR ABOUT 20 MINUTES,
UNTIL CHEESE MELTS AND VEGGIES SOFTEN.

TEACHER: WHAT IS A FIBULA?
CHILD: A SMALL LIE.

BAKED CORN PUDDING WITH A KICK

PARTNERS WELL WITH HAM OR ROAST PORK.

4 TBSP. BUTTER, DIVIDED	60 mL
2 CUPS FROZEN KERNEL CORN, THAWED	500 mL
1 CUP WHOLE MILK	250 mL
2 CUPS FINELY CHOPPED ONION	500 mL
6 GREEN ONIONS, CHOPPED	
1 TBSP. DICED SERRANO CHILI PEPPER	15 mL
4 LARGE EGGS	
1 TBSP. FLOUR	15 mL
¾ TSP. SALT	3 mL
½ TSP. PEPPER	2 mL
1½ CUPS GRATED PARMESAN CHEESE	375 mL

MELT 2 TBSP. (30 mL) BUTTER IN A LARGE FRYING PAN OVER MEDIUM-HIGH HEAT. ADD CORN AND SAUTÉ 5 MINUTES. ADD MILK; REDUCE HEAT TO MEDIUM. COVER AND SIMMER 5 MINUTES. TRANSFER TO A FOOD PROCESSOR; PURÉE UNTIL A COARSE CONSISTENCY. MELT REMAINING BUTTER IN THE SAME PAN. ADD ONIONS AND CHILI PEPPER; SAUTÉ ABOUT 4 MINUTES. REMOVE FROM HEAT AND STIR IN CORN PURÉE. COOL 15 MINUTES. PREHEAT OVEN TO 350°F (180°C). IN A SMALL BOWL BEAT EGGS, FLOUR, SALT AND PEPPER. STIR IN 1 CUP (250 mL) CHEESE. STIR EGG MIXTURE INTO CORN MIXTURE. TRANSFER TO A GREASED 7 X 11" (18 X 28 cm) GLASS BAKING DISH. SPRINKLE WITH REMAINING CHEESE AND BAKE UNTIL GOLDEN, ABOUT 40 MINUTES. TO REHEAT, BAKE FOR 25 MINUTES. SERVES 4-6.

RED CABBAGE

EXCELLENT WITH FOWL AND A MUST WITH WILD GAME!

3 LB. RED CABBAGE	1.5 kg
2 GREEN APPLES, PEELED & CHOPPED	
1 ONION, FINELY CHOPPED	
¼ CUP WHITE SUGAR	60 mL
¼ CUP VINEGAR	60 mL
2 TBSP. BACON FAT	30 mL
1 TSP. SALT	5 mL
FRESHLY GROUND PEPPER	
½ CUP BOILING WATER	125 mL

SHRED CABBAGE AND PLACE IN A LARGE SAUCEPAN WITH REMAINING INGREDIENTS. BRING TO A BOIL; REDUCE HEAT; COVER AND SIMMER FOR 1 HOUR. STIR OCCASIONALLY. SERVES 6-8.

IF WILE E. COYOTE HAD ENOUGH MONEY TO BUY ALL THAT ACME STUFF, WHY DIDN'T HE JUST BUY DINNER?

CREAMED ONIONS

THE WAY YOUR GRANDMOTHER MADE THEM.

12 BOILING ONIONS (SMALL)

CREAM SAUCE

3 TBSP. BUTTER	45 mL
3 TBSP. FLOUR	45 mL
2 CUPS MILK	500 mL
1/2 TSP. SALT	2 mL
PEPPER TO TASTE	
1/4 TSP. NUTMEG	1 mL
1/2 CUP CRACKER CRUMBS OR BREAD CRUMBS	125 mL
2 TBSP. BUTTER	30 mL
PARMESAN CHEESE	

PEEL ONIONS AND PLACE IN A POT WITH A LARGE AMOUNT OF BOILING SALTED WATER. BOIL, UNCOVERED, FOR 20-30 MINUTES, UNTIL TENDER BUT NOT FALLING APART. DRAIN AND TRANSFER ONIONS TO A BUTTERED CASSEROLE.

TO PREPARE CREAM SAUCE: MELT BUTTER IN A MEDIUM SAUCEPAN AND STIR IN FLOUR. WHEN BLENDED, ADD MILK SLOWLY WHILE STIRRING. COOK ON LOW HEAT UNTIL SAUCE THICKENS. ADD SALT, PEPPER AND NUTMEG. POUR SAUCE OVER ONIONS. COMBINE CRACKER CRUMBS AND BUTTER AND SPRINKLE OVER ONIONS. TOP WITH PARMESAN CHEESE. BEFORE SERVING, PREHEAT OVEN TO 350°F (180°C) AND BAKE FOR 15-20 MINUTES, UNTIL LIGHTLY BROWNED. SERVES 4.

CARAMELIZED ONION AND POTATO FLAN

EXCELLENT WITH HAM OR ROAST BEEF.

2 TBSP. BUTTER	30 mL
2 LARGE ONIONS, THINLY SLICED	
6-8 MEDIUM BAKER POTATOES, PEELED & THINLY SLICED	
SALT & FRESHLY GROUND PEPPER TO TASTE	
½-¾ LB. EMMENTHAL OR GRUYÈRE CHEESE, GRATED	250-340 g

IN A LARGE FRYING PAN OVER MEDIUM HEAT, SAUTÉ ONIONS IN BUTTER UNTIL DEEP GOLDEN BROWN, ABOUT 20 MINUTES. COOK SLOWLY TO CARAMELIZE. GREASE A 9 x 13" (23 x 33 cm) PAN OR LARGE ROUND BAKING DISH. LAYER HALF THE POTATO SLICES IN A SHINGLE FASHION AND SEASON. TOP WITH HALF THE ONIONS AND EMMENTHAL. REPEAT NEXT LAYER, ENDING WITH CHEESE. BAKE AT 350°F (180°C) FOR 50 MINUTES, OR UNTIL POTATOES ARE FORK-TENDER. CUT IN SQUARES OR WEDGES TO SERVE. SERVES 8.

DEAR GOD:
PLEASE SEND DENNIS CLARK TO A DIFFERENT CAMP THIS YEAR.

WHIPPED POTATO
WITH CELERY ROOT

CELERY ROOT DOES WONDERS FOR THE HUMBLE POTATO.

1 CELERY ROOT, PEELED & CHOPPED
4-5 BAKER POTATOES, PEELED & CUT
    INTO CHUNKS
2 TBSP. BUTTER   30 mL
3 TBSP. SOUR CREAM   45 mL
GRATED ZEST OF 1 ORANGE
SALT & FRESHLY GROUND PEPPER
    TO TASTE

COOK CELERY ROOT IN SIMMERING SALTED WATER UNTIL TENDER. DRAIN AND PURÉE IN FOOD PROCESSOR. COOK POTATOES IN SALTED WATER UNTIL TENDER. DRAIN AND MASH, MIXING IN BUTTER AND SOUR CREAM. ADD ORANGE ZEST TO MASHED CELERY ROOT, THEN ADD TO MASHED POTATOES. SEASON WITH SALT AND PEPPER. SERVES 6.

WILL CARROTS HELP YOU SEE IN THE DARK?
YES - BUT THEY SURE ARE HARD TO LIGHT!

POTATOES ROSTI

GREAT WITH STEAK, ROAST BEEF OR LAMB

POTATOES, SCRUBBED, UNPEELED
2 TBSP. BUTTER   30 mL
2 TBSP. VEGETABLE OIL   30 mL
SEASONING SALT TO TASTE

PREPARE POTATOES USING A MELON BALLER (ALLOW 8-10 BALLS PER PERSON). PREHEAT OVEN TO 350°F (180°C). ADD BUTTER AND OIL TO ROASTING PAN AND HEAT FOR 10 MINUTES; ADD POTATOES AND BAKE FOR 45 MINUTES, STIRRING OFTEN. DRAIN ON PAPER TOWEL. SPRINKLE WITH SALT. THESE MAY ALSO BE COOKED IN A FRYING PAN.

ANOTHER WAY:

USE SMALL NEW POTATOES, PLACE EACH ON A WOODEN SPOON AND SLICE, BUT NOT ALL THE WAY THROUGH. TOSS WITH MELTED BUTTER AND OIL. SPRINKLE WITH SEASONING SALT. BAKE AT 350°F (180°C) FOR 30 MINUTES, STIRRING OFTEN. THEY WILL FAN OUT WHILE COOKING - VERY CLEVER!

GIVE ME ABIGUITY OR GIVE ME SOMETHING ELSE.

ROASTED SWEET POTATO WEDGES

SERVE WITH HAM OR PORK ROAST.

3 SWEET POTATOES	
1 TBSP. OLIVE OIL	15 mL
1 TBSP. BROWN SUGAR	15 mL
½ TSP. CHILI POWDER	2 mL
½ TSP. SALT	2 mL
⅛-¼ TSP. CAYENNE PEPPER	0.5-1 mL

PREHEAT OVEN TO 400°F (200°C). PEEL POTATOES AND CUT INTO 1" (2.5 cm) WEDGES.

IN A LARGE BOWL, TOSS POTATOES WITH OIL. MIX SUGAR AND SEASONINGS TOGETHER. SPRINKLE ON POTATOES AND STIR UNTIL EVENLY COATED.

SPREAD ON A NON-STICK BAKING SHEET LARGE ENOUGH TO HOLD POTATOES WITHOUT OVERCROWDING.

ROAST POTATOES FOR 30 MINUTES, TURNING EVERY 10 MINUTES UNTIL TENDER AND BROWNED. SERVES 4.

THE ONLY TIME MY PRAYERS ARE NEVER ANSWERED IS ON THE GOLF COURSE. - BILLY GRAHAM

TURNIPS 'N' APPLES

EVERYBODY WHO TRIES THIS WANTS THE RECIPE - YOU'VE GOT IT!

1 LARGE TURNIP, PEELED & DICED	
1 TBSP. BUTTER	15 mL
2 APPLES	
1/4 CUP BROWN SUGAR	60 mL
PINCH OF CINNAMON	

TOPPING

1/3 CUP FLOUR	75 mL
1/3 CUP BROWN SUGAR	75 mL
2 TBSP. BUTTER	30 mL

BRING A LARGE POT OF WATER TO A BOIL AND COOK TURNIP UNTIL TENDER. DRAIN AND MASH TURNIP WITH BUTTER. PEEL AND SLICE APPLES. TOSS WITH BROWN SUGAR AND CINNAMON. IN A GREASED CASSEROLE, ARRANGE TURNIPS AND APPLES IN ALTERNATE LAYERS, BEGINNING AND ENDING WITH TURNIPS. MIX TOPPING INGREDIENTS UNTIL CRUMBLY. PAT ON TOP OF TURNIPS AND BAKE AT 350°F (180°C) FOR 1 HOUR. SERVES 6-8.

ITS GOOD SPORTSMANSHIP TO NOT PICK UP LOST GOLF BALLS WHILE THEY ARE STILL ROLLING.
- MARK TWAIN

PERFECT PARSNIPS

IF YOU ARE A DEVOTEE THESE ARE - PRESENTABLE, PALATABLE AND POSITIVELY A SNAP.

3 PARSNIPS, PEELED & SLICED IN MATCHSTICKS	
1 CARROT, PEELED & SLICED IN MATCHSTICKS	
3 TBSP. BUTTER	45 mL
1 TBSP. FRESH LEMON JUICE	15 mL
1 TBSP. FRESH DILL	15 mL
OR 1 TSP. (5 mL) DRIED DILL	

MELT BUTTER IN A FRYING PAN AND STIR-FRY PARSNIPS AND CARROTS OVER MEDIUM-HIGH HEAT FOR 3-4 MINUTES, UNTIL TENDER-CRISP. REMOVE TO A SERVING DISH AND SPRINKLE WITH LEMON JUICE AND DILL. SERVES 4.

A GRENADE THROWN INTO A KITCHEN IN FRANCE WOULD RESULT IN LINOLEUM BLOWNAPART.

OVEN-ROASTED
AUTUMN VEGETABLES

FOR A DIFFERENT FLAVOR, ADD A SPRINKLING OF FRESH HERBS (ROSEMARY, THYME OR MARJORAM) BEFORE SERVING.

1 LARGE SWEET POTATO, PEELED & CUT INTO 1" (2.5 cm) CUBES	
1 FENNEL BULB (1 LB./500 g), SCRUBBED, TRIMMED & CUT INTO WEDGES	
6 SMALL RED POTATOES, SCRUBBED & QUARTERED	
3-4 PARSNIPS, PEELED & CHOPPED	
4 LARGE SHALLOTS, PEELED & CUT INTO QUARTERS	
2 TBSP. OLIVE OIL	30 mL
1 TBSP. BALSAMIC VINEGAR	15 mL
1 TSP. COARSE SALT	5 mL
1 TBSP. BALSAMIC VINEGAR	15 mL

PREHEAT OVEN TO 425°F (220°C). IN A LARGE ROASTING PAN, TOSS SWEET POTATO, FENNEL, RED POTATOES, PARSNIPS AND SHALLOTS WITH OIL AND 1 TBSP. (15 mL) VINEGAR AND SALT. ROAST, UNCOVERED, FOR 30-35 MINUTES, STIRRING AND TOSSING ONCE OR TWICE, UNTIL VEGETABLES ARE LIGHTLY BROWNED AND TENDER.

PLACE ROASTED VEGETABLES IN A LARGE SERVING BOWL. SPRINKLE WITH 1 TBSP. (15 mL) VINEGAR. SERVES 4-6.

LEMON RISOTTO

WHEN YOU'RE WILLING TO FUSS . . .

1 TBSP. OLIVE OIL	15 mL
1½ CUPS SLICED SHIITAKE MUSHROOMS	375 mL
2 SHALLOTS OR GREEN ONIONS, THINLY SLICED	
2 GARLIC CLOVES, MINCED	
DASH OF PEPPER	
1 CUP ARBORIO OR SHORT-GRAIN RICE	250 mL
2 CUPS CHICKEN BROTH	500 mL
½ CUP DRY WHITE WINE OR WATER	125 mL
1 LARGE CARROT CUT INTO 1" (2.5 cm) MATCHSTICKS	
1 SMALL BUNCH ASPARAGUS SPEARS, CUT INTO 1" (2.5 cm) PIECES	
¼ CUP PARMESAN CHEESE	60 mL
2 TSP. GRATED LEMON ZEST	10 mL
FRESH BASIL OR PARSLEY (OPTIONAL)	

IN A LARGE SAUCEPAN, HEAT OIL AND COOK MUSHROOMS, SHALLOTS, GARLIC AND PEPPER UNTIL VEGETABLES ARE TENDER BUT NOT BROWN. ADD RICE AND COOK AND STIR 2 MINUTES MORE. STIR BROTH AND WINE INTO RICE MIXTURE AND BRING TO A BOIL. REDUCE HEAT; COVER AND SIMMER FOR 30 MINUTES (DO NOT LIFT COVER). REMOVE FROM HEAT. STIR IN CARROTS, ASPARAGUS, PARMESAN AND LEMON ZEST. COVER AND LET STAND FOR 5 MINUTES. ADD ADDITIONAL WATER, IF NECESSARY FOR THE DESIRED CONSISTENCY. GARNISH WITH BASIL OR PARSLEY. SERVES 8.

MUSHROOM BARLEY RISOTTO

USE A MIXTURE OF MUSHROOMS SUCH AS SHITAKE, CREMINI AND OYSTER TO GIVE A RICH FLAVOR.

1/4 CUP BUTTER, DIVIDED	60 mL
1/2 ONION, DICED	
SALT & PEPPER TO TASTE	
1 CUP PEARL OR POT BARLEY	250 mL
3 CUPS CHICKEN BROTH	750 mL
1 1/2 CUPS WATER	375 mL
4 CUPS CHOPPED MUSHROOMS	1 L
GRATED ZEST OF 1 LEMON	
1 TBSP. LEMON JUICE	15 mL
3 TBSP. CHOPPED FRESH PARSLEY	45 mL
1/3 CUP PINE NUTS, TOASTED	75 mL

IN A SAUCEPAN, MELT HALF OF THE BUTTER OVER MEDIUM HEAT. ADD ONION, SALT AND PEPPER; COOK AND STIR UNTIL ONION IS SOFTENED. STIR IN BARLEY AND COOK FOR 1 MINUTE. ADD BROTH AND WATER; BRING TO A BOIL. COVER, REDUCE HEAT AND SIMMER JUST UNTIL BARLEY IS TENDER AND LIQUID IS ABSORBED. REMOVE FROM HEAT; LET STAND FOR 5 MINUTES.

IN A FRYING PAN, MELT REMAINING BUTTER. ADD MUSHROOMS; COOK, STIRRING OCCASIONALLY, UNTIL NO LIQUID REMAINS.

PLACE MUSHROOMS OVER BARLEY AND SPRINKLE WITH LEMON ZEST AND JUICE. TOSS GENTLY WITH A FORK. SPRINKLE WITH PARSLEY AND PINE NUTS. A WONDERFUL ADDITION TO GRILLED MEAT OR FISH.

Crab Manicotti with Parmesan Cheese Sauce, page 148

Roasted Salmon Salad with Honey Mustard Vinaigrette, page 186

BASMATI RICE PILAF

"THE ROAD TO MOROCCO."

2 TBSP. BUTTER	30 mL
1 MEDIUM ONION, CHOPPED	
1/3 CUP SLIVERED ALMONDS	75 mL
1 CUP UNCOOKED BASMATI RICE	250 mL
1/2 CUP FINELY CHOPPED CARROTS	125 mL
1/3 CUP CURRANTS	75 mL
1 TSP. FINELY SHREDDED ORANGE PEEL	5 mL
1/4 TSP. GROUND CINNAMON	1 mL
1/4 TSP. GROUND BLACK PEPPER	1 mL
1/8-1/4 TSP. RED PEPPER FLAKES	0.5-1 mL
1 3/4 CUPS CHICKEN BROTH	425 mL
1/4 CUP WATER	60 mL

IN A MEDIUM SAUCEPAN, MELT BUTTER AND SAUTÉ ONION AND ALMONDS OVER MEDIUM HEAT UNTIL ONION IS TENDER AND ALMONDS ARE GOLDEN. STIR IN RICE. COOK AND STIR FOR 4 MINUTES. STIR IN CARROT, CURRANTS, ORANGE PEEL, CINNAMON, BLACK PEPPER, AND RED PEPPER FLAKES. CAREFULLY STIR BROTH AND WATER INTO RICE MIXTURE IN SAUCEPAN. BRING TO A BOIL AND REDUCE HEAT. SIMMER, COVERED, UNTIL LIQUID IS ABSORBED AND RICE IS TENDER (ABOUT 20 MINUTES). TRANSFER TO SERVING BOWL. SERVES 6.

A CHICKEN CROSSING THE ROAD IS
POULTRY IN MOTION.

OVEN BAKED WILD RICE

FABULOUS FLAVOR. MAKE IT IN THE MORNING AND BAKE IT WITH THE BEEF.

1½ CUPS WILD RICE	375 mL
½ CUP BUTTER	125 mL
4 OZ CAN WATER CHESTNUTS	115 mL
2 CUPS FRESH MUSHROOMS, SLICED	500 mL
3-10 OZ. CANS CONSOMMÉ, UNDILUTED	3-284 mL

SOAK RICE OVERNIGHT IN A GENEROUS AMOUNT OF WATER. DRAIN. MELT BUTTER IN A 2-QUART (2 L) CASSEROLE. ADD RICE, WATER CHESTNUTS AND MUSHROOMS AND STIR. POUR IN CONSOMMÉ. LET STAND UNTIL READY TO BAKE. BAKE AT 350°F (180°C) FOR 2-2½ HOURS. GREAT WITH BEEF. SERVES 8.

A THREE-LEGGED DOG WALKS INTO A SALOON IN THE OLD WEST. HE SLIDES UP TO THE BAR AND ANNOUNCES: "I'M LOOKING FOR THE MAN WHO SHOT MY PAW!"

FISH AND SEAFOOD

Crab Cakes with Roasted Red Pepper Aioli
Seared Scallops with Orzo Risotto
Mayan Grilled Shrimp
Ginger Shrimp Stir-Fry
with Sugar Snap Peas and Corn
Shrimp Stir-Fry
Shrimp with Artichokes
"The Ladies" Seafood Casserole
Quick Salmon Patties with
Lemon Caper Mayonnaise
Roasted Salmon Salad with
Honey Mustard Vinaigrette
Grilled Marinated Halibut
Wild West Salmon
Cedar Plank Salmon with Cucumber Dill Sauce
Layered Tuna Casserole

CRAB CAKES WITH
ROASTED RED PEPPER AIOLI

THESE CAN BE MADE ONE DAY AHEAD AND
COOKED JUST BEFORE SERVING. SERVE WARM WITH
ROASTED RED PEPPER AIOLI.

BÉCHAMEL SAUCE

2 TBSP. BUTTER	30 mL
2 TBSP. FLOUR	30 mL
1 CUP HOT MILK	250 mL
1 BAY LEAF	

1 LB. CRABMEAT OR MOCK CRAB	500 g
½ RED PEPPER, FINELY DICED	
2 GREEN ONIONS, DICED	
½ CUP FRESH BREADCRUMBS	125 mL
½ TSP. CAYENNE	2 mL
1½ TSP. LEMON JUICE	7 mL
DASH WORCESTERSHIRE SAUCE	
SALT & PEPPER TO TASTE	
1 CUP BREADCRUMBS	250 mL
¼ CUP BUTTER	60 mL

ROASTED RED PEPPER AIOLI

½ CUP ROASTED RED PEPPERS	125 mL
(FOUND IN YOUR DELI SECTION)	
½ CUP MAYONNAISE	125 mL
1 GARLIC CLOVE, MINCED	
1 TSP. LEMON JUICE	5 mL

MELT BUTTER IN A MEDIUM-SIZED SAUCEPAN AND
ADD FLOUR. MIX THOROUGHLY AND COOK OVER
MEDIUM HEAT FOR ABOUT 3 MINUTES. DO NOT
BROWN. GRADUALLY STIR HOT MILK INTO FLOUR

CRAB CAKES WITH
ROASTED RED PEPPER AIOLI

CONTINUED FROM PAGE 176.

MIXTURE UNTIL IT FORMS A SMOOTH SAUCE. ADD BAY LEAF AND COOK FOR JUST A FEW MINUTES. CHILL. REMOVE BAY LEAF FROM SAUCE. SQUEEZE ANY LIQUID FROM CRABMEAT AND ADD CRAB TO BÉCHAMEL SAUCE. IF USING MOCK CRAB, CHOP IN FOOD PROCESSOR. ADD RED PEPPER, ONION, BREADCRUMBS, CAYENNE, LEMON JUICE, WORCESTERSHIRE, SALT AND PEPPER TO SAUCE. MIX THOROUGHLY. COVER AND CHILL FOR 30 MINUTES OR OVERNIGHT.

FORM CRAB MIXTURE INTO 2" (5 cm) BALLS FOR APPETIZER-SIZED CAKES (LARGER FOR MAIN COURSE). ROLL IN BREADCRUMBS AND FLATTEN. MELT BUTTER AND BROWN EACH SIDE. MAKES 36 APPETIZERS.

TO MAKE AIOLI: PURÉE RED PEPPERS. ADD MAYONNAISE, GARLIC AND LEMON JUICE TO ROASTED RED PEPPER PURÉE. REFRIGERATE UNTIL SERVING.

IS IT MY IMAGINATION OR DO BUFFALO WINGS TASTE A LOT LIKE CHICKEN?

SEARED SCALLOPS
WITH ORZO RISOTTO

AWESOME WITH ASPARAGUS! AN ELEGANT
DINNER FOR 4.

ORZO RISOTTO

$1\frac{2}{3}$ CUPS ORZO	400 mL
1 TBSP. OLIVE OIL	15 mL
1 CUP DICED MUSHROOMS	250 mL
1/3 CUP DICED ONION	75 mL
1/3 CUP DICED SUN-DRIED TOMATOES	75 mL
1/3 CUP DICED RED PEPPER	75 mL
2 CUPS CHICKEN BROTH	500 mL
1/2 CUP FRESHLY GRATED PARMESAN CHEESE	125 mL
2 TBSP. CHOPPED PARSLEY	30 mL
1/2 CUP WHIPPING CREAM	125 mL

SCALLOPS

2 TBSP. OLIVE OIL	30 mL

16 LARGE ($3/4$ LB./340 g) NOVA SCOTIA
     SCALLOPS (LARGE SHRIMP ARE AN
     EXCELLENT SUBSTITUTE)
SALT & FRESHLY GROUND PEPPER TO TASTE
FRESHLY GRATED PARMESAN CHEESE

TO MAKE RISOTTO: COOK ORZO ACCORDING TO
PACKAGE DIRECTIONS AND SET ASIDE.

IN A LARGE HEAVY POT, HEAT OIL AND SAUTÉ
MUSHROOMS, ONION, SUN-DRIED TOMATOES AND
RED PEPPER UNTIL SOFT. ADD BROTH AND BRING
TO A BOIL.

SEARED SCALLOPS
WITH ORZO RISOTTO

CONTINUED FROM PAGE 178.

STIR IN ORZO, PARMESAN AND PARSLEY. ADD CREAM AND SIMMER GENTLY, STIRRING FREQUENTLY, UNTIL MIXTURE IS CREAMY BUT NOT RUNNY, ABOUT 20 MINUTES.

HEAT OIL IN A VERY HOT PAN. SEASON SCALLOPS WITH SALT AND PEPPER AND SEAR UNTIL BROWN ON OUTSIDE BUT JUST OPAQUE IN THE MIDDLE.

SPRINKLE PARMESAN OVER RISOTTO AND TOP WITH SCALLOPS. SERVES 4.

MURPHY'S RULES OF GOLF:

SOMETIMES IT SEEMS THAT YOUR CUP MOVETH OVER.

THE REASON THAT YOUR REAL SWING IS NOT AS GOOD AS YOUR PRACTICE SWING IS THAT YOU ARE TERRIBLE.

GOLF BALLS ARE LIKE EGGS. THEY'RE WHITE, THEY'RE SOLD BY THE DOZEN, AND A WEEK LATER YOU HAVE TO BUY MORE.

MAYAN GRILLED SHRIMP

EXCELLENT SERVED AS AN APPETIZER OR AN ENTRÉE.

WOODEN SKEWERS
2 LBS. LARGE SHRIMP IN THE SHELL .... 1 kg

TEQUILA LIME MARINADE

¼ CUP FRESH LIME JUICE	60 mL
¼ CUP TEQUILA	60 mL
2 SHALLOTS, FINELY CHOPPED	
2 GARLIC CLOVES, MINCED	
2 TSP. GROUND CUMIN	10 mL
SALT & GROUND PEPPER	
½ CUP OLIVE OIL	125 mL

SOAK SKEWERS IN WATER FOR AT LEAST 30 MINUTES.

THREAD 4 SHRIMP ON EACH SKEWER. LAY IN A SINGLE LAYER IN A SHALLOW GLASS DISH.

TO MAKE MARINADE: WHISK TOGETHER LIME JUICE, TEQUILA, SHALLOTS, GARLIC, CUMIN, AND SALT AND PEPPER TO TASTE. SLOWLY ADD OIL, WHISKING UNTIL COMBINED. TASTE FOR SEASONING.

POUR MARINADE OVER SHRIMP AND LET MARINATE FOR AT LEAST 30 MINUTES, OR UP TO 4 HOURS IN THE REFRIGERATOR.

HEAT BARBECUE TO MEDIUM HEAT. GRILL SHRIMP ABOUT 2 MINUTES ON EACH SIDE, JUST UNTIL PINK. SERVES 8.

GINGER SHRIMP STIR-FRY
WITH SUGAR SNAP PEAS AND CORN

1 LB. UNCOOKED LARGE SHRIMP, PEELED & DEVEINED	500	g

MARINADE

2 TBSP. CANOLA OIL	30	mL
1 TBSP. PEELED MINCED FRESH GINGER	15	mL
2 LARGE GARLIC CLOVES, MINCED		
1/2 TSP. SALT	2	mL
1/4 TSP. RED PEPPER FLAKES	1	mL

1 LB. SUGAR SNAP PEAS	500	g
1 CUP FRESH OR FROZEN CORN KERNELS	250	mL
1/2 CUP DICED SWEET RED PEPPER	125	mL
3 GREEN ONIONS, DIAGONALLY SLICED		
2 TSP. TOASTED SESAME SEEDS	10	mL
BASMATI RICE, FRESH CILANTRO & SOY SAUCE		

COMBINE SHRIMP, OIL, GINGER, GARLIC, SALT AND RED PEPPER FLAKES IN A MEDIUM BOWL. REFRIGERATE FOR 1 HOUR. HEAT LARGE NON-STICK FRYING PAN OVER HIGH HEAT. ADD SHRIMP MIXTURE, SAUTÉ UNTIL SHRIMP ARE JUST OPAQUE ABOUT 2 MINUTES. TRANSFER TO A BOWL. ADD A LITTLE OIL TO WOK; ADD PEAS, CORN, PEPPERS AND ONIONS. STIR-FRY UNTIL VEGGIES ARE TENDER-CRISP, ABOUT 3 MINUTES. RETURN SHRIMP AND JUICES TO WOK; STIR-FRY 1 MINUTE LONGER. SEASON WITH SALT AND PEPPER. SPRINKLE WITH SESAME SEEDS. SERVE OVER STEAMED RICE MIXED WITH CHOPPED FRESH CILANTRO. PASS THE SOY SAUCE. SERVES 4.

SHRIMP STIR-FRY

GET OUT YOUR STOPWATCH!!

2 TBSP. SESAME OIL	30 mL
1 GARLIC CLOVE, MINCED	
½ TSP. MINCED FRESH GINGER	2 mL
24-36 PEELED SHRIMP	
A HANDFUL OF SNOW PEAS	
2 CUPS BROCCOLI FLORETS	500 mL
2 STALKS CELERY, SLICED DIAGONALLY	
1 SMALL WHITE ONION, SLIVERED	
1 RED BELL PEPPER, SLICED	
2 CUPS FRESH BEAN SPROUTS	500 mL
½ CUP OYSTER SAUCE	125 mL
1 TBSP. SOY SAUCE	15 mL
1 TBSP. LIQUID HONEY	15 mL
¼ CUP WHITE WINE	60 mL

HEAT SESAME OIL IN A WOK OR FRYING PAN OVER MEDIUM HEAT. SAUTÉ GARLIC AND GINGER FOR 30 SECONDS. ADD SHRIMP AND COOK FOR 30 SECONDS. ADD VEGGIES AND STIR-FRY UNTIL TENDER-CRISP - ABOUT 3 MINUTES. STIR IN OYSTER SAUCE, SOY SAUCE, HONEY AND WINE. TOSS TOGETHER FOR 2 MINUTES. SERVE WITH RICE. SERVES 4.

HASTE CUISINE: FAST FRENCH FOOD.

SHRIMP WITH ARTICHOKES

EXCELLENT CASSEROLE - GREAT SAUCE!

SAUCE

2 TBSP. BUTTER	30 mL
2 TBSP. FLOUR	30 mL
1/2 TSP. BLACK PEPPER	2 mL
1/4 TSP. CAYENNE PEPPER	1 mL
2 CUPS HALF & HALF CREAM	500 mL
1 TBSP. KETCHUP	15 mL
1 TBSP. WORCESTERSHIRE SAUCE	15 mL
3 TBSP. LEMON JUICE	45 mL
3 TBSP. SHERRY	45 mL

12 OZ. JAR MARINATED ARTICHOKE HEARTS, DRAINED & COARSELY CHOPPED	340 g
2 LBS. MEDIUM SHRIMP, PEELED, DEVEINED, TAIL OFF	1 kg
1 CUP GRATED SHARP CHEDDAR CHEESE	250 mL

TO MAKE SAUCE: MELT BUTTER IN A SAUCEPAN; STIR IN FLOUR, PEPPER AND CAYENNE. ADD CREAM; COOK OVER LOW HEAT, STIRRING UNTIL THICKENED. STIR IN KETCHUP, WORCESTERSHIRE, LEMON JUICE AND SHERRY.

PREHEAT OVEN TO 400°F (200°C). IN A SHALLOW 9 x 13" (23 x 33 cm) BAKING DISH, LAYER ARTICHOKES AND SHRIMP. POUR SAUCE OVER AND SPRINKLE WITH CHEESE. (COVER AND REFRIGERATE IF MAKING AHEAD. UNCOVER AND BRING TO ROOM TEMPERATURE BEFORE BAKING.) BAKE FOR 20-30 MINUTES, OR UNTIL SHRIMP ARE PINK AND CHEESE IS MELTED. SERVE ON RICE WITH A GREEN SALAD. SERVES 8-10.

"THE LADIES"
SEAFOOD CASSEROLE

ASSEMBLE EARLY IN THE MORNING AND YOU'RE FREE TO ORGANIZE YOURSELF WITH LAST-MINUTE DETAILS. FRESH SEAFOOD IS BEST.

⅓ CUP BUTTER	75 mL
⅓ CUP FLOUR	75 mL
2 TSP. PREPARED MUSTARD	10 mL
1 TBSP. GRATED ONION	15 mL
1 TBSP. WORCESTERSHIRE SAUCE	15 mL
½ TSP. PAPRIKA	2 mL
½ TSP. SALT	2 mL
¼ TSP. TABASCO SAUCE	1 mL
3 CUPS MILK	750 mL
6 OZ. GRUYÈRE CHEESE, CUBED	170 g
2 CUPS MEDIUM SHRIMP	500 mL
2 CUPS CRABMEAT	500 mL
½ CUP SLICED RIPE OLIVES	125 mL
1 TBSP. LEMON JUICE	15 mL

IN A LARGE SAUCEPAN, MELT BUTTER OVER LOW HEAT. BLEND IN FLOUR, MUSTARD, ONION, WORCESTERSHIRE, PAPRIKA, SALT AND TABASCO. GRADUALLY ADD MILK, STIRRING CONSTANTLY UNTIL THICKENED. ADD CHEESE AND STIR UNTIL MELTED. REMOVE FROM HEAT AND BLEND IN SEAFOOD AND OLIVES. POUR INTO A LARGE CASSEROLE AND BRUSH WITH LEMON JUICE. MAY BE REFRIGERATED AT THIS POINT. BAKE AT 350°F (180°C) FOR 30 MINUTES, OR UNTIL BUBBLY. DELICIOUS SERVED OVER RICE WITH A GREEN SALAD AND WARM ROLLS.

QUICK SALMON PATTIES WITH LEMON CAPER MAYONNAISE

THE LEMON CAPER MAYO IS MARVELOUS!

2-7½ OZ. CANS RED SALMON (LEFTOVER COOKED SALMON IS EVEN BETTER)	2-213 g
1 TBSP. CHOPPED FRESH PARSLEY	15 mL
2 GREEN ONIONS, CHOPPED	
1 STALK CELERY, FINELY DICED	
1 CUP DRY BREADCRUMBS	250 mL
1 TSP. LEMON PEPPER OR BLACK PEPPER	5 mL
½ TSP. SALT	2 mL
2 EGGS, BEATEN	
1 CUP DRY BREADCRUMBS	250 mL
2 TSP. VEGETABLE OIL	10 mL
2 TSP. BUTTER	10 mL

LEMON CAPER MAYONNAISE

½ CUP MAYONNAISE	125 mL
2 TBSP. FRESH LEMON JUICE	30 mL
1 TBSP. SMALL CAPERS	15 mL
1 TBSP. CHOPPED FRESH DILL OR 1 TSP. (5 mL) DRIED	15 mL
DASH CAYENNE PEPPER	

DRAIN SALMON; PLACE IN BOWL AND FLAKE WITH A FORK. ADD PARSLEY, ONION, CELERY, BREAD-CRUMBS, LEMON PEPPER, SALT AND EGGS; BLEND WELL. DIVIDE INTO 4 BALLS AND ROLL IN BREAD-CRUMBS; FLATTEN INTO PATTIES. IN A LARGE FRYING PAN, HEAT OIL AND BUTTER OVER MEDIUM HEAT. COOK PATTIES, TURNING ONCE, UNTIL CRISP AND GOLDEN.

TO MAKE LEMON CAPER MAYONNAISE: COMBINE INGREDIENTS; COVER; REFRIGERATE UNTIL SERVING.

ROASTED SALMON SALAD
WITH HONEY MUSTARD VINAIGRETTE
DELICIOUS AND HEALTHY TOO!

HONEY MUSTARD VINAIGRETTE

½ CUP BALSAMIC VINEGAR	125 mL
½ CUP WATER	125 mL
2 TBSP. DRIED CRANBERRIES	30 mL
8 DRIED APRICOTS, SLICED	
2 TSP. DIJON MUSTARD	10 mL
2 TSP. HONEY	10 mL
1 TBSP. OLIVE OIL	15 mL

SALAD

1 LB. SALMON FILLET, CUT INTO 4 EQUAL PORTIONS	500 g
½ TSP. SALT	2 mL
¼ TSP. PEPPER	1 mL
8 CUPS SPINACH LEAVES, STEMS REMOVED & WASHED	2 L
2 CUPS SLICED YELLOW PEPPERS	500 mL
2 CUPS SLICED RED PEPPERS	500 mL
3 TBSP. CHOPPED TOASTED PECANS	45 mL

TO MAKE VINAIGRETTE: IN A SMALL SAUCEPAN, COMBINE BALSAMIC VINEGAR, WATER, CRANBERRIES AND APRICOTS. SET PAN OVER MEDIUM-HIGH HEAT AND BRING TO A BOIL. SIMMER FOR 5 MINUTES. STRAIN AND RESERVE LIQUID AND FRUITS. COMBINE LIQUID WITH MUSTARD, HONEY AND OIL. SET ASIDE.

ROASTED SALMON SALAD
WITH HONEY MUSTARD VINAIGRETTE
CONTINUED FROM PAGE 186.

CONTINUED FROM PAGE 186.

PREHEAT OVEN TO 425°F (220°C). LIGHTLY COAT A BAKING SHEET WITH COOKING SPRAY. SEASON SALMON FILLETS WITH SALT AND PEPPER AND TRANSFER THEM TO BAKING SHEET. BAKE FOR 5-7 MINUTES, UNTIL FORK-TENDER.

DIVIDE SPINACH AMONG 4 PLATES. TOP WITH YELLOW AND RED PEPPERS. PLACE A COOKED SALMON FILLET ON TOP OF EACH SALAD AND SPRINKLE WITH TOASTED PECANS. DRIZZLE DRESSING OVER AND ADD SOME OF THE RESERVED FRUIT. (PICTURED ON PAGE 172.)

AN OLDER WOMAN WILL NEVER WAKE YOU IN THE MIDDLE OF THE NIGHT TO ASK WHAT YOU THINK. THEY DON'T CARE WHAT YOU THINK.

GRILLED MARINATED HALIBUT

MARINADE

¼ TSP. BLACK PEPPER	1 mL
¼ TSP. SALT	1 mL
¼ TSP. PAPRIKA	1 mL
1 TSP. FENNEL SEED, CRUSHED	5 mL
2 TBSP. TERIYAKI SAUCE	30 mL
2 TBSP. OLIVE OIL	30 mL
JUICE OF 2 LIMES	
4 LIME WEDGES	

4 HALIBUT STEAKS, CUT 1" (2.5 cm) THICK

TO MAKE MARINADE: COMBINE ALL INGREDIENTS. POUR MARINADE OVER HALIBUT IN A SHALLOW DISH. REFRIGERATE 1 HOUR. GRILL OVER MEDIUM-HIGH HEAT (OR UNDER BROILER) 5 MINUTES EACH SIDE, OR UNTIL FISH IS JUST OPAQUE IN MIDDLE. SERVE WITH STEAMED BASMATI RICE, SESAME SPINACH, PAGE 155, AND DILL AND PARMESAN TOMATOES, PAGE 157. (PICTURED OPPOSITE.)

BORROW MONEY FROM PESSIMISTS - THEY DON'T EXPECT IT BACK.

Grilled Marinated Halibut, page 188
Sesame Spinach, page 155

Braised Lamb Shanks with Lentils, page 220

WILD WEST SALMON

SCRUMPTIOUS COMPANY FARE FOR THE BARBECUE SEASON

1 WHOLE SALMON, BUTTERFLIED (SEE METHOD)

MARINADE

1 TBSP. BROWN SUGAR	15 mL
½ CUP RYE WHISKEY	125 mL
1 TBSP. MOLASSES	15 mL
½ CUP VEGETABLE OIL	125 mL
2 TBSP. SOY SAUCE	30 mL
1 TBSP. EACH SALT & PEPPER	15 mL
2 GARLIC CLOVES, MINCED	

TO PREPARE SALMON, REMOVE HEAD, TAIL AND FINS FROM SALMON. RUN A SHARP KNIFE DOWN BACKBONE UNTIL SALMON OPENS FLAT. REMOVE BACKBONE. PLACE FLESH-SIDE DOWN IN A LARGE DISH.

COMBINE MARINADE INGREDIENTS; MIX WELL AND POUR OVER SALMON. COVER AND MARINATE OVERNIGHT IN REFRIGERATOR.

WHEN READY TO GRILL, REMOVE SALMON FROM MARINADE AND PLACE SKIN-SIDE DOWN ON HEAVY FOIL. BARBECUE UNTIL FLESH IS OPAQUE AND FLAKES EASILY, 20-30 MINUTES. SERVE WITH CRUSTY ROLLS.

CEDAR PLANK SALMON
WITH CUCUMBER DILL SAUCE

1 UNTREATED CEDAR PLANK

2 SHALLOTS, DICED
10 GARLIC CLOVES, MINCED
3 TBSP. SNIPPED FRESH DILL 45 mL
3 TBSP. CHOPPED FRESH THYME 45 mL
2 TBSP. CHOPPED FRESH CILANTRO 30 mL
2 TBSP. GRATED LEMON ZEST 30 mL
3 TBSP. FRESH LEMON JUICE 45 mL
2 GREEN ONIONS, CHOPPED
1 TSP. OLIVE OIL 5 mL
3-4 LB. SALMON FILLET 1.5-2 kg
SALT & FRESHLY GROUND PEPPER
    TO TASTE

CUCUMBER DILL SAUCE

1/4 ENGLISH CUCUMBER, FINELY CHOPPED
1/4 TSP. SALT 1 mL
1 CUP PLAIN YOGURT 250 mL
1/2 CUP SOUR CREAM 125 mL
1 TSP. LEMON JUICE 5 mL
PEPPER TO TASTE
3 GREEN ONIONS, FINELY CHOPPED,
    WHITE PART ONLY
2 TSP. CHOPPED FRESH DILL OR 10 mL
    1 TSP. (5 mL) DRIED

SOAK CEDAR PLANK IN WATER FOR SEVERAL
HOURS.

CEDAR PLANK SALMON
WITH CUCUMBER DILL SAUCE

CONTINUED FROM PAGE 192.

IN A SMALL GLASS BOWL, COMBINE SHALLOTS, GARLIC, DILL, THYME, CILANTRO, LEMON ZEST AND JUICE, GREEN ONIONS AND OIL. COVER AND PLACE IN REFRIGERATOR FOR AT LEAST 1 HOUR TO ALLOW FLAVORS TO GET ACQUAINTED.

PLACE SALMON ON CEDAR PLANK AND SPRINKLE WITH SALT AND PEPPER. COVER WITH HERB MIXTURE. SET PLANK ON BARBECUE AND CLOSE LID. BAKE FOR 30 MINUTES ON MEDIUM HEAT, UNTIL FISH FLAKES EASILY WITH A FORK.

TO PREPARE CUCUMBER DILL SAUCE: TOSS CUCUMBER WITH SALT AND LET STAND FOR 15 MINUTES.

COMBINE YOGURT, SOUR CREAM, LEMON JUICE, PEPPER, ONION AND DILL.

DRAIN WATER FROM CUCUMBER AND ADD TO YOGURT MIXTURE. SERVES 8.

THE PROBLEM WITH THE GENE POOL IS THAT THERE IS NO LIFEGUARD.

LAYERED TUNA CASSEROLE

DOWN-HOME COOKIN'! A TASTY FAMILY CASSEROLE THAT TAKES ABOUT 20 MINUTES TO PREPARE, 30 MINUTES TO COOK AND HOW LONG IT TAKES TO EAT IS UP TO YOU!

2-6½ OZ. CANS CHUNK-STYLE TUNA, PACKED IN WATER	2-184 g
3 CUPS UNCOOKED EGG NOODLES	750 mL
½ CUP CHOPPED CELERY	125 mL
⅓ CUP FINELY CHOPPED GREEN ONIONS	75 mL
⅔ CUP SOUR CREAM	150 mL
2 TSP. DRY MUSTARD	10 mL
½ CUP MAYONNAISE	125 mL
½ TSP. THYME	2 mL
¼ TSP. SALT	1 mL
1 MEDIUM ZUCCHINI, SLICED	
½ CUP GRATED MOZZARELLA CHEESE	125 mL
½ CUP GRATED CHEDDAR CHEESE	125 mL
1 TOMATO, CHOPPED (OPTIONAL)	

DRAIN AND FLAKE TUNA. SET ASIDE. COOK NOODLES ACCORDING TO PACKAGE DIRECTIONS. DRAIN; RINSE IN HOT WATER. COMBINE TUNA, NOODLES, CELERY AND ONIONS. BLEND TOGETHER SOUR CREAM, MUSTARD, MAYONNAISE, THYME AND SALT AND MIX INTO TUNA MIXTURE. SPOON HALF OF THIS MIXTURE INTO A GREASED 2-QUART (2 L) CASSEROLE. TOP WITH HALF THE ZUCCHINI. REPEAT LAYERS AND TOP WITH GRATED CHEESES. BAKE AT 350°F (180°C) FOR 30-40 MINUTES. TOP WITH CHOPPED TOMATO. SERVES 8.

CHICKEN

Skewers of Sticky Garlic Chicken
Thai Grilled Chicken
Chicken Burritos
Chicken Scallopini with Lemon-Caper Glaze
Spicy Orange Chicken Stir-Fry
Jerk Chicken with Pineapple-Rum Glaze
Chicken Curry
Sweet 'n' Sour Chicken
Chicken, Artichoke and Wild Rice Casserole
Chicken Stew with Dumplings
Yummy Chicken
No-Fuss Moroccan Chicken
Roasted Thighs 'n' Peppers
Thigh Chicken
Pheasant Pie in Herb Pastry

SKEWERS OF STICKY GARLIC CHICKEN

PREPARE THE NIGHT BEFORE AND COOK WHEN YOU WANT THEM. GREAT AS A MEAL OR APPETIZER.

12-10" (25 cm) WOODEN SKEWERS

GARLIC HONEY MARINADE

3 GARLIC CLOVES, CRUSHED	
2 TBSP. HONEY	30 mL
1/4 CUP KETCHUP	60 mL
1/4 CUP WORCESTERSHIRE SAUCE	60 mL
2 TSP. DIJON MUSTARD	10 mL
2 TSP. TABASCO SAUCE	10 mL
SALT & PEPPER TO TASTE	

3 SKINLESS, BONELESS CHICKEN BREASTS, CUT IN THIN STRIPS

SOAK SKEWERS IN WATER AT LEAST 30 MINUTES.

TO MAKE MARINADE: COMBINE ALL INGREDIENTS.

TOSS CHICKEN IN MARINADE AND STIR UNTIL WELL COATED. TRANSFER TO A NON-METALLIC DISH; COVER AND MARINATE OVERNIGHT.

PREHEAT BROILER TO HIGH. THREAD CHICKEN ONTO SKEWERS. ARRANGE ON A FOIL-LINED BAKING SHEET AND BROIL FOR 6-7 MINUTES, TURNING OCCASIONALLY, UNTIL WELL BROWNED AND COOKED THROUGH. THESE CAN ALSO BE GRILLED ON THE BARBECUE FOR 5-6 MINUTES.

THAI GRILLED CHICKEN

SERVE WITH THAI NOODLE SALAD, PAGE 101.

MARINADE

1/3 CUP FRESH BASIL	75 mL
1/3 CUP FRESH MINT	75 mL
1/3 CUP FRESH CILANTRO	75 mL
3 TBSP. PEELED, CHOPPED GINGER	45 mL
2-3 GARLIC CLOVES	
1 1/2 TBSP. SOY SAUCE	22 mL
1 1/2 TBSP. FISH SAUCE	22 mL
1 1/2 TBSP. VEGETABLE OIL	22 mL
1 1/2 TBSP. BROWN SUGAR	22 mL
1 ANAHEIM PEPPER, CHOPPED	

6 SKINLESS, BONELESS CHICKEN
BREAST HALVES (2 LBS./1 kg)

TO MAKE MARINADE: PROCESS ALL INGREDIENTS IN FOOD PROCESSOR OR BLENDER UNTIL FINELY CHOPPED.

ARRANGE CHICKEN IN A GLASS BAKING DISH. POUR MARINADE OVER. COVER AND REFRIGERATE SEVERAL HOURS OR OVERNIGHT. REMOVE CHICKEN FROM MARINADE AND GRILL UNTIL CHICKEN IS NO LONGER PINK IN THE MIDDLE.

EXPERIENCE IS SOMETHING YOU DON'T GET UNTIL JUST AFTER YOU NEED IT.

CHICKEN BURRITOS

4 BONELESS CHICKEN BREASTS,
    SLICED IN THIN STRIPS
1 TBSP. OLIVE OIL   15 mL
2 CUPS SOUR CREAM   500 mL
4 OZ. CAN CHOPPED GREEN CHILIES   115 g
1 CUP GRATED MONTEREY JACK CHEESE   250 mL
8 MEDIUM FLOUR TORTILLAS
1 CUP GRATED SHARP CHEDDAR CHEESE   250 mL
½ HEAD LETTUCE, SHREDDED
2 TOMATOES, DICED
4 GREEN ONIONS, CHOPPED
RIPE OLIVES, SLICED

GUACAMOLE

2 AVOCADOS, PEELED & MASHED
JUICE OF ½ LEMON
1 TBSP. CHILI POWDER   15 mL
¼ TSP. CAYENNE PEPPER   1 mL
1 TBSP. WORCESTERSHIRE SAUCE   15 mL
1 GARLIC CLOVE, MINCED
2 DROPS TABASCO SAUCE

SAUTÉ CHICKEN IN OIL UNTIL JUST DONE. REMOVE FROM HEAT. STIR IN 1 CUP (250 mL) SOUR CREAM, CHILIES AND JACK CHEESE. FILL TORTILLAS AND FOLD OVER BURRITO-STYLE. PLACE SIDE BY SIDE IN LIGHTLY GREASED CASSEROLE. SPRINKLE WITH CHEDDAR. BAKE AT 350°F (180°C) FOR 20 MINUTES, OR UNTIL CHEESE MELTS. REMOVE FROM OVEN; TOP WITH GUACAMOLE, REMAINING SOUR CREAM, LETTUCE, TOMATOES, ONIONS AND OLIVES.

TO MAKE GUACAMOLE: COMBINE ALL INGREDIENTS.

CHICKEN SCALOPPINE WITH LEMON-CAPER GLAZE

4 BONELESS, SKINLESS CHICKEN BREAST HALVES	
2 TBSP. DIJON MUSTARD	30 mL
2 EGGS	
1 CUP DRY BREADCRUMBS	250 mL
½ TSP. POULTRY SEASONING	2 mL
½ TSP. GARLIC POWDER	2 mL
½ TSP. SEASONING SALT	2 mL
2 TBSP. OLIVE OIL	30 mL
¼ CUP CHICKEN BROTH	60 mL
2 TBSP. FRESH LEMON JUICE	30 mL
4 TSP. CAPERS	20 mL
¼ TSP. SALT	1 mL
4 THIN LEMON SLICES	
FRESH PARSLEY, CHOPPED	

PLACE CHICKEN BREASTS BETWEEN WAX PAPER; LIGHTLY POUND TO ⅓" (1 cm) THICK. WHISK MUSTARD AND EGGS TOGETHER. SET ASIDE. COMBINE BREADCRUMBS, POULTRY SEASONING, GARLIC POWDER AND SEASONING SALT; SPREAD ON WAX PAPER. DIP CHICKEN IN EGG MIXTURE AND COAT WITH CRUMB MIXTURE. HEAT HALF THE OIL AND ADD HALF THE CHICKEN. SAUTÉ FOR 5 MINUTES EACH SIDE, OR UNTIL NO LONGER PINK INSIDE. REMOVE TO PLATE AND KEEP WARM. REPEAT WITH REMAINING CHICKEN. IN THE SAME PAN, ADD BROTH, LEMON JUICE, CAPERS AND SALT; BRING TO A BOIL, SCRAPING BROWN BITS FROM PAN. ADD LEMON SLICES AND PARSLEY. SPOON LEMON GLAZE OVER CHICKEN. SERVES 4.

SPICY ORANGE CHICKEN STIR-FRY

We like the simplicity of this recipe - and the orange flavor!

MARINADE

1 TBSP. SOY SAUCE	15 mL
1 TBSP. DRY SHERRY	15 mL
1 TBSP. OYSTER SAUCE	15 mL
2 TSP. GRATED ORANGE ZEST	10 mL

4 BONELESS, SKINLESS CHICKEN BREAST
     HALVES, CUT INTO ½" (1.3 cm) CUBES
2 RED PEPPERS
1 SMALL ZUCCHINI
1 LARGE ONION

SPICY ORANGE SAUCE

JUICE OF 1 ORANGE	
¼ CUP DRY SHERRY	60 mL
1 TBSP. OYSTER SAUCE	15 mL
1 TBSP. SESAME OIL	15 mL
2-4 TSP. ASIAN CHILI SAUCE	10-20 mL
1 TBSP. CORNSTARCH	15 mL

3 TBSP. COOKING OIL	45 mL

4 GARLIC CLOVES, MINCED
1" (2.5 cm) PIECE FRESH GINGERROOT,
    PEELED & CHOPPED

TO MAKE MARINADE: COMBINE ALL INGREDIENTS.
ADD CHICKEN TO MARINADE AND MARINATE
15 MINUTES AT ROOM TEMPERATURE.

SPICY ORANGE CHICKEN STIR-FRY

CONTINUED FROM PAGE 200.

SEED AND STEM PEPPERS. CUT INTO 1/2" (1.3 cm) CUBES. CUT ZUCCHINI LENGTHWISE (DON'T PEEL) INTO 4 STRIPS. CUT EACH STRIP CROSSWISE INTO 1/2" (1.3 cm) PIECES. PEEL ONION AND CUT INTO THIN WEDGES. CUT EACH WEDGE IN HALF. COMBINE VEGGIES IN BOWL.

YOU'RE PROBABLY WONDERING WHY YOU HAVE TO CUT EVERYTHING INTO UNIFORM SIZES! NOT ONLY DO THE INGREDIENTS COOK EVENLY, THEY LOOK CAREFULLY CONSIDERED. VERY ZEN!

TO MAKE SPICY ORANGE SAUCE: COMBINE ORANGE JUICE, SHERRY, OYSTER SAUCE, SESAME OIL, CHILI SAUCE AND CORNSTARCH IN A SMALL BOWL. SET ASIDE.

PLACE A WOK OR HEAVY FRYING PAN OVER HIGH HEAT. WHEN WOK BECOMES HOT, ADD 2 TBSP. (30 mL) OIL. WHEN OIL SMOKES, ADD CHICKEN AND STIR 2 MINUTES. REMOVE TO PLATE. ADD REMAINING 1 TBSP. (15 mL) OIL WITH GARLIC AND GINGER. STIR FOR 5 SECONDS. ADD VEGGIES AND STIR 2 MINUTES. ADD SPICY ORANGE SAUCE AND CHICKEN AND STIR UNTIL SAUCE THICKENS. SERVE IMMEDIATELY WITH STEAMED RICE. SERVES 4.

JERK CHICKEN WITH PINEAPPLE-RUM GLAZE

GREAT FOR GRILLING - IN SHORTS OR A PARKA - IT'S THAT GOOD!

RUB

1 TBSP. DARK BROWN SUGAR	15 mL
1½ TSP. COARSE SALT	7 mL
1 TSP. CORIANDER	5 mL
½ TSP. FRESHLY GROUND PEPPER	2 mL
½ TSP. DRIED THYME	2 mL
½ TSP. ONION POWDER	2 mL
½ TSP. ALLSPICE	2 mL
½ TSP. CINNAMON	2 mL
¼-½ TSP. CAYENNE PEPPER	1-2 mL

8-10 CHICKEN LEGS, RINSED & PATTED DRY	
1½ TBSP. VEGETABLE OIL	22 mL
2 GARLIC CLOVES, MINCED	
2 GREEN ONIONS, MINCED	

PINEAPPLE-RUM GLAZE

¼ CUP BUTTER	60 mL
¼ CUP PACKED DARK BROWN SUGAR	60 mL
¼ CUP DARK RUM	60 mL
¼ CUP PINEAPPLE JUICE	60 mL

TO MAKE RUB: COMBINE SUGAR, SALT, CORIANDER, PEPPER, THYME, ONION POWDER, ALLSPICE, CINNAMON AND CAYENNE.

PLACE CHICKEN IN A 9 X 13" (23 X 33 cm) PAN AND DRIZZLE WITH OIL, RUBBING IT OVER THE CHICKEN ON ALL SIDES.

JERK CHICKEN WITH PINEAPPLE-RUM GLAZE

CONTINUED FROM PAGE 202.

SPRINKLE THE RUB, GARLIC AND ONIONS ON THE CHICKEN, PATTING SEASONINGS INTO MEAT WITH YOUR FINGERS. REFRIGERATE AT LEAST 1 HOUR.

TO MAKE GLAZE: COMBINE BUTTER, SUGAR, RUM AND PINEAPPLE JUICE IN A HEAVY SAUCEPAN. SIMMER 7-10 MINUTES OVER MEDIUM-HIGH HEAT.

OIL THE GRILL AND HEAT BARBECUE TO HIGH. ARRANGE CHICKEN ON GRILL. BRUSH WITH GLAZE AND COOK, TURNING REGULARLY, UNTIL BROWN AND NO LONGER PINK INSIDE. SERVE DRIZZLED WITH ANY REMAINING GLAZE.

I LOVE MEN WHO CAN MAKE THINGS. HOW MUCH DO YOU MAKE?

CHICKEN CURRY

4 LBS. BONELESS, SKINLESS CHICKEN BREASTS (APPROX. 8 BREASTS) CUT CROSSWISE IN ½" (1.3 cm) SLICES	2 kg
3 TBSP. OIL	45 mL
3 CUPS CHOPPED ONION	750 mL
¼ CUP MINCED FRESH GINGER	60 mL
3 CLOVES GARLIC, MINCED	
3 TBSP. CURRY POWDER (MORE IF YOU WANT IT HOTTER)	45 mL
1 TSP. CUMIN	5 mL
¼ TSP. CINNAMON	1 mL
2 TBSP. FLOUR	30 mL
1 CUP PLAIN YOGURT	250 mL
3 TBSP. TOMATO PASTE	45 mL
3 CUPS CHICKEN BROTH	750 mL
1 CUP APPLESAUCE	250 mL
12 OZ. PKG. FROZEN PEAS	340 g
½ CUP SOUR CREAM	125 mL
½ CUP COCONUT MILK	125 mL

CONDIMENTS

MANGO CHUTNEY, DICED CUCUMBER, DICED BANANAS, CURRANTS, SHREDDED COCONUT & CHOPPED PEANUTS

IN A LARGE FRYING PAN, BROWN CHICKEN IN OIL; REMOVE AND SET ASIDE. ADD ONION AND SAUTÉ UNTIL GOLDEN. ADD GINGER AND GARLIC AND SAUTÉ ABOUT 1 MINUTE. ADD CURRY, CUMIN AND CINNAMON AND MIX WELL. COOK FOR 1 MINUTE. ADD FLOUR, YOGURT AND TOMATO PASTE, WHISKING UNTIL SAUCE IS SMOOTH.

CHICKEN CURRY

CONTINUED FROM PAGE 204.

POUR IN BROTH AND APPLESAUCE AND SIMMER, UNCOVERED, UNTIL MIXTURE THICKENS (APPROXIMATELY 30 MINUTES). ADD BROWNED CHICKEN (AND ANY JUICE), FROZEN PEAS, SOUR CREAM AND COCONUT MILK. SIMMER ANOTHER 15 MINUTES. SERVE OVER BASMATI RICE WITH A VARIETY OF CONDIMENTS. SERVES 6-8.

SWEET 'N' SPEEDY CHICKEN

FAST AND TASTY! SERVES 4 DEPENDING ON THE SIZE OF YOUR THIGHS!

6 CHICKEN THIGHS, BONELESS, SKIN ON OR OFF	
SALT & PEPPER TO TASTE	
¼ CUP JALAPEÑO PEPPER JELLY	60 mL
2 TSP. LIQUID HONEY	10 mL
1 TSP. DIJON MUSTARD	5 mL

PREHEAT OVEN TO 425°F (220°C). LINE A 9 X 13" (23 X 33 cm) BAKING DISH WITH FOIL. SALT AND PEPPER CHICKEN AND PLACE IN A DISH. COMBINE JELLY, HONEY AND MUSTARD AND SPREAD OVER CHICKEN. BAKE FOR 30 MINUTES, UNCOVERED. BASTE AT LEAST ONCE DURING COOKING. SERVE OVER RICE. SERVES 4.

CHICKEN, ARTICHOKE AND WILD RICE CASSEROLE

AN "ENTERTAINING" CASSEROLE.

3 CUPS WATER	750 mL
1 CUP WILD RICE	250 mL
½ TSP. SALT	2 mL
1 TBSP. BUTTER	15 mL
1 CUP CHOPPED ONION	250 mL
1 CUP THINLY SLICED CELERY	250 mL
1 CUP SHREDDED CARROT	250 mL
1¾ CUPS CHICKEN BROTH	425 mL
2 CUPS LIGHT CREAM	500 mL
¼ CUP FLOUR	60 mL
¾ TSP. SALT	3 mL
2 TBSP. SHERRY	30 mL
FRESHLY GROUND PEPPER	
3 CUPS COOKED CUBED CHICKEN	750 mL
14 OZ. CAN ARTICHOKES, DRAINED & CHOPPED	398 mL
⅓ CUP TOASTED SLICED ALMONDS	75 mL

IN A MEDIUM-SIZED SAUCEPAN, BRING WATER TO A BOIL. STIR IN RICE AND SALT. COVER AND SIMMER 45-55 MINUTES, OR UNTIL RICE IS TENDER BUT STILL CHEWY. DRAIN RICE IN A COLANDER. MELT BUTTER IN A LARGE FRYING PAN OVER MEDIUM HEAT. ADD ONION, CELERY AND CARROT; COOK 10 MINUTES, STIRRING OCCASIONALLY, UNTIL SOFTENED. ADD BROTH TO VEGGIES IN FRYING PAN AND BRING TO A BOIL.

CHICKEN, ARTICHOKE AND WILD RICE CASSEROLE

CONTINUED FROM PAGE 206.

IN A BOWL, WHISK CREAM AND FLOUR UNTIL SMOOTH. GRADUALLY WHISK INTO BOILING BROTH. ADD SALT, SHERRY AND PEPPER. BRING TO A BOIL. REDUCE HEAT AND SIMMER 5 MINUTES, STIRRING OCCASIONALLY. ADD RICE TO SAUCE. ADD CHICKEN AND ARTICHOKES TO SAUCE AND MIX WELL. POUR MIXTURE INTO A SHALLOW 2½-3-QUART (2-3 L) BAKING DISH. COVER AND BAKE AT 350°F (180°C) FOR 35-40 MINUTES, OR UNTIL HOT AND BUBBLY. SPRINKLE WITH ALMONDS. SERVES 8-10.

IF YOU THINK IT'S HARD TO MEET NEW PEOPLE, TRY PICKING UP THE WRONG GOLF BALL. - JACK LEMMON.

CHICKEN STEW WITH DUMPLINGS

HERE IT IS - THAT OLD STANDARD - AND IT'S EXACTLY WHAT YOU'D EXPECT - COMFORT FOOD!

THE STEW

5 CUPS CHICKEN BROTH	1.25 L
14 CHICKEN THIGHS, SKINNED	2 kg
7 MEDIUM CARROTS, PEELED & CUT IN CHUNKS	
4 POTATOES, PEELED & CUT IN 1" (2.5 cm) CUBES	
2 CUPS BOILING ONIONS, PEELED	500 mL
3 TBSP. BUTTER	45 mL
3 STALKS CELERY, CHOPPED	
1 ONION, CHOPPED	
8 OZ. SMALL BUTTON MUSHROOMS	250 g
1/3 CUP FLOUR	75 mL
1/2-1 TSP. DRIED THYME OR TARRAGON	2-5 mL
SALT & PEPPER TO TASTE	
1/2 CUP FROZEN PEAS	125 mL
1/4 CUP WHIPPING CREAM	60 mL

THE DUMPLINGS

1 1/2 CUPS FLOUR	375 mL
2 TSP. BAKING POWDER	10 mL
1/2 TSP. SALT	2 mL
2/3 CUP MILK	150 mL
2 TBSP. OIL	30 mL
1 EGG, SLIGHTLY BEATEN	
1 TBSP. CHOPPED PARSLEY (OPTIONAL)	15 mL

TO MAKE STEW: IN A LARGE DUTCH OVEN, BRING BROTH TO A BOIL. ADD CHICKEN, COVER AND SIMMER OVER MEDIUM-LOW HEAT FOR 30 MINUTES. TRANSFER TO A PLATE AND LET COOL.

CHICKEN STEW WITH DUMPLINGS

CONTINUED FROM 208.

CUT MEAT INTO BITE-SIZE PIECES. ADD CARROTS AND POTATOES TO BROTH; COVER AND COOK FOR 10 MINUTES. ADD ONIONS AND SIMMER, COVERED, UNTIL ONIONS ARE TENDER, ABOUT 5 MINUTES. TRANSFER VEGETABLES TO A PLATE. POUR BROTH INTO A LARGE MEASURING CUP, ADDING MORE BROTH IF NECESSARY TO MAKE 5 CUPS (1.25 L). USING THE SAME POT, MELT BUTTER AND COOK CELERY, ONION AND MUSHROOMS, STIRRING OFTEN, UNTIL SOFTENED. ADD FLOUR, THYME, SALT AND PEPPER. COOK AND STIR FOR 1 MINUTE. GRADUALLY WHISK IN BROTH AND BRING TO A BOIL, STIRRING. REDUCE HEAT TO MEDIUM-LOW; SIMMER, STIRRING OFTEN, FOR ABOUT 5 MINUTES. RETURN CHICKEN AND JUICES TO POT. STIR IN VEGETABLE MIXTURE, PEAS AND CREAM.

TO MAKE DUMPLINGS: IN A MEDIUM BOWL, COMBINE FLOUR, BAKING POWDER AND SALT. MIX MILK, OIL AND EGG TOGETHER AND ADD TO FLOUR MIXTURE. STIR UNTIL DRY INGREDIENTS ARE JUST MOISTENED. DROP DUMPLING DOUGH BY ROUNDED TABLESPOONFULS ONTO BOILING STEW, LEAVING SPACE AROUND EACH. REDUCE HEAT, COVER TIGHTLY (DON'T PEEK!) AND SIMMER 15 MINUTES, OR UNTIL DUMPLINGS ARE FLUFFY AND NO LONGER DOUGHY ON BOTTOM. SERVES 8.

YUMMY CHICKEN

THE NAME SAYS IT ALL!

¼ CUP FLOUR	50 mL
2 TSP. SALT	10 mL
¼ TSP. PEPPER	1 mL
DASH OF THYME	
¼ CUP MELTED BUTTER	60 mL
3-4 LBS. CUT-UP CHICKEN	1.5-2 kg
4 GREEN ONIONS, CHOPPED	
½ CUP SLICED MUSHROOMS	125 mL
2 TBSP. LEMON JUICE	30 mL
1 TSP. SUGAR	5 mL
1 TSP. SALT	5 mL
⅓ CUP APPLE JUICE	75 mL

MIX FLOUR, SALT, PEPPER AND THYME IN A PLASTIC BAG. SHAKE CHICKEN IN FLOUR MIXTURE TO COAT WELL. MELT BUTTER IN A LARGE FRYING PAN AND BROWN CHICKEN. REMOVE CHICKEN TO A CASSEROLE. ADD GREEN ONIONS AND MUSHROOMS TO FRYING PAN. COVER AND SIMMER FOR 3 MINUTES. ADD TO CASSEROLE. COMBINE LEMON JUICE, SUGAR, SALT AND APPLE JUICE. POUR OVER CHICKEN AND BAKE AT 325°F (160°C) FOR 1 HOUR. SERVES 6.

MY MIND WORKS LIKE LIGHTNING: ONE BRILLIANT FLASH AND IT'S GONE.

NO-FUSS MOROCCAN CHICKEN

SERVE WITH RICE OR COUSCOUS.

2 TBSP. VEGETABLE OIL	30	mL
1½ LBS. BONELESS, SKINLESS CHICKEN BREAST HALVES	750	g
½ CUP CHOPPED ONION	125	mL
1 GARLIC CLOVE, MINCED		
2 CUPS SALSA	500	mL
½ CUP WATER	125	mL
¼ CUP CURRANTS	60	mL
2 TBSP. LIQUID HONEY	30	mL
1½ TSP. CUMIN	7	mL
1 TSP. CINNAMON	5	mL
½ CUP TOASTED SLIVERED ALMONDS	125	mL

PREHEAT OVEN TO 325°F (160°C). HEAT OIL IN A LARGE FRYING PAN AND BROWN CHICKEN. PLACE CHICKEN IN A BAKING DISH. LIGHTLY SAUTÉ ONION AND GARLIC. SPOON OVER CHICKEN. COMBINE SALSA, WATER, CURRANTS, HONEY, CUMIN AND CINNAMON. POUR OVER CHICKEN. COVER AND BAKE FOR 1 HOUR. SPRINKLE WITH ALMONDS. SERVES 4.

I CHILD-PROOFED MY HOME BUT THEY STILL GET IN.

ROASTED THIGHS 'N' PEPPERS

THIS RECIPE GOES TOGETHER IN MINUTES.

8 CHICKEN THIGHS (ABOUT 1½ LBS.)	750	g
4-6 GARLIC CLOVES, HALVED		
3-4 NEW POTATOES, QUARTERED		
1 RED PEPPER, SEEDED, CUT LENGTHWISE INTO A ½" (1.3 cm) STRIPS		
1 GREEN PEPPER, SEEDED, CUT LENGTHWISE INTO ½" (1.3 cm) STRIPS		
1 ONION, CUT INTO WEDGES		
½ TSP. DRIED THYME	2 mL	
SALT & FRESHLY GROUND PEPPER TO TASTE		
1-2 TBSP. OLIVE OIL	15-30 mL	

PREHEAT OVEN TO 425°F (220°C). IN A 9 x 13" (23 x 33 cm) BAKING DISH, LIGHTLY COATED WITH COOKING SPRAY, TOSS ALL INGREDIENTS WITH OIL AND SPREAD IN A SINGLE LAYER. ROAST, UNCOVERED, UNTIL VEGETABLES ARE TENDER-CRISP, ABOUT 30 MINUTES. TURN CHICKEN AND VEGETABLES AND COOK UNTIL CHICKEN IS NO LONGER PINK IN THE CENTER, 15-20 MINUTES LONGER. ARRANGE ON A HEATED PLATTER AND SERVE IMMEDIATELY.

IF ALL IS LOST, WHERE IS IT?

THIGH CHICKEN

A MILD-FLAVORED CASSEROLE, BUT IF YOU REALLY WANT TO "THAI" ONE ON - ADD MORE HOT CHILI SAUCE.

2 TBSP. VEGETABLE OIL	30 mL
2 LBS. CHICKEN THIGHS, SKIN REMOVED	1 kg
1 MEDIUM ONION, CHOPPED	
1 GARLIC CLOVE, MINCED	
1 TSP. CORIANDER	5 mL
1 TSP. CUMIN	5 mL
1 TSP. SALT	5 mL
2 TSP. GRATED FRESH GINGER	10 mL
2-3 TSP. SWEET HOT ORIENTAL CHILI SAUCE	10-15 mL
2 TBSP. SOY SAUCE	30 mL
2 TBSP. PEANUT BUTTER	30 mL
14 OZ. CAN COCONUT MILK	398 mL
1 TSP. GRATED LIME ZEST	5 mL
JUICE OF 1 LIME	

IN A DUTCH OVEN, HEAT OIL AND BROWN CHICKEN, ABOUT 15 MINUTES. SET ASIDE IN A LARGE CASSEROLE. SAUTÉ ONION AND GARLIC AND COOK UNTIL TENDER. STIR IN CORIANDER, CUMIN, SALT, GINGER, CHILI SAUCE, SOY SAUCE AND PEANUT BUTTER. ADD COCONUT MILK AND STIR TO BLEND. POUR SAUCE OVER CHICKEN; COVER AND COOK FOR 1 HOUR AT 325°F (160°C). JUST BEFORE SERVING, STIR IN LIME ZEST AND JUICE. SERVE OVER RICE.

PHEASANT PIE IN HERB PASTRY

AN OLD FAVORITE WITH OUR NEW HERB PASTRY OR FROZEN PUFF PASTRY.

THE BROTH

2 PHEASANTS	
6 CUPS WATER	1.5 L
1 TSP. SALT	5 mL
1 MEDIUM ONION, PEELED & CUT IN HALF	
4 WHOLE CLOVES	
2 BAY LEAVES	
10 PEPPERCORNS	

THE SAUCE

3 TBSP. BUTTER	45 mL
¼ CUP FLOUR	60 mL
2 CUPS PHEASANT BROTH	500 mL
½ CUP WHIPPING CREAM	125 mL
3 MEDIUM CARROTS, SLICED	
8 OZ. MUSHROOMS, QUARTERED	250 g
SALT & PEPPER TO TASTE	
1 CUP PEAS, FRESH OR FROZEN	250 mL
HERB CRUST PASTRY (PAGE 216)	
OR 7 OZ. (200 g) PKG. FROZEN	
PUFF PASTRY, ROOM TEMPERATURE	

TO MAKE BROTH: CUT PHEASANTS INTO QUARTERS, WASH AND PLACE IN A LARGE POT (DON'T FORGET THE NECKS.!). ADD WATER AND SALT AND BRING TO A BOIL. ADD ONION, CLOVES, BAY LEAVES AND PEPPERCORNS. SIMMER 1 HOUR, OR UNTIL MEAT IS TENDER. REMOVE MEAT, SET ASIDE AND LET COOL. STRAIN AND RESERVE BROTH.

PHEASANT PIE IN HERB PASTRY

CONTINUED FROM PAGE 214.

TO MAKE SAUCE: MELT BUTTER IN A SAUCEPAN OVER MEDIUM HEAT. ADD FLOUR AND COOK FOR A FEW MINUTES, STIRRING CONSTANTLY. WHISK IN BROTH AND BRING TO BOIL. ADD CREAM, CARROTS AND MUSHROOMS AND SIMMER FOR 15 MINUTES. SPRINKLE WITH SALT AND PEPPER. ADD PEAS AND REMOVE FROM HEAT.

PREHEAT OVEN TO 400°F (200°C). REMOVE PHEASANT MEAT FROM BONES AND DISCARD SKIN. CUT MEAT INTO PIECES AND PLACE IN A 4-QUART (4 L) CASSEROLE. POUR SAUCE OVER PHEASANT. ROLL OUT HERB PASTRY (PAGE 216) TO 1/8" (3 mm) THICKNESS. COVER CASSEROLE WITH PASTRY AND MAKE SEVERAL SLASHES ON TOP. PLACE IN OVEN FOR 30 MINUTES, OR UNTIL PASTRY IS GOLDEN BROWN. SERVE WITH WILD RICE OR BOILED NEW POTATOES. SERVES 6.

I STARTED WITH NOTHING AND I HAVE MOST OF IT LEFT.

HERB PASTRY

GREAT FOR CHICKEN PIE TOO!

2½ CUPS FLOUR	625 mL
2 TBSP. CHOPPED FRESH PARSLEY	30 mL
1 TBSP. CHOPPED FRESH THYME	15 mL
1 TSP. SALT	5 mL
1 TSP. SUGAR	5 mL
½ CUP CHILLED UNSALTED BUTTER, CUT INTO ½" (1.3 cm) PIECES	125 mL
½ CUP CHILLED SOLID VEGETABLE SHORTENING, CUT INTO ½" (1.3 cm) PIECES	125 mL
6½ TBSP. (ABOUT) ICE WATER	97 mL

BLEND FLOUR, PARSLEY, THYME, SALT AND SUGAR IN FOOD PROCESSOR UNTIL HERBS ARE VERY FINELY CHOPPED. ADD BUTTER AND SHORTENING. BLEND UNTIL MIXTURE RESEMBLES COARSE MEAL. TRANSFER MIXTURE TO LARGE BOWL. USING A FORK, MIX ENOUGH ICE WATER INTO FLOUR MIXTURE TO FORM MOIST CLUMPS. GATHER DOUGH INTO A BALL; FLATTEN INTO A RECTANGLE. COVER AND CHILL 30 MINUTES (THIS CAN BE MADE UP TO 2 DAYS AHEAD. KEEP CHILLED BUT LET DOUGH SOFTEN SLIGHTLY BEFORE ROLLING OUT.) ROLL PASTRY TO REQUIRED THICKNESS. THIS MAKES 2 CRUSTS.

LAMB

Rack of Lamb with Herb and Mustard Crust
Leg of Lamb with Red Currant Sauce
Braised Lamb Shanks with Lentils

PORK

Balsamic Honey Tenderloin
Roast Pork Loin with Apple Topping
Island Pork Tenderloin Salad
Adobo Stew
Tourtière with Mushroom Sauce
Chop Suey
Patio Ribs
Sweet 'n' Sour Chili Ribs
Baked Ham with Maple Glaze
Ham Baked in Beer
Ham Casserole

BEEF

Châteaubriand with Cognac Sauce
Beef Bourguignon
Cowboy Pot Roast with Yams
and Jalapeño Ketchup
Ginger's Beef Stroganoff
Tex-Mex Fajitas
The Best Darn Chili Around
Saturday Night Special
Playoff Casserole
Braised Short Ribs

RACK OF LAMB
WITH HERB AND MUSTARD CRUST

2 SLICES BREAD, TORN INTO PIECES	
2 TBSP. CHOPPED FRESH PARSLEY	30 mL
1 TBSP. CHOPPED FRESH ROSEMARY	15 mL
2 TBSP. CHOPPED FRESH BASIL	30 mL
1 GARLIC CLOVE, MINCED	
OLIVE OIL	
2 RACKS OF 8 LAMB CHOPS	
3 TBSP. DIJON MUSTARD	45 mL

FRESH MINT PESTO

2 CUPS FRESH MINT	500 mL
1/4 CUP CHOPPED ONION	60 mL
1/4 CUP LIME JUICE	60 mL
2 TBSP. WHITE WINE VINEGAR	30 mL
2 TBSP. SUGAR	30 mL
1/4 CUP CHOPPED PARSLEY	60 mL

PLACE BREAD, PARSLEY, ROSEMARY, BASIL AND GARLIC IN FOOD PROCESSOR. PULSE TO MAKE FINE CRUMBS. HEAT OIL IN A HEAVY FRYING PAN; SEAR LAMB ON ALL SIDES. BRUSH MUSTARD OVER LAMB, PRESS INTO CRUMBS. THIS CAN BE DONE AHEAD OF TIME. PREHEAT OVEN TO 400°F (200°C). ROAST FOR 20-30 MINUTES FOR MEDIUM-RARE. REMOVE FROM OVEN AND REST LAMB FOR 5 MINUTES BEFORE CARVING INTO CHOPS. ALLOW 4 CHOPS PER PERSON. SERVES 4.

TO MAKE MINT PESTO: COMBINE INGREDIENTS IN BLENDER AND PURÉE. CHILL AND SERVE WITH LAMB.

LEG OF LAMB
WITH RED CURRANT SAUCE

4-5 LB. LEG OF LAMB	2-2.5 kg
1 TBSP. GIN	15 mL
2 TSP. SALT	10 mL
1/2 TSP. DRY MUSTARD	2 mL
1/4 TSP. PEPPER	1 mL

RED CURRANT SAUCE

1/2 CUP RED CURRANT JELLY	125 mL
1 CUP WATER	250 mL
1/4 TSP. SALT	1 mL
1/4 CUP GIN	60 mL
3 TBSP. FLOUR	45 mL
1/4 CUP WATER	60 mL

PLACE LAMB ON A RACK IN ROASTING PAN, FAT SIDE UP. COMBINE GIN, SALT, MUSTARD AND PEPPER TO MAKE A PASTE; SPREAD OVER LAMB. ROAST AT 350°F (180°C) FOR 2½ HOURS, OR UNTIL MEAT THERMOMETER READS 180°F (90°C). SET ON A PLATTER AND COVER WITH FOIL.

TO MAKE SAUCE: REMOVE EXCESS FAT FROM ROASTING PAN. BLEND JELLY INTO PAN JUICES. ADD WATER AND HEAT OVER MEDIUM-LOW HEAT UNTIL JELLY MELTS. STIR IN SALT AND GIN. BLEND FLOUR IN WATER AND STIR INTO SAUCE. STIR UNTIL SAUCE BOILS AND THICKENS. POUR INTO GRAVY BOAT AND SERVE WITH LAMB. SERVE WITH WHIPPED POTATO WITH CELERY ROOT, PAGE 163, AND STIR-FRIED SUGAR SNAP PEAS, PAGE 154.

BRAISED LAMB SHANKS WITH LENTILS

A HEARTY MID-WINTER MEAL OF TENDER LAMB AND RICH FLAVORFUL JUICES.

6 LAMB SHANKS (ABOUT 4½ LBS.)	2.25 kg
1 TSP. SALT	5 mL
1 TSP. PEPPER	5 mL
2 TBSP. OLIVE OIL	30 mL
1 LARGE ONION, THINLY SLICED	
2¼ CUPS BEEF BROTH	550 mL
2 CUPS RED WINE	500 mL
¼ CUP TOMATO PASTE	60 mL
3 GARLIC CLOVES, MINCED	
2 TBSP. MINCED FRESH ROSEMARY LEAVES	30 mL
2 TBSP. PACKED BROWN SUGAR	30 mL
2 TBSP. WORCESTERSHIRE SAUCE	30 mL
2 TBSP. RED WINE VINEGAR	30 mL
1½ CUPS LENTILS, RINSED & DRAINED	375 mL
FRESH ROSEMARY SPRIGS	

PREHEAT OVEN TO 350°F (180°C). PAT LAMB SHANKS DRY WITH PAPER TOWELS, THEN SPRINKLE BOTH SIDES WITH HALF OF THE SALT AND PEPPER. HEAT OIL IN A LARGE FRYING PAN OVER MEDIUM-HIGH HEAT. COOK LAMB SHANKS, A FEW AT A TIME, FOR 3-5 MINUTES, TURNING OFTEN, UNTIL BROWNED ON ALL SIDES. REMOVE TO A ROASTING PAN AND ARRANGE IN A SINGLE LAYER AFTER BROWNING EACH BATCH.

BRAISED LAMB SHANKS WITH LENTILS

CONTINUED FROM PAGE 220.

CONTINUED FROM PAGE 220.

REDUCE HEAT TO MEDIUM AND ADD ONION TO OIL REMAINING IN FRYING PAN. COOK, STIRRING OFTEN, FOR 4-6 MINUTES, UNTIL ONION IS GOLDEN BROWN. STIR IN 2 CUPS (500 mL) BROTH, WINE, TOMATO PASTE, GARLIC, ROSEMARY, SUGAR, WORCESTERSHIRE, VINEGAR AND REMAINING SALT AND PEPPER. BRING TO A BOIL OVER HIGH HEAT, STIRRING TO SCRAPE UP ANY BROWN BITS FROM BOTTOM OF FRYING PAN. POUR CONTENTS OVER LAMB SHANKS AND COVER ROASTING PAN TIGHTLY WITH FOIL. TRANSFER TO OVEN AND COOK FOR 30 MINUTES.

TURN SHANKS OVER AND STIR LENTILS INTO COOKING JUICES. RE-COVER WITH FOIL AND COOK AT LEAST 1 HOUR, OR UNTIL LAMB SHANKS AND LENTILS ARE VERY TENDER. IF LENTIL MIXTURE SEEMS TOO THICK, ADD A LITTLE OF THE REMAINING BEEF BROTH, HEATING IT BEFORE ADDING TO ROASTING PAN. TASTE AND ADJUST SEASONING IF NECESSARY. SPOON ALL INTO A SHALLOW SERVING DISH AND GARNISH WITH FRESH ROSEMARY. SERVES 6. (PICTURED ON PAGE 190.)

— BALSAMIC HONEY TENDERLOIN —

MARINATED AND SEARED, THIS PORK IS JUICY AND DELICIOUS. MY HUSBAND SAYS, "IS THIS ALL YOU KNOW HOW TO MAKE?"

MARINADE

2 TBSP. LIQUID HONEY	30 mL
2 TBSP. GRAINY MUSTARD	30 mL
2 TBSP. BALSAMIC VINEGAR	30 mL
1 TBSP. OLIVE OIL	15 mL
1 GARLIC CLOVE, MINCED	
SALT & PEPPER TO TASTE	

2 PORK TENDERLOINS

TO MAKE MARINADE: IN A LARGE BOWL, COMBINE INGREDIENTS.

ADD PORK TO MARINADE AND TURN TO COAT. MARINATE IN REFRIGERATOR FOR UP TO 24 HOURS.

REMOVE PORK FROM MARINADE AND RESERVE LIQUID. PLACE PORK ON GREASED GRILL OVER MEDIUM-HIGH HEAT. BRUSH WITH MARINADE. CLOSE LID AND COOK, TURNING AND BASTING OCCASIONALLY, FOR ABOUT 18 MINUTES, OR UNTIL INSIDE HAS JUST A HINT OF PINK. TRANSFER PORK TO CUTTING BOARD AND LET SIT FOR 5 MINUTES. CUT INTO 1/3" (1 cm) THICK SLICES. SERVE WITH NEW POTATOES, FRESH GREEN BEANS, AND SPINACH SALAD WITH PEARS, BRIE AND RASPBERRIES, PAGE 93. SERVES 4-6.

Island Pork Tenderloin Salad, page 226

Chocolate Raspberry Truffle Squares, page 270

ROAST PORK LOIN
WITH APPLE TOPPING

MUSTARD CARAWAY RUB

½ TSP. SUGAR	2 mL
2 TBSP. FLOUR	30 mL
1½ TSP. SALT	7 mL
1 TSP. DRY MUSTARD	5 mL
1 TSP. CARAWAY SEEDS	5 mL
¼ TSP. BLACK PEPPER	1 mL
¼ TSP. GROUND SAGE	1 mL

4-5 LB. PORK LOIN ROAST	2-2.2 kg

TOPPING

1½ CUPS APPLESAUCE (OR MINCED APPLE)	375 mL
½ CUP BROWN SUGAR	125 mL
¼ TSP. CINNAMON	1 mL
¼ TSP. MACE	1 mL
¼ TSP. SALT	1 mL
SMALL AMOUNT OF WATER FOR GRAVY	

TO MAKE RUB: COMBINE INGREDIENTS AND RUB INTO PORK. PLACE FAT SIDE UP IN A ROASTING PAN AND BAKE AT 325°F (160°C) FOR 1½ HOURS.

TO PREPARE TOPPING: COMBINE INGREDIENTS AND SPREAD OVER ROAST. BAKE 1 HOUR LONGER, ADDING A LITTLE WATER TO PAN TO MAKE EXCELLENT GRAVY.

ISLAND PORK TENDERLOIN SALAD

THE SUPERB FLAVOR OF JERK PORK - THE PERFECT DINNER FOR A SUMMER'S DAY. THIS RECIPE LOOKS INVOLVED BUT IT'S NOT.

PORK

2 TSP. SALT	10 mL
½ TSP. BLACK PEPPER	2 mL
1 TSP. GROUND CUMIN	5 mL
1 TSP. CHILI POWDER	5 mL
1 TSP. CINNAMON	5 mL
2-3 PORK TENDERLOINS (2½-3 LBS. TOTAL)	1-1.5 kg
2 TBSP. OLIVE OIL	30 mL

GLAZE

1 CUP PACKED DARK BROWN SUGAR	250 mL
2 TBSP. FINELY CHOPPED GARLIC	30 mL
1 TBSP. TABASCO	15 mL

VINAIGRETTE

3 TBSP. FRESH LIME JUICE	45 mL
1 TBSP. FRESH ORANGE JUICE	15 mL
1 TBSP. DIJON MUSTARD	15 mL
1 TSP. CURRY POWDER	5 mL
¼ TSP. BLACK PEPPER	1 mL
½ CUP OLIVE OIL	125 mL

SALAD

3 NAVEL ORANGES, PEELED, WHITE PITH REMOVED	
6 CUPS BABY SPINACH, TRIMMED	1.5 L
4 CUPS THINLY SLICED NAPA CABBAGE	1 L
1 RED PEPPER, IN THIN STRIPS	
½ CUP GOLDEN RAISINS	125 mL
2 FIRM-RIPE AVOCADOS, PEELED & CUT DIAGONALLY INTO THIN SLICES	

ISLAND PORK TENDERLOIN SALAD

CONTINUED FROM PAGE 226.

TO PREPARE PORK: PREHEAT OVEN TO 350°F (180°C). COMBINE SALT, PEPPER, CUMIN, CHILI POWDER AND CINNAMON. COAT PORK WITH SPICES. HEAT OIL IN OVENPROOF FRYING PAN OVER MODERATELY HIGH HEAT; BROWN PORK, TURNING OFTEN. LEAVE IN PAN.

TO MAKE GLAZE: COMBINE INGREDIENTS AND PAT ONTO TOPS OF TENDERLOINS. ROAST IN MIDDLE OF OVEN FOR ABOUT 20 MINUTES. LET STAND AT ROOM TEMPERATURE FOR 10 MINUTES.

TO MAKE VINAIGRETTE: WHISK TOGETHER JUICES, MUSTARD, CURRY POWDER AND PEPPER. ADD OIL IN A STREAM, WHISKING THOROUGHLY.

FOR THE SALAD: CUT ORANGES CROSSWISE INTO THIN SLICES. TOSS SPINACH, CABBAGE, PEPPERS AND RAISINS IN A LARGE BOWL WITH ½ CUP (125 mL) VINAIGRETTE.

TO ASSEMBLE SALAD: CUT PORK AT A 45° ANGLE INTO ½" (1.3 cm) SLICES. LINE A LARGE PLATTER WITH DRESSED SALAD. ARRANGE SLICED PORK, ORANGES AND AVOCADO IN ROWS ON TOP. DRIZZLE SOME VINAIGRETTE OVER AVOCADO AND ORANGES. POUR JUICES FROM FRYING PAN OVER PORK. (PICTURED ON PAGE 223.)

ADOBO STEW

A PHILIPPINE STEW FOR COMPANY - THE SWEET
AND SOUR FLAVOR APPEALS TO EVERYONE. SERVE
OVER RICE. GOOD CROCKPOT RECIPE. THIS STEW
FREEZES WELL.

2 CUPS PEARL ONIONS	500 mL
3 LBS. LEAN BONELESS PORK SHOULDER BUTT	1.5 kg
1 TBSP. VEGETABLE OIL	15 mL
2 MEDIUM ONIONS, CHOPPED	
6 CARROTS, CUT IN THICK CHUNKS	
4 GARLIC CLOVES, MINCED	
1 TSP. FINELY CHOPPED GINGER ROOT	5 mL
3 BAY LEAVES	
3 WHOLE CLOVES	
1 CINNAMON STICK	
FRESHLY GROUND PEPPER TO TASTE	
2 CUPS WATER	500 mL
1/2 CUP RICE OR CIDER VINEGAR	125 mL
1/2 CUP SOY SAUCE	125 mL
4 TSP. CORNSTARCH MIXED WITH 2 TBSP. (30 mL) WATER	20 mL
2 CELERY STALKS, SLICED INTO THIN 1" (2.5 cm) STRIPS	

PARBOIL PEARL ONIONS FOR 3 MINUTES. PLUNGE
INTO COLD WATER, CUT OFF ENDS AND POP
ONIONS OUT OF THEIR SKINS. SET ASIDE.

TRIM FAT FROM PORK AND CUT INTO BITE-SIZED
CUBES. IN A DUTCH OVEN, HEAT OIL OVER
MEDIUM-HIGH HEAT AND BROWN PORK IN
3 BATCHES. TRANSFER TO A BOWL.

ADOBO STEW

CONTINUED FROM PAGE 228.

REDUCE HEAT TO MEDIUM AND SAUTÉ CHOPPED ONIONS, CARROTS, GARLIC, GINGER, BAY LEAVES, CLOVES, CINNAMON AND PEPPER, STIRRING UNTIL ONIONS ARE GOLDEN, ABOUT 6 MINUTES.

STIR IN WATER, VINEGAR AND SOY SAUCE; BRING TO A BOIL AND STIR TO SCRAPE UP BROWN BITS.

RETURN PORK AND ANY ACCUMULATED JUICES TO POT. COVER AND BAKE AT 325°F (160°C) FOR 2 HOURS. CHECK AFTER 1 HOUR AND ADD WATER IF NEEDED. DISCARD BAY LEAVES AND CINNAMON STICK. ADD CORNSTARCH MIXTURE, CELERY AND RESERVED PEARL ONIONS AND STIR GENTLY - YOU TOOK SO MUCH TROUBLE TO PEEL THE ONIONS, YOU DON'T WANT THEM TO FALL APART! RETURN TO OVEN FOR 15 MINUTES. DINNER'S READY! SERVES 6.

RETIREMENT: TWICE AS MUCH HUSBAND AND HALF AS MUCH MONEY.

TOURTIÈRE WITH MUSHROOM SAUCE

A CHRISTMAS EVE TRADITION AND A PERFECT GIFT. SAVE TIME AND YOUR SANITY - MAKE AHEAD AND FREEZE.

ENOUGH PASTRY FOR 3, 2-CRUST PIES

1½ LBS. LEAN GROUND PORK	750	g
1½ LBS. LEAN GROUND BEEF	750	g
1½ CUPS FINELY CHOPPED ONION	375	mL
1 TSP. THYME	5	mL
1 TSP. SAGE	5	mL
1 TSP. DRY MUSTARD	5	mL
2 TSP. SALT	10	mL
½ CUP CHOPPED FRESH PARSLEY	125	mL
2 GARLIC CLOVES, MINCED		
PEPPER TO TASTE		
1 CUP WATER	250	mL
1 CUP BREAD CRUMBS OR 2 CUPS (500 mL) MASHED POTATOES	250	mL

MUSHROOM SAUCE

2 TBSP. BUTTER	30	mL
3 CUPS SLICED MUSHROOMS	750	mL
½ CUP SLICED ONIONS	125	mL
2 TBSP. BUTTER	30	mL
2 TSP. FLOUR	10	mL
1 CUP BEEF BROTH	250	mL
½ CUP DRY RED WINE	125	mL

TO MAKE PIES: IN A FRYING PAN, LIGHTLY BROWN MEAT. DRAIN OFF FAT. ADD ONION AND STIR IN SEASONINGS. ADD WATER, COVER AND SIMMER FOR 15 MINUTES, OR UNTIL MOST OF LIQUID IS ABSORBED BUT MIXTURE IS STILL MOIST.

TOURTIÈRE WITH MUSHROOM SAUCE

CONTINUED FROM PAGE 230.

ADD BREAD CRUMBS. LET COOL. SPOON FILLING INTO PASTRY-LINED 9" (23 cm) PIE PLATES. COVER WITH TOP CRUSTS, SEAL AND FLUTE EDGES. MAY BE FROZEN AT THIS POINT. CUT SLASHES ON TOP TO RELEASE STEAM. BAKE AT 425°F (220°C) FOR 15 MINUTES, REDUCE HEAT TO 350°F (180°C) AND BAKE FOR 30 MINUTES, OR UNTIL WELL BROWNED. THIS RECIPE CAN ALSO BE MADE AS AN APPETIZER USING TART SHELLS.

TO MAKE MUSHROOM SAUCE: MELT BUTTER IN A LARGE FRYING PAN AND SAUTÉ MUSHROOMS AND ONIONS FOR 10 MINUTES. REMOVE TO A PLATE. MELT BUTTER AND BLEND FLOUR AND A FEW TABLESPOONS OF BROTH INTO PAN JUICES. STIR IN REMAINING BROTH AND WINE. BRING TO A BOIL UNTIL SAUCE THICKENS. ADD MUSHROOMS AND ONIONS TO SAUCE. SERVE WARM WITH TOURTIÈRE.

MY WIFE COMES WITH INSTRUCTIONS - LOTS OF INSTRUCTIONS.

CHOP SUEY

A YUMMY WAY TO USE UP LEFTOVERS.

3 TBSP. SOY SAUCE	45 mL
1 TBSP. BROWN SUGAR	15 mL
2 CUPS SLICED LEFTOVER ROAST	500 mL
PORK, BEEF OR CHICKEN	
2 TBSP. CORNSTARCH	30 mL
1 CUP WATER	250 mL
¼ CUP VEGETABLE OIL	60 mL
1 MEDIUM ONION, SLICED	
2 GARLIC CLOVES, MINCED	
1 GREEN OR RED PEPPER, SLICED	
3 CELERY STALKS, SLICED	
2 CUPS MUSHROOMS, SLICED	500 mL
SALT & PEPPER TO TASTE	
2 CUPS FRESH BEAN SPROUTS	500 mL

COMBINE SOY SAUCE, BROWN SUGAR AND MIX WITH MEAT. LET STAND FOR 15 MINUTES. MIX CORNSTARCH WITH WATER AND SET ASIDE. NOW, YOU'RE READY TO START COOKING.

IN A WOK OR FRYING PAN OVER HIGH HEAT, HEAT OIL; ADD ONION; STIR FOR 2 MINUTES. ADD GARLIC AND SLICED VEGETABLES; STIR FOR 2 MINUTES. ADD MEAT MIXTURE; STIR FOR 2 MINUTES. ADD CORNSTARCH MIXTURE; STIR FOR 2 MINUTES. ADD BEAN SPROUTS; STIR FOR 2 MINUTES. NOW YOU'RE STIR CRAZY BUT DINNER'S READY! SERVE OVER RICE AND PASS THE SOY SAUCE. SERVES 6-8.

PATIO RIBS

STICKY RIBS - "DEE-RISHUS GRAMMA! ALSO GREAT AS AN APPETIZER.

4 LBS. (3-4 RACKS) PORK BACK SPARERIBS	2 kg

SAUCE

½ CUP HOISIN SAUCE	125 mL
½ CUP OYSTER SAUCE	125 mL
3 TBSP. HOT CHILI SAUCE	45 mL
2 TBSP. LIQUID HONEY	30 mL

REMOVE SKIN FROM UNDERSIDE OF RIBS. TO TENDERIZE RIBS, SLICE EACH RACK IN HALF AND ADD TO A LARGE POT OF BOILING WATER. BOIL GENTLY UNTIL RIBS ARE FORK-TENDER, ABOUT 45 MINUTES. DRAIN.

TO MAKE SAUCE: STIR HOISIN, OYSTER, HOT CHILI SAUCE AND HONEY TOGETHER.

GENEROUSLY COAT RIBS WITH SAUCE ON BOTH SIDES. WHEN READY TO BARBECUE, SPRAY GRILL WITH OIL AND COOK RIBS OVER MEDIUM HEAT, BASTING WITH SAUCE AND TURNING OFTEN UNTIL WELL GLAZED, ABOUT 15 MINUTES. SERVES 4.

I CAN'T BE OVERDRAWN - I STILL HAVE SOME CHECKS!

SWEET 'N' SOUR CHILI RIBS

THE AROMA OF THESE RIBS WILL BRING YOUR FAMILY RUNNING.

4 LBS. PORK RIBS	2 kg

SAUCE

¾ CUP BROWN SUGAR	175 mL
½ CUP KETCHUP	125 mL
½ CUP WHITE VINEGAR	125 mL
2 TBSP. WORCESTERSHIRE SAUCE	30 mL
1 TSP. CHILI POWDER	5 mL
¾ CUP WATER	175 mL
1 ONION, DICED	

PARBOIL RIBS IN A LARGE POT FOR 30-45 MINUTES. PLACE RIBS IN A LARGE SHALLOW BAKING PAN.

TO MAKE SAUCE: IN A MEDIUM BOWL, COMBINE INGREDIENTS.

POUR SAUCE OVER RIBS. BAKE, UNCOVERED, AT 250°F (120°C) FOR 3 HOURS. SERVES 4-6.

I CAME FROM A FAMILY OF 8 KIDS - I WAS 18 BEFORE I FOUND OUT MACARONI WASN'T MEAT.

BAKED HAM WITH MAPLE GLAZE

SERVE WITH BAKED CORN PUDDING WITH A KICK,
PAGE 159, AND PATRICK'S SALAD, PAGE 99.

5-6 LB. HAM, BONE-IN	2.5-3 kg
WHOLE CLOVES	

MAPLE GLAZE

2 CUPS ORANGE JUICE	500 mL
½ CUP MAPLE SYRUP	125 mL
¼ CUP MARMALADE	60 mL
2 TBSP. DIJON MUSTARD	30 mL

PREHEAT OVEN TO 325°F (160°C). USING A SHARP
KNIFE, REMOVE SKIN FROM HAM. SCORE FAT
DIAGONALLY IN DIAMOND DESIGN. STUD TOP OF
HAM WITH CLOVES. PLACE HAM ON A WIRE RACK
IN A ROASTING PAN LINED WITH FOIL.

TO MAKE GLAZE: COMBINE INGREDIENTS IN A
MEDIUM SAUCEPAN. BRING TO A BOIL AND SIMMER
FOR 5 MINUTES, UNTIL WELL BLENDED.

BAKE HAM FOR 2-3 HOURS. POUR ¼ CUP (60 mL)
OF GLAZE OVER HAM EVERY HALF-HOUR OR SO.

GOLF IS A GAME INVENTED BY THE SAME PEOPLE
WHO THINK MUSIC COMES OUT OF A BAGPIPE.

HAM BAKED IN BEER

YOUR FAMILY WILL WONDER WHERE THE COMPANY IS!

5 LB. HAM, BONE-IN	2.5 kg
1 CAN GINGER ALE	355 mL
WHOLE CLOVES	

BEER MARINADE

1 CUP MOLASSES	250 mL
2 TSP. DRY MUSTARD	10 mL
1 TSP. PEPPER	5 mL
1 CUP BEER	250 mL

PREHEAT OVEN TO 325°F (160°C). USING A SHARP KNIFE, REMOVE SKIN FROM HAM. SCORE FAT DIAGONALLY IN DIAMOND DESIGN. SOAK HAM IN GINGER ALE FOR AT LEAST 2 HOURS TO REMOVE EXCESS SALT. DRAIN. STUD TOP OF HAM WITH CLOVES. PLACE HAM IN MIDDLE OF A LARGE PIECE OF FOIL IN A SHALLOW ROASTING PAN.

TO MAKE MARINADE: COMBINE INGREDIENTS.

POUR MARINADE OVER HAM, THEN COVER COMPLETELY WITH FOIL SO JUICES DON'T ESCAPE. BAKE FOR 20 MINUTES PER POUND. SERVE WITH CARMELIZED ONION AND POTATO FLAN ON PAGE 162.

HAM CASSEROLE

THAT'S IT FOR THE LEFTOVER HAM!

2 TBSP. BUTTER	30 mL
½ CUP CHOPPED ONION	125 mL
3 TBSP. FLOUR	45 mL
SALT & PEPPER TO TASTE	
1¼ CUPS MILK	300 mL
½ CUP SHREDDED SWISS CHEESE	125 mL
2 CUPS CUBED COOKED HAM	500 mL
(OR MORE)	
1 CUP CUBED COOKED POTATOES	250 mL
1½ CUPS SOFT BREADCRUMBS	375 mL
2 TBSP. BUTTER	30 mL

IN A FRYING PAN, MELT BUTTER AND SAUTÉ ONION. BLEND IN FLOUR, SALT AND PEPPER. SLOWLY ADD MILK; STIR CONSTANTLY AND COOK UNTIL THICKENED. ADD CHEESE AND STIR UNTIL MELTED. ADD HAM AND POTATOES AND MIX GENTLY. POUR INTO A CASSEROLE. SPRINKLE WITH BREADCRUMBS AND DOT WITH BUTTER. PREHEAT OVEN TO 400°F (200°C) AND BAKE FOR 30 MINUTES. SERVES 6.

THERE'S A SPECIAL TRICK I DO WITH FAT-FREE FOOD. I THROW IT AWAY.

CHÂTEAUBRIAND WITH COGNAC SAUCE

IF YOU'RE GOING ALL OUT BUT WANT TO STAY IN . . .

2, 2½ LBS. EACH BEEF TENDERLOINS	2, 1.25 kg
5 MEDIUM GARLIC CLOVES, FINELY SLIVERED	
2½ TBSP. OLIVE OIL	37 mL

COGNAC MUSTARD SAUCE

1½ TBSP. BUTTER	22 mL
4 MEDIUM SHALLOTS, MINCED	
2 CUPS BEEF STOCK	500 mL
2 TBSP. COGNAC OR BRANDY	30 mL
2 TBSP. DIJON MUSTARD	30 mL
½ CUP BUTTER, CUT INTO 8 PIECES	125 mL
3 TBSP. CHOPPED, FRESH PARSLEY	45 mL
SALT & FRESHLY GROUND PEPPER TO TASTE	

CUT ¾" (2 cm) DEEP SLITS IN MEAT. INSERT GARLIC SLIVERS INTO SLITS. PREHEAT OVEN TO 450°F (230°C). IN LARGE FRYING PAN, HEAT OIL; BROWN MEAT ON ALL SIDES. PLACE MEAT ON A RACK IN ROASTING PAN. SET FRYING PAN ASIDE. ROAST MEAT TO DESIRED DONENESS, ABOUT 40 MINUTES FOR MEDIUM-RARE. LET STAND FOR 10 MINUTES.

CHÂTEAUBRIAND WITH COGNAC SAUCE

CONTINUED FROM PAGE 238.

TO MAKE SAUCE: MELT 1½ TBSP. (22 mL) BUTTER IN FRYING PAN. ADD SHALLOTS AND SAUTÉ UNTIL SOFTENED. STIR IN STOCK, SCRAPING UP BROWN BITS. BRING TO A BOIL AND COOK UNTIL REDUCED BY HALF. ADD COGNAC AND BOIL 1 MINUTE. REDUCE HEAT TO LOW. WHISK IN MUSTARD THEN BUTTER, 1 PIECE AT A TIME. STIR IN PARSLEY. SEASON WITH SALT AND PEPPER.

CARVE MEAT IN ½" (1.3 cm) SLICES. SPOON SAUCE OVER AND SERVE IMMEDIATELY WITH A VARIETY OF FRESH GARDEN VEGETABLES AND YOUR BEST BEAUJOLAIS. SERVES 12.

THERE ARE TWO THEORIES ABOUT ARGUING WITH WOMEN. NEITHER ONE WORKS.

BEEF BOURGUIGNON

TREAT YOUR COMPANY TO A TASTE OF BURGUNDY.

½ LB. THICK-SLICED BACON, DICED	250 g
3 LBS. BEEF CHUCK, CUT INTO 1" (2.5 cm) PIECES	1.5 kg
1 CUP CHOPPED ONIONS	250 mL
SALT & PEPPER TO TASTE	
3 TBSP. FLOUR	45 mL
3 CUPS DRY RED WINE	750 mL
3 CUPS BEEF STOCK	750 mL
2 TBSP. TOMATO PASTE	30 mL
½-1 TBSP. CHOPPED FRESH ROSEMARY OR ½ TSP. (2 mL) DRIED ROSEMARY OR THYME	7-15 mL
4 LARGE CARROTS, PEELED & CUT INTO 1½" (4 cm) PIECES	
2 CUPS WHITE PEARL ONIONS	500 mL
1 TBSP. BUTTER	15 mL
8 OZ. FRESH MUSHROOMS, SLICED LENGTHWISE	250 g
1 TBSP. RED CURRANT JELLY	15 mL
2 TBSP. CHOPPED FRESH PARSLEY	30 mL

PREHEAT OVEN TO 350°F (180°C). IN A DUTCH OVEN, SAUTÉ BACON UNTIL CRISP. REMOVE AND DRAIN ON PAPER TOWELS. SET ASIDE. POUR OFF DRIPPINGS EXCEPT FOR 1 TBSP. (15 mL). OVER MEDIUM-HIGH HEAT, SAUTÉ BEEF, A FEW PIECES AT A TIME, UNTIL BROWNED ON ALL SIDES. ADD ONION, SPRINKLE WITH SALT, PEPPER AND FLOUR. COOK OVER HIGH HEAT, STIRRING CONSTANTLY, FOR 5 MINUTES.

BEEF BOURGUIGNON

CONTINUED FROM PAGE 240.

STIR IN WINE, STOCK, TOMATO PASTE, BACON AND ROSEMARY. BRING TO A BOIL. COVER AND TRANSFER TO THE OVEN. BAKE 2 HOURS, OR UNTIL MEAT IS TENDER.

BRING A SMALL POT OF WATER TO A BOIL; COOK CARROTS UNTIL TENDER, 5-7 MINUTES. RINSE UNDER COLD WATER; DRAIN AND SET ASIDE. MAKE AN X IN THE ROOT END OF EACH ONION AND PUT INTO BOILING WATER. COOK 5 MINUTES. RINSE UNDER COLD WATER AND DRAIN. MELT BUTTER IN A SMALL FRYING PAN; ADD MUSHROOMS AND SAUTÉ OVER MEDIUM HEAT FOR 10 MINUTES.

WHEN MEAT IS COOKED, TRANSFER DUTCH OVEN TO A BURNER; ADD CARROTS, ONIONS, MUSHROOMS AND CURRANT JELLY. HEAT THROUGH, ABOUT 7 MINUTES. SERVE IN BOWLS, GARNISHED WITH CHOPPED PARSLEY. A BAGUETTE IS A MUST WITH THIS MEAL. SERVES 6.

WITH HER MARRIAGE, SHE GOT A NEW NAME AND - A DRESS.

COWBOY POT ROAST
WITH YAMS AND JALAPEÑO KETCHUP

SERVE WITH HOMEMADE BISCUITS. THE BEST POT ROAST WE'VE TASTED IN YEARS. YAHOO!

JALAPEÑO KETCHUP

3 JALAPEÑO PEPPERS, STEMMED, SEEDED & DICED	
¼ CUP MINCED ONION	60 mL
2 GARLIC CLOVES, MINCED	
1½ CUPS WATER	375 mL
2 TBSP. BROWN SUGAR	30 mL
1½ TSP. CUMIN	7 mL
4½ OZ. TOMATO PASTE	123 g
SALT & FRESHLY GROUND PEPPER	

POT ROAST

½ CUP FLOUR	125 mL
1 TSP. SALT	5 mL
1 TSP. FRESHLY GROUND PEPPER	5 mL
4-6 LB. CHUCK ROAST	2-3 kg
½ CUP VEGETABLE OIL	125 mL
3 CARROTS, PEELED & CUT IN CHUNKS	
3 YAMS OR SWEET POTATOES, PEELED & CUT INTO 2" (5 cm) PIECES	
1 MEDIUM ONION, CUT IN QUARTERS	
4 GARLIC CLOVES, MINCED	
2 CUPS BEEF STOCK	500 mL

TO MAKE JALAPEÑO KETCHUP: PLACE PEPPERS, ONION, GARLIC AND WATER IN A SAUCEPAN. BRING TO A BOIL OVER HIGH HEAT AND SIMMER FOR 15 MINUTES, OR UNTIL PEPPERS HAVE ABSORBED

COWBOY POT ROAST
WITH YAMS AND JALAPEÑO KETCHUP
CONTINUED FROM PAGE 242.

SOME LIQUID AND BECOME SOFT. REMOVE PEPPER MIXTURE WITH SLOTTED SPOON TO FOOD PROCESSOR. RESERVE LIQUID. TO FOOD PROCESSOR, ADD BROWN SUGAR, CUMIN, TOMATO PASTE, SALT, PEPPER AND ¼ CUP (60 mL) RESERVED LIQUID. PURÉE, ADDING MORE PEPPER LIQUID, IF NEEDED, TO REACH DESIRED THICKNESS. ADD SALT AND PEPPER AND MORE BROWN SUGAR IF DESIRED.

MIX TOGETHER FLOUR, SALT AND PEPPER. DREDGE ROAST IN FLOUR MIXTURE.

HEAT OIL IN LARGE OVENPROOF POT. SEAR ROAST FOR 4 MINUTES ON EACH SIDE, OR UNTIL WELL BROWNED.

ADD JALAPEÑO KETCHUP, CARROTS, YAMS, ONION AND GARLIC TO POT. COOK FOR 5 MINUTES. ADD BEEF STOCK; COVER AND BRING TO A BOIL. PLACE POT IN 300°F (150°C) OVEN AND COOK FOR 2½-3 HOURS, OR UNTIL BEEF IS VERY TENDER. SERVES 6-8.

GINGER'S BEEF STROGANOFF

2 TBSP. BUTTER	30 mL
1 LB. BEEF SIRLOIN, CUT AGAINST GRAIN INTO THIN STRIPS	500 g
1 CUP SLICED FRESH MUSHROOMS	250 mL
½ CUP CHOPPED ONION	125 mL
1 GARLIC CLOVE, MINCED	

SAUCE

3 TBSP. BUTTER	45 mL
3 TBSP. FLOUR	45 mL
½ TSP. SALT	2 mL
1 TBSP. TOMATO PASTE	15 mL
10 OZ. CAN BEEF BROTH	284 mL
1 CUP SOUR CREAM	250 mL
2 TBSP. SHERRY	30 mL

COOKED BROAD NOODLES FOR 4-6

IN A FRYING PAN, MELT BUTTER AND BROWN MEAT QUICKLY. REMOVE TO A CASSEROLE. REDUCE PAN HEAT AND ADD MUSHROOMS, ONIONS AND GARLIC (ADD MORE BUTTER IF NECESSARY). COOK 3-4 MINUTES, UNTIL ONION IS TRANSLUCENT. REMOVE AND ADD TO CASSEROLE.

TO MAKE SAUCE: MELT BUTTER IN FRYING PAN; ADD FLOUR, SALT AND TOMATO PASTE. SLOWLY STIR IN BROTH; COOK AND STIR UNTIL THICKENED. ADD SAUCE TO CASSEROLE AND STIR.

WHEN READY TO SERVE, ADD SOUR CREAM AND SHERRY TO CASSEROLE; BAKE AT 275°F (130°C) FOR ½ HOUR, OR UNTIL WARMED THROUGH. SERVE OVER BROAD NOODLES. SERVES 4-6 - BUT CAN BE EASILY DOUBLED.

TEX-MEX FAJITAS

OLÉ YOUSE GRINGOS!!

2 LBS. FLANK STEAK OR 3 CHICKEN   1 kg
     BREASTS, SKINNED, BONED & HALVED

MARINADE

½ CUP VEGETABLE OIL	125 mL
⅓ CUP LIME JUICE	75 mL
⅓ CUP RED WINE VINEGAR	75 mL
(ELIMINATE FOR CHICKEN)	
⅓ CUP CHOPPED ONION	75 mL
1 TSP. SUGAR	5 mL
1 TSP. OREGANO	5 mL
SALT & PEPPER TO TASTE	
¼ TSP. CUMIN	1 mL
2 GARLIC CLOVES, MINCED	

6 LARGE FLOUR TORTILLAS

TOPPINGS

ONION SLICES, SAUTÉED
GREEN & RED PEPPER STRIPS, SAUTÉED
SHREDDED LETTUCE
GUACAMOLE, SOUR CREAM & SALSA

TO MAKE MARINADE: COMBINE INGREDIENTS IN A
SHALLOW CASSEROLE. SCORE BOTH SIDES OF
STEAK; ADD TO MARINADE; COVER AND MARINATE
IN REFRIGERATOR FOR SEVERAL HOURS. REMOVE
FROM MARINADE AND BARBECUE. SLICE IN THIN
STRIPS ACROSS THE GRAIN. WRAP IN WARM
TORTILLAS WITH ONIONS, PEPPERS AND ANY OR
ALL OF THE TOPPINGS. SERVES 6 GRINGOS.

THE BEST DARN CHILI AROUND

MAKE A DAY OR SO AHEAD, THE FLAVOR IMPROVES AND SO DO THE REVIEWS.

6 OZ. HOT ITALIAN CHICKEN SAUSAGE	170	g
2 CUPS CHOPPED ONION	500	mL
1 CUP CHOPPED GREEN PEPPER	250	mL
8 GARLIC CLOVES, MINCED		
1 LB. GROUND SIRLOIN	500	g
1 JALAPEÑO PEPPER, SEEDED & CHOPPED		
2 TBSP. CHILI POWDER	30	mL
2 TBSP. BROWN SUGAR	30	mL
1 TBSP. GROUND CUMIN	15	mL
3 TBSP. TOMATO PASTE	45	mL
1 TSP. DRIED OREGANO	5	mL
SALT & PEPPER TO TASTE		
2 BAY LEAVES		
1¼ CUPS MERLOT OR OTHER RED WINE	300	mL
2-28 OZ. CANS WHOLE TOMATOES WITH JUICE, CHOPPED	2-796	mL
2-14 OZ. CANS KIDNEY BEANS, DRAINED	2-398	mL

SOUR CREAM
CHEDDAR CHEESE, SHREDDED
GREEN ONIONS, CHOPPED

HEAT A LARGE DUTCH OVEN OVER MEDIUM-HIGH HEAT. REMOVE CASINGS FROM SAUSAGE. ADD SAUSAGE, ONION, GREEN PEPPER, GARLIC, BEEF AND JALAPEÑO TO POT; COOK ABOUT 8 MINUTES, OR UNTIL SAUSAGE AND BEEF ARE BROWNED, STIRRING TO CRUMBLE.

THE BEST DARN CHILI AROUND

CONTINUED FROM PAGE 246.

ADD CHILI POWDER, BROWN SUGAR, CUMIN, TOMATO PASTE, OREGANO, SALT, PEPPER AND BAY LEAVES. COOK FOR 1 MINUTE, STIRRING CONSTANTLY. STIR IN WINE, TOMATOES AND KIDNEY BEANS; BRING TO A BOIL. COVER; REDUCE HEAT AND SIMMER FOR 1 HOUR, STIRRING OCCASIONALLY.

UNCOVER AND COOK FOR 30 MINUTES, STIRRING OCCASIONALLY. DISCARD BAY LEAVES. GARNISH EACH SERVING WITH A DOLLOP OF SOUR CREAM, A SPRINKLING OF CHEDDAR CHEESE AND GREEN ONIONS. SERVES 8-10.

TEACHER: NAME THE FOUR SEASONS.
CHILD: SALT, PEPPER, MUSTARD AND VINEGAR.

SATURDAY NIGHT SPECIAL

... OR SUNDAY ... OR MONDAY ... OR TUESDAY

½ LB. SPAGHETTI, BROKEN IN PIECES	250	g
1 LB. GROUND BEEF	500	g
1 SMALL ONION, CHOPPED		
1 GREEN PEPPER, CHOPPED		
1 CUP FRESH MUSHROOMS, SLICED	250 mL	
12 OZ. CAN KERNEL CORN OR 1 CUP	341 mL	
(250 mL) FROZEN CORN		
1 CUP GRATED CHEDDAR CHEESE	250 mL	
10 OZ. CAN TOMATO SOUP	284 mL	
14 OZ. CAN TOMATOES	398 mL	
¾ TSP. SALT	3 mL	
½ TSP. CHILI POWDER	2 mL	
½ TSP. WORCESTERSHIRE SAUCE	2 mL	

IN A POT, BRING SALTED WATER TO A BOIL AND COOK SPAGHETTI UNTIL TENDER. DRAIN. IN A FRYING PAN, BROWN BEEF AND ONION. ADD GREEN PEPPER AND MUSHROOMS AND COOK UNTIL TENDER. IN A LARGE CASSEROLE, COMBINE BEEF MIXTURE WITH THE OTHER INGREDIENTS AND MIX WELL. BAKE AT 325°F (160°C) FOR 45 MINUTES. SERVE WITH FRENCH BREAD AND A TOSSED SALAD. SERVES 6-8.

THE TROUBLE WITH LIFE IS THERE'S NO BACKGROUND MUSIC.

PLAYOFF CASSEROLE

A.K.A. CHOP, CHOP CASSEROLE - IT'S IN - IT'S OUT - IT'S IN - IT'S OUT - SORRY LINDA - YOU LOSE!

BENIGN: WHAT YOU GONNA BE WHEN YOU IS DONE BEING EIGHT.

BRAISED SHORT RIBS

MAKE THIS A DAY AHEAD. NOT ONLY WILL THE FLAVORS BE MELLOW . . . SO WILL YOU!!!

1/3 CUP FLOUR	75 mL
SALT & PEPPER TO TASTE	
1/2 TSP. PAPRIKA	2 mL
3-4 LBS. BEEF SHORT RIBS, BONE-IN	1.5-2 kg
2 TBSP. VEGETABLE OIL	30 mL
2 MEDIUM ONIONS	
1/2 CUP TOMATO SAUCE	125 mL
1/2 CUP BARBECUE SAUCE	125 mL
2 TBSP. MOLASSES	30 mL
2 TBSP. CIDER VINEGAR	30 mL

COMBINE FLOUR, SALT, PEPPER AND PAPRIKA. TRIM EXCESS FAT FROM RIBS. DREDGE RIBS IN FLOUR MIXTURE AND BROWN IN OIL ON ALL SIDES. REMOVE TO CASSEROLE.

CHOP ONION INTO LARGE CHUNKS AND PLACE ON TOP OF BROWNED RIBS.

WHISK TOMATO SAUCE, BARBECUE SAUCE, MOLASSES AND CIDER VINEGAR TOGETHER IN A SAUCEPAN. BRING TO A BOIL AND POUR OVER RIBS AND ONIONS. COVER AND BAKE AT 275°F (130°C) FOR 3-4 HOURS.

ON A COOL FALL NIGHT YOUR FAMILY WILL DELIGHT IN THE TASTE OF BARBECUE. SERVE WITH MASHED POTATOES AND A GREEN VEGETABLE. SERVES 4.

COOKIES

Lemon Shortbread Cookies
Aunt Mary's Sugar Cookies
Sensational Pecan Sables
Wafer Puffs
French Button Cookies
Ginger Cookies
Mrs. Smith's Oatcakes
Oatmeal Crispies
Toffee Cranberry Crisps
Skor Bar Cookies
Better-Than-Mom's Oatmeal Cookies
Carrot Hermits
The "Best" Chocolate Chip Cookies

SQUARES

Brownies
Chewy Chocolate Peanut Bars
Chocolate Raspberry Truffle Squares
Brandied Cranberry Apricot Bars
Dream Slice
Krispie Granola Bars
Salted Peanut Bars

— LEMON SHORTBREAD COOKIES —

THE CHRISTMAS BAKING LIST JUST INCREASED BY ONE! HIDE THEM BEFORE THE CHILDREN DISCOVER YOUR NEW BEST RECIPE!

¾ CUP BUTTER, SOFTENED	175 mL
⅓ CUP ICING (CONFECTIONER'S) SUGAR	75 mL
1 TSP. GRATED LEMON ZEST	5 mL
1 TBSP. FRESH LEMON JUICE	15 mL
1¼ CUPS FLOUR	300 mL
½ CUP CORNSTARCH	125 mL

FROSTING

¾ CUP ICING SUGAR	175 mL
¼ CUP BUTTER, SOFTENED	60 mL
1 TSP. GRATED LEMON ZEST	5 mL
1 TSP. FRESH LEMON JUICE	5 mL

IN A LARGE BOWL, CREAM BUTTER AND SUGAR. MIX IN LEMON ZEST AND JUICE. ADD FLOUR AND CORNSTARCH; MIX THOROUGHLY. DIVIDE DOUGH IN HALF. SHAPE EACH HALF INTO A 1" (2.5 cm) ROLL. WRAP IN PLASTIC WRAP AND REFRIGERATE FOR AT LEAST 1 HOUR, OR UNTIL READY TO BAKE. PREHEAT OVEN TO 350°F (180°C). USING A SHARP KNIFE, CUT ROLLS INTO ¼" (6 mm) SLICES. PLACE EACH SLICE 2" (5 cm) APART ON UNGREASED COOKIE SHEETS. BAKE FOR 8-12 MINUTES, OR UNTIL SET. DO NOT BROWN. COOL COMPLETELY. TO MAKE ICING: IN A SMALL BOWL COMBINE SUGAR, BUTTER, LEMON ZEST AND JUICE. BEAT UNTIL LIGHT AND FLUFFY. FROST COOLED COOKIES. MAKES 4 DOZEN.

AUNT MARY'S SUGAR COOKIES

THE KIDS CAN DECORATE THESE FOR A SPECIAL OCCASION - HALLOWEEN, CHRISTMAS, VALENTINE'S DAY OR BIRTHDAYS. AUNT MARY WOULD BE PROUD!

2 CUPS WHITE SUGAR	500 mL
2 CUPS BUTTER, ROOM TEMPERATURE	500 mL
4 EGGS, BEATEN	
½ TSP. LEMON EXTRACT	2 mL
5 CUPS FLOUR	1.25 L
2 TSP. CREAM OF TARTAR	10 mL
1 TSP. BAKING SODA	5 mL
SUGAR FOR SPRINKLING	

IN A LARGE BOWL, CREAM SUGAR AND BUTTER. ADD BEATEN EGGS AND LEMON EXTRACT. SIFT DRY INGREDIENTS; ADD TO EGG MIXTURE. MIX WELL. CHILL FOR 15 MINUTES; ROLL ON GENEROUSLY FLOURED SURFACE TO ⅛-¼" (3-6 mm) THICK. CUT WITH A 3" (8 cm) COOKIE CUTTER AND SPRINKLE WITH SUGAR. PLACE ON UNGREASED COOKIE SHEETS AND BAKE AT 350°F (180°C) FOR 10-12 MINUTES, UNTIL EDGES ARE LIGHT BROWN. MAKES 9 DOZEN COOKIES.

CONSCIOUSNESS: THAT ANNOYING TIME BETWEEN NAPS.

SENSATIONAL PECAN SABLES

SABLE IS THE FRENCH WORD FOR SAND, WHICH BEST DESCRIBES THEIR DELICATE CRUMBLY TEXTURE.

¾ CUP PECANS, TOASTED	175 mL
2 TBSP. ICING (CONFECTIONER'S) SUGAR	30 mL
1¼ CUPS FLOUR	300 mL
½ TSP. SALT	2 mL
¼ TSP. BAKING POWDER	1 mL
½ CUP BUTTER, SOFTENED	125 mL
⅔ CUP ICING (CONFECTIONER'S) SUGAR	150 mL
½ TSP. VANILLA	2 mL
1 LARGE EGG, SEPARATED	

32 PECAN HALVES

PULSE TOASTED PECANS WITH 2 TBSP. (30 mL) SUGAR IN A FOOD PROCESSOR UNTIL FINELY GROUND. WHISK TOGETHER FLOUR, SALT, AND BAKING POWDER IN A BOWL. IN A LARGE BOWL, BEAT BUTTER, SUGAR AND VANILLA WITH AN ELECTRIC MIXTURE AT HIGH SPEED UNTIL PALE AND FLUFFY. ADD EGG YOLK AND BEAT WELL. ADD FLOUR MIXTURE AND GROUND-PECAN MIXTURE AND BEAT AT LOW SPEED UNTIL JUST COMBINED. (DOUGH WILL BE CRUMBLY BUT WILL HOLD TOGETHER WHEN SQUEEZED.)

PREHEAT OVEN TO 325°F (160°C). HALVE DOUGH. ROLL OUT 1 PIECE, BETWEEN 2 SHEETS OF WAX PAPER, ¼" (6 mm) THICK, ABOUT A 9" (23 cm) ROUND. CUT OUT AS MANY ROUNDS AS POSSIBLE WITH A 2" (5 cm) COOKIE CUTTER AND ARRANGE

SENSATIONAL PECAN SABLES

CONTINUED FROM PAGE 254.

ABOUT 2" (5 cm) APART ON LARGE UNGREASED COOKIE SHEETS. ROLL OUT AND CUT REMAINING DOUGH IN SAME MANNER.

BEAT EGG WHITE UNTIL FROTHY, THEN LIGHTLY BRUSH TOPS OF EACH ROUND. PUT A PECAN HALF ON TOP OF EACH ROUND AND BRUSH PECAN LIGHTLY WITH EGG WHITE. BAKE COOKIES IN THE MIDDLE OF THE OVEN UNTIL TOPS ARE PALE GOLDEN, 15-20 MINUTES. COOL COOKIES ON COOKIE SHEETS FOR 2 MINUTES, THEN TRANSFER COOKIES TO RACKS TO COOL COMPLETELY.

STORE IN AN AIRTIGHT CONTAINER. MAKES ABOUT 2½ DOZEN.

A CLEAR CONSCIENCE IS USUALLY THE SIGN OF A BAD MEMORY.

WAFER PUFFS

THESE LITTLE SANDWICH COOKIES MELT IN YOUR MOUTH AND PUFF UP YOUR CHEEKS!

1 CUP BUTTER	250 mL
2 CUPS FLOUR	500 mL
½ CUP WHIPPING CREAM	125 mL
SOME WHITE SUGAR	A BIT

FILLING

¼ CUP BUTTER	60 mL
½ TSP. VANILLA	2 mL
1 EGG YOLK	
1½-2 CUPS ICING (CONFECTIONER'S) SUGAR	375-500 mL

IN A MEDIUM BOWL, CUT BUTTER INTO FLOUR TO FORM A CRUMBLY MIXTURE. ADD CREAM AND MIX LIGHTLY. ROLL OUT DOUGH TO ¼" (6 mm) AND CUT OUT IN 1" (2.5 cm) CIRCLES. PRICK WITH A FORK AND SUGAR BOTH SIDES. PLACE ON UNGREASED COOKIE SHEETS AND BAKE AT 375°F (190°C) FOR 7-9 MINUTES.

TO MAKE FILLING: BEAT BUTTER, VANILLA AND EGG YOLK TOGETHER. ADD ENOUGH SUGAR TO MAKE A VERY CREAMY BUT FAIRLY STIFF ICING. SPREAD FILLING BETWEEN 2 COOKIES TO MAKE SANDWICHES.

Diddle Diddle Dumplings, page 296

Plum Upside-Down Cakes with Mascarpone Cream, page 310

FRENCH BUTTON COOKIES

YOU __MUST__ MAKE THESE!

1 CUP BUTTER, ROOM TEMPERATURE	250 mL
2/3 CUP PACKED BROWN SUGAR	150 mL
1 LARGE EGG	
1 TSP. VANILLA	5 mL
2½ CUPS FLOUR	625 mL
1 TSP. SALT	5 mL
½ CUP TURBINADO✳ OR REGULAR SUGAR	125 mL

COMBINE BUTTER AND BROWN SUGAR IN A BOWL AND BEAT ON HIGH SPEED UNTIL FLUFFY. ADD EGG AND VANILLA AND BEAT TO COMBINE. ADD FLOUR AND SALT AND BEAT ON LOW SPEED UNTIL FLOUR IS INCORPORATED. ROLL DOUGH INTO THREE LOGS 1½" (4 cm) IN DIAMETER. WRAP IN PLASTIC WRAP AND REFRIGERATE UNTIL FIRM, AT LEAST 1 HOUR. PREHEAT OVEN TO 350°F (180°C). LINE A COOKIE SHEET WITH PARCHMENT PAPER. ROLL COOKIE LOGS IN SUGAR, COATING EVENLY, AND SLICE INTO ¼" (6 mm) ROUNDS. PLACE COOKIES ABOUT 1" (2.5 cm) APART ON COOKIE SHEETS. USING A SKEWER, POKE 4 HOLES (LIKE BUTTON HOLES) IN EACH COOKIE. BAKE FOR 15-20 MINUTES, UNTIL GOLDEN BROWN. REMOVE FROM OVEN AND LET COOL COMPLETELY ON WIRE RACKS.

✳TURBINADO SUGAR IS STEAM-CLEANED RAW SUGAR. THE COARSE CRYSTALS ARE BLOND-COLORED, WITH A DELICATE MOLASSES FLAVOR.

GINGER COOKIES

SPICY AND CHEWY!

1½ CUPS SHORTENING	375 mL
2 CUPS SUGAR	500 mL
2 EGGS, BEATEN	
¼ CUP MOLASSES	60 mL
4 CUPS FLOUR	1 L
4 TSP. BAKING SODA	20 mL
½ TSP. SALT	2 mL
4 TSP. GROUND GINGER	20 mL
2 TSP. GROUND CINNAMON	10 mL
2 TSP. GROUND CLOVES	10 mL
¼ TSP. GROUND WHITE PEPPER (OPTIONAL)	1 mL
SUGAR	

IN A LARGE BOWL, CREAM SHORTENING AND SUGAR TOGETHER. BEAT EGGS AND MOLASSES TOGETHER AND BLEND WITH CREAMED SUGAR MIXTURE. COMBINE FLOUR, BAKING SODA, SALT, GINGER, CINNAMON, CLOVES AND WHITE PEPPER. ADD DRY INGREDIENTS TO CREAMED MIXTURE AND BLEND WELL. CHILL FOR 1 HOUR. SHAPE DOUGH INTO 1" (2.5 cm) BALLS AND ROLL IN SUGAR. PREHEAT OVEN TO 350°F (180°C). PLACE BALLS ON UNGREASED COOKIE SHEETS 2" (5 cm) APART AND BAKE FOR 8-9 MINUTES. MAKES ABOUT 6 DOZEN SPICY COOKIES!

THE ONLY THING BETTER THAN A DRY MARTINI IS TWO DRY MARTINIS.

MRS. SMITH'S OATCAKES

A TIMELESS SCOTTISH RECIPE. THEY'RE GOOD ON THEIR OWN OR WITH FRUIT AND CHEESE!

3 CUPS FLOUR	750 mL
3 CUPS ROLLED OATS (NOT INSTANT)	750 mL
1 CUP SUGAR	250 mL
2 TSP. SALT	10 mL
1 TSP. BAKING SODA	5 mL
1½ CUPS LARD	375 mL
¾ CUP WATER	175 mL

ROLLED OATS

IN A LARGE BOWL, MIX DRY INGREDIENTS TOGETHER. CUT IN LARD WITH A PASTRY BLENDER. ADD WATER. USING YOUR HANDS, FORM DOUGH INTO A BALL. PLACE DOUGH ON A CLEAN WORKING SURFACE SPREAD WITH MORE ROLLED OATS AND ROLL TO ¼" (6 mm) THICKNESS. CUT INTO 2" (5 cm) SQUARES; PLACE ON LIGHTLY GREASED COOKIE SHEETS. BAKE AT 375°F (190°C) FOR 20-25 MINUTES. COOL AND STORE IN AN AIRTIGHT CONTAINER. MAKES 6 DOZEN.

HE'S SUCH A DIPLOMAT, HIS FAVORITE COLOR IS PLAID.

OATMEAL CRISPIES

YOU MUST TRY THESE - THEY'RE VERY MORE-ISH!

1 CUP BUTTER, SOFTENED	250 mL
1/2 CUP SUGAR	125 mL
1 CUP FLOUR	250 mL
1 1/2 CUPS ROLLED OATS	375 mL

ICING (CONFECTIONER'S) SUGAR

PREHEAT OVEN TO 350°F (180°C). IN A LARGE BOWL, BEAT BUTTER AND SUGAR TOGETHER UNTIL CREAMY. COMBINE FLOUR AND ROLLED OATS. MIX INTO CREAMED MIXTURE. SHAPE DOUGH INTO MEDIUM-SIZED BALLS AND PLACE ABOUT 3" (8 cm) APART ON UNGREASED COOKIE SHEETS. FLATTEN WITH A FORK DIPPED IN WATER. BAKE FOR 10 MINUTES. COOL BEFORE REMOVING FROM COOKIE SHEETS.

WHEN COMPLETELY COOL, GENEROUSLY DUST WITH ICING SUGAR. MAKES 3 DOZEN COOKIES.

IT MAY BE THAT YOUR SOLE PURPOSE IN LIFE IS SIMPLY TO SERVE AS A WARNING TO OTHERS.

TOFFEE CRANBERRY CRISPS

IF YOU'RE A CHEWY COOKIE FAN, FIRE UP THE OVEN - YOU'RE GOING TO ENJOY THESE!

1 CUP BUTTER	250 mL
3/4 CUP SUGAR	175 mL
3/4 CUP PACKED BROWN SUGAR	175 mL
1 EGG	
1 TSP. VANILLA	5 mL
2 CUPS FLOUR	500 mL
1½ CUPS ROLLED OATS	375 mL
1 TSP. BAKING SODA	5 mL
¼ TSP. SALT	1 mL
1½ CUPS DRIED CRANBERRIES	375 mL
1 CUP TOFFEE BITS (CHECK THE BAKING SECTION OF YOUR SUPERMARKET)	250 mL

CREAM TOGETHER BUTTER AND SUGARS. BEAT IN EGG AND VANILLA. COMBINE FLOUR, OATS, BAKING SODA AND SALT; GRADUALLY ADD TO CREAMED MIXTURE. MIX IN CRANBERRIES AND TOFFEE BITS. PLACE TEASPOONFULS OF DOUGH 2" (5 cm) APART ON GREASED COOKIE SHEETS. DON'T MAKE THEM TOO LARGE - THEY SPREAD! BAKE AT 350°F (180°C) FOR 10 MINUTES, UNTIL GOLDEN BROWN. COOL ON A WIRE RACK. MAKES 5 DOZEN.

EAT A LIVE TOAD IN THE MORNING AND NOTHING WORSE WILL HAPPEN TO YOU FOR THE REST OF THE DAY.

SKOR BAR COOKIES

CHEWY TREATS FOR YOUR FAVORITE PEOPLE.

1 CUP BUTTER	250 mL
3/4 BROWN SUGAR	175 mL
1/2 CUP SUGAR	125 mL
1 EGG	
2 TBSP. MILK	30 mL
2 TSP. VANILLA	10 mL
1 3/4 CUPS FLOUR	425 mL
3/4 CUP ROLLED OATS	175 mL
1 TSP. BAKING SODA	5 mL
1/4 TSP. SALT	1 mL
4 SKOR BARS OR ANY CRUNCHY TOFFEE CHOCOLATE-COATED BARS, BROKEN INTO SMALL PIECES	4-39 g
1 CUP SLIVERED ALMONDS, TOASTED	250 mL

PREHEAT OVEN TO 350°F (180°C). CREAM BUTTER, SUGARS, EGG, MILK AND VANILLA IN A LARGE BOWL. BEAT UNTIL LIGHT AND CREAMY. COMBINE FLOUR, OATS, BAKING SODA AND SALT. ADD TO CREAMED MIXTURE AND BLEND WELL. STIR IN SKOR BAR PIECES AND ALMONDS. DROP DOUGH BY TEASPOONFULS ON GREASED COOKIE SHEETS. (LEAVE ROOM FOR SPREADING - THE COOKIES, NOT YOU!) BAKE FOR 8-10 MINUTES, OR UNTIL GOLDEN. COOL SLIGHTLY, THEN REMOVE TO A COOLING RACK.

NEVER PUT BOTH FEET IN YOUR MOUTH AT THE SAME TIME. YOU WON'T HAVE A LEG TO STAND ON.

BETTER-THAN-MOM'S OATMEAL COOKIES

TALK ABOUT RAVES!

1 CUP BUTTER	250 mL
1 CUP SUGAR	250 mL
1 CUP BROWN SUGAR	250 mL
2 LARGE EGGS	
2 TSP. VANILLA	10 mL
1½ CUPS FLOUR	375 mL
1⅛ TSP. BAKING SODA	5.5 mL
1 TSP. SALT	5 mL
1 TSP. CINNAMON	5 mL
½ TSP. MACE	2 mL
½ TSP. NUTMEG	2 mL
½ TSP. GROUND CLOVES	2 mL
3 CUPS ROLLED OATS	750 mL
1 CUP CHOPPED WALNUTS OR PECANS	250 mL
1 CUP GOLDEN RAISINS	250 mL

IN A LARGE BOWL, CREAM BUTTER AND SUGARS UNTIL LIGHT AND FLUFFY. BEAT IN EGGS AND VANILLA. IN A MEDIUM-SIZED BOWL, COMBINE FLOUR, SODA, SALT, CINNAMON, MACE, NUTMEG AND CLOVES. GRADUALLY ADD DRY INGREDIENTS TO CREAMED MIXTURE, MIXING UNTIL COMPLETELY BLENDED. MIX IN OATS, NUTS AND RAISINS. PREHEAT OVEN TO 350°F (180°C). LIGHTLY GREASE COOKIE SHEETS AND DROP TEASPOONFULS OF DOUGH ABOUT 2" (5 cm) APART. FLATTEN SLIGHTLY. BAKE FOR 8-10 MINUTES FOR A SOFT COOKIE, 12 MINUTES FOR A CRUNCHY COOKIE. COOL ON WIRE RACK. MAKES ABOUT 4 DOZEN COOKIES.

CARROT HERMITS

AS HEALTHY AS A COOKIE CAN BE.

½ CUP BUTTER, SOFTENED	125 mL
½ CUP BROWN SUGAR	125 mL
1 EGG	
1 TSP. VANILLA	5 mL
¾ CUP COARSELY GRATED CARROT	175 mL
½ CUP SHREDDED COCONUT	125 mL
1¼ CUPS FLOUR	300 mL
½ TSP. BAKING POWDER	2 mL
½ TSP SALT	2 mL
½ TSP. CINNAMON	2 mL
¼ TSP. NUTMEG	1 mL
PINCH CLOVES	
¾ CUP RAISINS	175 mL
¾ CUP CHOPPED PECANS	175 mL

PREHEAT OVEN TO 350°F (180°C). CREAM BUTTER
WITH BROWN SUGAR UNTIL FLUFFY. BEAT IN EGG.
STIR IN VANILLA, CARROT AND COCONUT. COMBINE
FLOUR, BAKING POWDER, SALT, CINNAMON, NUTMEG
AND CLOVES. STIR INTO CREAMED MIXTURE. STIR
IN RAISINS AND PECANS. LINE BAKING SHEETS
WITH PARCHMENT PAPER. DROP LARGE
SPOONFULS OF DOUGH ONTO BAKING SHEETS.
BAKE FOR 10-12 MINUTES, OR UNTIL BROWNED.
MAKES 2½ DOZEN COOKIES.

WHO DO PILGRIMS PANTS FALL DOWN? BECAUSE THEY
WEAR THEIR BUCKLES ON THEIR HATS.

THE "BEST" CHOCOLATE CHIP COOKIE

EVERYONE HAS A FAVORITE . . . THIS IS OURS!

2¼ CUPS FLOUR	550 mL
½ TSP. BAKING SODA	2 mL
1 CUP BUTTER, ROOM TEMPERATURE	250 mL
½ CUP SUGAR	125 mL
1 CUP BROWN SUGAR, PACKED	250 mL
1 TSP. SALT	5 mL
2 TSP. VANILLA	10 mL
2 LARGE EGGS	
2 CUPS SEMISWEET CHOCOLATE CHIPS	500 mL

PREHEAT OVEN TO 350°F (180°C). IN A SMALL BOWL, WHISK TOGETHER FLOUR AND BAKING SODA AND SET ASIDE. IN A LARGE BOWL, BEAT BUTTER AND SUGARS ON MEDIUM SPEED UNTIL LIGHT AND FLUFFY. REDUCE SPEED TO LOW AND ADD SALT, VANILLA AND EGGS. BEAT FOR ABOUT 1 MINUTE, UNTIL WELL MIXED. ADD FLOUR MIXTURE AND BEAT UNTIL JUST COMBINED. STIR IN CHOCOLATE CHIPS. ON A PARCHMENT-COVERED COOKIE SHEET, DROP HEAPING SPOONFULS OF DOUGH ABOUT 2" (5 cm) APART. BAKE FOR 10-12 MINUTES. REMOVE FROM OVEN AND LET COOL ON BAKING SHEETS ABOUT 2 MINUTES. TRANSFER TO WIRE RACK AND COOL COMPLETELY. MAKES 3-4 DOZEN.

BROWNIES

OUR "BEST"!

1 CUP SUGAR	250 mL
1/3 CUP BUTTER	75 mL
PINCH OF SALT	
2 EGGS, BEATEN	
1/4 CUP COCOA POWDER	60 mL
2/3 CUP FLOUR	150 mL
1/3 CUP MILK OR CREAM	75 mL
1 TSP. VANILLA	5 mL
1/2 CUP CHOPPED WALNUTS OR PECANS	125 mL

MOCHA ICING

3 TBSP. COCOA POWDER	45 mL
2 TBSP. BUTTER, SOFTENED	30 mL
3 TBSP. COFFEE (LIQUID)	45 mL
2 TSP. VANILLA	10 mL
ICING (CONFECTIONER'S) SUGAR	

PREHEAT OVEN TO 350°F (180°C). IN A LARGE BOWL, CREAM TOGETHER SUGAR AND BUTTER. STIR IN SALT, EGGS, COCOA, FLOUR, MILK, VANILLA AND WALNUTS. POUR INTO A GREASED 8" (20 cm) SQUARE PAN AND BAKE FOR 20-25 MINUTES, OR UNTIL A KNIFE COMES OUT CLEAN WHEN INSERTED IN THE CENTER. COOL ON A WIRE RACK.

TO MAKE ICING: BEAT COCOA, BUTTER, COFFEE, VANILLA AND ENOUGH ICING SUGAR TO REACH DESIRED CONSISTENCY. SPREAD ON COOLED BROWNIES. THIS RECIPE DOUBLES WELL. USE A 9 x 13" (23 x 33 cm) PAN.

CHEWY CHOCOLATE
PEANUT BARS

TASTES LIKE ALMOND ROCA AND MAKES ENOUGH
TO TREAT ABOUT FIVE DOZEN CONNOISSEURS.

2 CUPS ROLLED OATS	500	mL
1 CUP GRAHAM WAFER CRUMBS	250	mL
3/4 CUP BROWN SUGAR	175	mL
1/4 TSP. BAKING SODA	1	mL
1/2 CUP SALTED PEANUTS	125	mL
1/2 CUP CORN SYRUP	125	mL
1/2 CUP BUTTER, MELTED	125	mL
1 TSP. VANILLA	5	mL
6 OZ. PKG. SEMISWEET CHOCOLATE CHIPS	170	g
1/2 CUP PEANUT BUTTER	125	mL

PREHEAT OVEN TO 375°F (190°C). GREASE A
15 X 10" (38 X 25 cm) EDGED COOKIE SHEET. IN
A LARGE BOWL, COMBINE OATS, CRUMBS, SUGAR,
BAKING SODA AND PEANUTS. MIX WELL. COMBINE
CORN SYRUP WITH MELTED BUTTER AND VANILLA.
STIR INTO OAT MIXTURE AND MIX WELL. PRESS
INTO PAN AND BAKE FOR 15 MINUTES. MELT
CHOCOLATE CHIPS AND PEANUT BUTTER
TOGETHER IN A DOUBLE BOILER. SPREAD OVER
WARM, BAKED BARS. COOL 10 MINUTES IN PAN
AND CUT INTO 2 X 1" (5 X 2.5 cm) BARS.
REFRIGERATE TO SET CHOCOLATE. MAKES
5 DOZEN BARS.

CHOCOLATE RASPBERRY TRUFFLE SQUARES

DROP DEAD DELICIOUS!

BROWNIE BASE

3-1 OZ. SQUARES UNSWEETENED CHOCOLATE	90	g
1/3 CUP BUTTER	75	mL
1/4 CUP RASPBERRY JAM	60	mL
2 EGGS		
1 CUP SUGAR	250	mL
1 TSP. VANILLA	5	mL
1/2 CUP FLOUR	125	mL

TOPPING

2 TBSP. WHIPPING CREAM	30	mL
2 TBSP. RASPBERRY JAM	30	mL
2 TBSP. BUTTER	30	mL
4-1 OZ. SQUARES SEMISWEET CHOCOLATE, CHOPPED	120	g
1 CUP FRESH RASPBERRIES	250	mL

TO MAKE BASE: PREHEAT OVEN TO 350°F (180°C). LINE AN 8" (20 cm) SQUARE PAN WITH FOIL; GREASE AND SET ASIDE. COMBINE CHOCOLATE, BUTTER AND JAM IN A SAUCEPAN. STIR OVER LOW HEAT UNTIL SMOOTH. REMOVE FROM HEAT. BEAT EGGS IN A LARGE BOWL UNTIL FOAMY. MIX IN SUGAR, VANILLA AND CHOCOLATE MIXTURE. STIR IN FLOUR, JUST UNTIL BLENDED. SPREAD BATTER EVENLY IN PAN AND BAKE FOR 20-35 MINUTES, OR UNTIL SET.

CHOCOLATE RASPBERRY TRUFFLE SQUARES

CONTINUED FROM PAGE 270.

COOL COMPLETELY IN PAN ON A RACK.

TO MAKE TOPPING: COMBINE, CREAM, JAM AND BUTTER IN A SAUCEPAN. HEAT TO A SIMMER, STIRRING CONSTANTLY UNTIL MELTED. REMOVE FROM HEAT AND ADD CHOCOLATE, STIRRING UNTIL SMOOTH. LET STAND UNTIL COOL BUT STILL SOFT, ABOUT 30 MINUTES. SPREAD TOPPING OVER BROWNIE BASE. IMMEDIATELY TOP WITH RASPBERRIES AND CHILL UNTIL COLD. CUT INTO SMALL SQUARES. (PICTURED ON PAGE 224).

MOTHER TO TEENAGE DAUGHTER: "TONIGHT WAS YOUR LITTLE BROTHER'S TURN TO CHOOSE THE MEAL. WE'RE HAVING GUM."

BRANDIED CRANBERRY APRICOT BARS

NOT TOO SWEET - GOOD CHRISTMAS BAKING.

CRUST

1 CUP FLOUR	250 mL
1/3 CUP PACKED BROWN SUGAR	75 mL
1/3 CUP BUTTER	75 mL

THE FRUIT

1/3 CUP GOLDEN RAISINS	75 mL
1/3 CUP DARK RAISINS	75 mL
1/3 CUP DRIED CRANBERRIES	75 mL
1/3 CUP CHOPPED DRIED APRICOTS	75 mL
1/3 CUP BRANDY OR WATER	75 mL

FILLING

2 EGGS	
1 CUP PACKED BROWN SUGAR	250 mL
1/3 CUP FLOUR	75 mL
1 TSP. VANILLA	5 mL
1/3 CUP CHOPPED PECANS	75 mL

ICING (CONFECTIONER'S) SUGAR

TO MAKE CRUST: COMBINE FLOUR AND SUGAR; CUT IN BUTTER UNTIL MIXTURE IS CRUMBLY. PRESS INTO AN UNGREASED 9" (23 cm) SQUARE PAN AND BAKE AT 350°F (180°C) FOR 15-20 MINUTES, UNTIL GOLDEN.

BRANDIED CRANBERRY APRICOT BARS

CONTINUED FROM PAGE 272.

TO PREPARE FRUIT: PLACE ALL INGREDIENTS IN A SAUCEPAN, BRING TO A BOIL AND REMOVE FROM HEAT. LET STAND FOR 20 MINUTES. DRAIN.

TO MAKE FILLING: BEAT EGGS, ADD BROWN SUGAR, FLOUR AND VANILLA, MIXING WELL. STIR IN PECANS AND COOLED FRUIT.

TO ASSEMBLE: POUR FILLING OVER CRUST AND BAKE FOR 35-40 MINUTES. COVER WITH FOIL FOR THE LAST 10 MINUTES OF BAKING - THE TOP BECOMES VERY BROWN. WHEN COOL, SIFT ICING SUGAR OVER TOP. CUT INTO BARS.

I'M GIVING UP EXERCISE DUE TO ILLNESS AND FATIGUE; I'M SICK AND TIRED OF IT.

DREAM SLICE

ALWAYS A HIT - ADD TO YOUR CHRISTMAS BAKING.

CRUST

1⅓ CUPS FLOUR	325 mL
1 TBSP. SUGAR	15 mL
¾ CUP BUTTER	175 mL

FILLING

2 EGGS	
1 CUP BROWN SUGAR	250 mL
1 TSP. VANILLA	5 mL
3 TBSP. FLOUR	45 mL
1 TSP. BAKING POWDER	5 mL
PINCH OF SALT	
1 CUP SHREDDED COCONUT	250 mL
⅔ CUP CHOPPED WALNUTS	150 mL
¼ CUP SNIPPED GLACÉ CHERRIES	60 mL

BUTTER ICING

¼ CUP BUTTER, ROOM TEMPERATURE	60 mL
2½ CUPS ICING (CONFECTIONER'S) SUGAR	625 mL
3 TBSP. CREAM	45 mL

TO MAKE CRUST: PREHEAT OVEN TO 350°F (180°C). COMBINE FLOUR AND SUGAR. CUT IN BUTTER WITH PASTRY BLENDER UNTIL CRUMBLY. PRESS FIRMLY INTO A LIGHTLY GREASED 8" (20 cm) SQUARE PAN. BAKE FOR 20 MINUTES.

TO MAKE FILLING: BEAT EGGS IN A LARGE BOWL, GRADUALLY ADD SUGAR AND VANILLA. MIX FLOUR, BAKING POWDER AND SALT TOGETHER, THEN ADD TO SUGAR MIXTURE. ADD REMAINING INGREDIENTS. SPREAD OVER CRUST.

DREAM SLICE

CONTINUED FROM PAGE 274.

RETURN TO OVEN - LOWER TEMPERATURE TO 300°F (150°C). BAKE FOR 25-30 MINUTES, UNTIL TOP IS SET AND LIGHTLY BROWN. COOL

TO MAKE ICING: .BEAT INGREDIENTS TOGETHER AND SPREAD OVER COOLED SQUARE. FREEZES WELL.

KRISPIE GRANOLA BARS

GREAT FOR GOLFERS, TRAIL RIDERS AND SNACKIN'!

2½ CUPS RICE KRISPIES	625 mL
1 CUP DRIED APRICOTS, QUARTERED	250 mL
1¼ CUPS OATMEAL	300 mL
1¼ CUPS SUNFLOWER SEEDS, TOASTED	300 mL
½ CUP BROWN SUGAR	125 mL
¾ CUP HONEY	175 mL
¾ CUP PEANUT BUTTER, SUPER CHUNKY	175 mL

IN A MEDIUM BOWL, MIX RICE KRISPIES, APRICOTS, OATMEAL AND SUNFLOWER SEEDS. LINE A 10 X 15" (25 X 38 cm) PAN WITH PLASTIC WRAP. IN A LARGE POT, OVER LOW HEAT, MELT BROWN SUGAR, HONEY AND PEANUT BUTTER UNTIL BUBBLY. STIR SO IT WON'T BURN. STIR IN RICE KRISPIE MIXTURE. POUR INTO PAN AND PRESS DOWN. COOL. REMOVE PLASTIC WRAP AND CUT INTO SQUARES. KEEP REFRIGERATED.

SALTED PEANUT BARS

BOY - ARE THESE GOOD!!

CRUST

1½ CUPS FLOUR	375 mL
¾ CUP PACKED BROWN SUGAR	175 mL
½ TSP. SALT	2 mL
½ CUP BUTTER, ROOM TEMPERATURE	125 mL
3 CUPS SALTED PEANUTS	750 mL

TOPPING

½ CUP CORN SYRUP	125 mL
2 TBSP. BUTTER	30 mL
1 TBSP. WATER	15 mL
1 CUP BUTTERSCOTCH CHIPS	250 mL

PREHEAT OVEN TO 350°F (180°C). COMBINE CRUST INGREDIENTS AND BLEND WELL. PRESS INTO AN UNGREASED 10 x 15" (25 x 38 cm) PAN. BAKE FOR 12 MINUTES. SPRINKLE PEANUTS OVER CRUST. IN A SMALL SAUCEPAN, COMBINE TOPPING INGREDIENTS, BRING TO BOIL AND COOK FOR 2 MINUTES, STIRRING CONSTANTLY. POUR OVER NUTS AND RETURN TO OVEN FOR 15 MINUTES, UNTIL GOLDEN. COOL COMPLETELY BEFORE CUTTING. MAKES 48 BARS.

RESPONDEZ S'IL VOUS PLAID: HONK IF YOU'RE SCOTTISH.

DESSERTS

Icebox Pudding
Peanut Butter Rice Krispies Ice-Cream Sandwiches
Toffee Crunch Ice-Cream Cake
Pumpkin Crème Brûlée
Triple Chocolate Cheesecake
Vanilla Panna Cotta
Angel Mocha Torte
Lemon Meringue Pie
French Lemon Pie
Pumpkin Chiffon Pie
Old-Fashioned Butter Tarts
Spiced Pecan Whiskey Tart
Fruit Poof
Diddle Diddle Dumplings
Little Sticky Toffee Puddings
Lemon Pudding
Apple Cobbler with Cheddar-Biscuit Topping
Rhubarb Cobbler
Fruit Crisp with Oat Crumble Crust
Apple Crisp with Toffee Sauce
Cajun Bread Pudding
with Rum Sauce and Soft Cream
Plum Upside-Down Cakes with Mascarpone Cream
Chocolate Volcanoes with Raspberry Coulis
Berry-Topped Chocolate Torte
Black Magic Cake
Armenian Orange Cake
Orange Chiffon Cake
Fresh Apple Cake

ICEBOX PUDDING

Light and delicious. A family favorite for at least three generations - which is probably why it's called icebox pudding!

½ cup graham wafer crumbs	125 mL
1 cup whipping cream	250 mL
3 eggs, separated	
1 cup sugar, divided	250 mL
1 tbsp. gelatin (1 pkg)	15 mL
Juice of 1 lemon	
Juice of 1 orange	
¼ cup graham wafer crumbs	60 mL

Spread ½ cup (125 mL) graham wafer crumbs in bottom of an 8½ x 4½ x 2½" (22 x 11 x 6 cm) loaf pan. Whip cream until stiff. In another bowl, beat egg whites until stiff. Gradually add ½ cup (125 mL) sugar and continue beating. In a large bowl, beat egg yolks with remaining sugar until lemon colored. Soften gelatin in lemon and orange juices and add to yolk mixture. Gently fold in egg whites. Fold in whipped cream and pour into loaf pan. Sprinkle with remaining graham wafer crumbs. Freeze at least 4 hours or overnight.

At least 1 hour before serving, loosen edges and invert onto serving plate. Leave in refrigerator.

PEANUT BUTTER RICE KRISPIE ICE-CREAM SANDWICHES

KEEP THESE IN YOUR FREEZER FOR A SUMMER TREAT!

1 CUP LIGHT CORN SYRUP	250 mL
1 CUP SMOOTH PEANUT BUTTER	250 mL
6 CUPS RICE KRISPIES	1.5 L
1 QT. VANILLA ICE CREAM, SLIGHTLY SOFTENED	1 L

LINE BOTTOM AND SIDES OF A 9 X 13" (23 X 33 cm) BAKING DISH WITH FOIL, LEAVING SOME OVERLAP. IN A LARGE BOWL, MIX CORN SYRUP AND PEANUT BUTTER UNTIL WELL BLENDED. ADD CEREAL AND STIR UNTIL WELL COATED. SPREAD HALF OF MIXTURE IN BAKING DISH. SPREAD ICE CREAM OVER TOP AND FREEZE UNTIL FIRM, ABOUT 30 MINUTES. SPREAD REMAINING CEREAL MIXTURE OVER TOP, WRAP WELL WITH PLASTIC WRAP AND FREEZE AGAIN UNTIL FIRM, AT LEAST 30 MINUTES. USE FOIL OVERLAP TO TRANSFER TO A CUTTING BOARD, DISCARD FOIL AND CUT INTO BARS. MAKES 32 BARS.

I'M NOT CHEAP, BUT I AM ON SPECIAL THIS MONTH.

TOFFEE CRUNCH
ICE-CREAM CAKE

A GOOD SUMMERTIME BIRTHDAY CAKE!

CAKE

1¼ CUPS CRUSHED CHOCOLATE WAFERS	300 mL
⅓ CUP BUTTER	75 mL
2 QTS. VANILLA (OR COFFEE) ICE CREAM, SOFTENED	2 L
4-8 OZ. SKOR CHOCOLATE BARS, CRUSHED	4-250 g
1¼ CUPS UNSALTED PEANUTS, COARSELY CHOPPED	300 mL

TOFFEE SAUCE

½ CUP BUTTER	125 mL
1 CUP PACKED BROWN SUGAR	250 mL
½ CUP HALF & HALF CREAM	125 mL
1 TSP. VANILLA	5 mL

TO MAKE CAKE: GREASE A 9 X 13" (23 X 33 cm) PAN OR A 10" (25 cm) SPRINGFORM PAN. COMBINE WAFER CRUMBS AND BUTTER AND PRESS INTO BOTTOM OF PAN. PLACE IN FREEZER FOR 15 MINUTES. SPREAD HALF OF THE ICE CREAM OVER CRUST. SPRINKLE WITH CRUSHED SKOR BARS AND PRESS INTO ICE CREAM LAYER. CAREFULLY SPREAD REMAINING ICE CREAM OVER CRUMBS. SPRINKLE WITH PEANUTS AND FREEZE FOR 2-3 HOURS.

TOFFEE CRUNCH
ICE-CREAM CAKE

CONTINUED FROM PAGE 280.

TO MAKE SAUCE: IN A SMALL SAUCEPAN, MELT BUTTER OVER LOW HEAT. STIR IN BROWN SUGAR AND CREAM. COOK AND STIR CONSTANTLY OVER LOW HEAT UNTIL SUGAR HAS DISSOLVED. REMOVE FROM HEAT AND ADD VANILLA.

TO SERVE: REMOVE CAKE FROM PAN AND CUT INTO SLICES. POUR WARM OR COLD TOFFEE SAUCE OVER EACH SERVING.

WHAT DO YOU CALL CHEESE THAT ISN'T YOURS?
NACHO CHEESE!

PUMPKIN CRÈME BRÛLÉE

ANOTHER THANKSGIVING FINALE FAVORITE! COOL
AND STYLISH - IT NEVER FEELS LIKE TOO MUCH.
AND - IN THE TRUE SPIRIT OF THE HOLIDAY
SEASON - YOU CAN MAKE IT 2 DAYS AHEAD!

3 CUPS WHIPPING CREAM	750 mL
8 EGG YOLKS	
3/4 CUP CANNED PUMPKIN	175 mL
1/3 CUP SUGAR	75 mL
1/2 TSP. CINNAMON	2 mL
1/4 TSP. GROUND CLOVES	1 mL
1/4 TSP. GINGER	1 mL
1/4 TSP. NUTMEG	1 mL
1 1/2 TSP. VANILLA	7 mL
1/2 CUP PACKED BROWN SUGAR	125 mL

IN A SAUCEPAN, HEAT CREAM OVER MEDIUM-HIGH
HEAT UNTIL STEAMING. IN A BOWL, WHISK
TOGETHER EGG YOLKS, PUMPKIN, SUGAR, CINNAMON,
CLOVES, GINGER AND NUTMEG. GRADUALLY WHISK
IN CREAM. WHISK IN VANILLA. SKIM OFF FOAM.
DIVIDE AMONG 8, 6-OZ. (170 mL) RAMEKINS OR
CUSTARD CUPS. PLACE IN 2 LARGE SHALLOW
PANS AND POUR IN ENOUGH BOILING WATER TO
COME HALFWAY UP SIDES OF RAMEKINS.

BAKE AT 350°F (180°C) FOR 30-35 MINUTES, OR
UNTIL EDGES ARE SET AND CENTER IS STILL
JIGGLY. A KNIFE INSERTED IN THE CENTER
SHOULD COME OUT CREAMY.

PUMPKIN CRÈME BRÛLÉE

CONTINUED FROM PAGE 282.

REMOVE RAMEKIN FROM WATER AND LET COOL ON RACKS. COVER AND REFRIGERATE UNTIL SET (ABOUT 2 HOURS).

PLACE RAMEKINS ON A RIMMED BAKING SHEET AND PAT TOPS DRY WITH A PAPER TOWEL. SPRINKLE BROWN SUGAR EVENLY OVER TOPS AND BROIL 6" (15 cm) FROM HEAT UNTIL SUGAR BUBBLES AND DARKENS. WATCH CAREFULLY AS THEY CAN BURN. REFRIGERATE AGAIN, UNCOVERED, FOR AT LEAST 30 MINUTES, OR UNTIL READY TO SERVE.

I DON'T KNOW HOW I GOT OVER THE HILL WITHOUT GETTING TO THE TOP.

TRIPLE CHOCOLATE CHEESECAKE

YOU MIGHT BE FULL TO THE BRIM AND VERY WELL FED, BUT YOU'LL FIND ROOM FOR THIS TREAT AND "WADDLE" OFF TO BED!

CHOCOLATE CRUST

1½ CUPS CHOCOLATE WAFER CRUMBS	375 mL
¼ CUP BUTTER, MELTED	60 mL
3 TBSP. SUGAR	45 mL
¼ TSP. CINNAMON	1 mL

CHOCOLATE FILLING

½ CUP SOUR CREAM	125 mL
2 TSP. VANILLA	10 mL
1 TSP. ESPRESSO POWDER OR INSTANT COFFEE GRANULES	5 mL
8-1 OZ. BITTERSWEET CHOCOLATE SQUARES	250 g
3-8 OZ. PKGS. CREAM CHEESE, ROOM TEMPERATURE	3-250 g
3 TBSP. COCOA POWDER	45 mL
¼ TSP. SALT	1 mL
1 CUP SUGAR	250 mL
3 LARGE EGGS	

TO MAKE CRUST: PREHEAT OVEN TO 400°F (200°C). PLACE WAFER CRUMBS IN A MEDIUM BOWL. ADD BUTTER, SUGAR AND CINNAMON. BLEND WELL. PAT MIXTURE INTO A 9" (23 cm) SPRINGFORM PAN AND PUSH CRUMBS UP SIDES ABOUT 1" (2.5 cm). BAKE FOR 10 MINUTES. SET ON A RACK TO COOL. TURN OVEN DOWN TO 300°F (150°C).

TRIPLE CHOCOLATE CHEESECAKE

CONTINUED FROM PAGE 284.

TO MAKE FILLING: IN SMALL BOWL MIX SOUR CREAM, VANILLA AND ESPRESSO. STIR UNTIL COFFEE IS DISSOLVED. IN A DOUBLE BOILER, MELT CHOCOLATE, STIRRING UNTIL SMOOTH. LET COOL.

IN LARGE BOWL, BEAT CREAM CHEESE, COCOA AND SALT UNTIL SMOOTH AND FLUFFY. ADD SUGAR AND BEAT UNTIL WELL BLENDED. POUR IN MELTED CHOCOLATE AND BEAT AGAIN. ADD SOUR CREAM MIXTURE AND MIX THOROUGHLY. ADD EGGS 1 AT A TIME, BEATING AFTER EACH ADDITION. (DON'T MIX TOO MUCH OR CAKE WILL BE TOO PUFFY.) POUR BATTER OVER COOLED CRUST AND SMOOTH TOP WITH A SPATULA.

*PLACE IN MIDDLE OF OVEN AND BAKE FOR 60-70 MINUTES. THE CENTER SHOULD BARELY JIGGLE WHEN NUDGED. SET ON RACK AND COOL TO ROOM TEMPERATURE. REFRIGERATE TO CHILL THOROUGHLY. CAKE CAN ALSO BE FROZEN. PLACE IN FREEZER, UNCOVERED, UNTIL TOP IS COLD AND FIRM. THEN WRAP IN 2 LAYERS OF PLASTIC WRAP AND 1 LAYER OF FOIL.

TO SERVE: RUN METAL SPATULA UNDER BOTTOM CRUST AND SLIDE CAKE ONTO SERVING PLATE. USE A WARM KNIFE TO MAKE CLEAN CUTS.

*TO AVOID CRACKING: BEFORE BAKING, WRAP OUTSIDE AND BOTTOM OF PAN WITH FOIL AND PLACE A PAN OF WATER ON RACK DIRECTLY BELOW CAKE. SERVES 12 GRATEFUL GUESTS.

VANILLA PANNA COTTA

YOU'LL NEVER MAKE ANYTHING ELSE THAT'S THIS GOOD AND THIS EASY! THE TEXTURE IS LIKE VELVET!

1 TBSP. GELATIN (1 ENV.)	15 mL
½ CUP MILK	125 mL
3 CUPS WHIPPING CREAM	750 mL
½ CUP MILK	125 mL
½ CUP SUGAR	125 mL
1 TSP. VANILLA	5 mL

GARNISH

MANGO, PINEAPPLE, RASPBERRIES, KIWI FRUIT,
     PEACHES

IN A LARGE BOWL, ADD GELATIN TO COLD MILK AND LET SOFTEN. IN A SAUCEPAN, COMBINE CREAM, MILK, SUGAR AND VANILLA AND BRING TO A BOIL. POUR OVER GELATIN MIXTURE; STIR UNTIL COMPLETELY DISSOLVED. SET BOWL OVER VERY COLD WATER AND CHILL ½ HOUR, STIRRING OCCASIONALLY, UNTIL ALMOST SET. POUR INTO 8, ½ CUP (125 mL) RAMEKINS AND REFRIGERATE. COVER WITH PLASTIC WRAP IF MAKING THE NIGHT BEFORE. TO SERVE, QUICKLY DIP RAMEKINS IN WARM WATER TO LOOSEN SIDES. INVERT ONTO INDIVIDUAL SERVING PLATES AND SHAKE TO RELEASE. CUT FRUIT INTO SMALL PIECES AND ARRANGE ON EACH PLATE AROUND PANNA COTTA. SERVES 8.

ANGEL MOCHA TORTE

A CLASSIC ENTERTAINING DESSERT.

MERINGUES

1 CUP SLICED ALMONDS	250 mL
4 EGG WHITES	
PINCH OF SALT	
1 CUP BROWN SUGAR	250 mL

MOCHA FILLING

1 CUP WHIPPING CREAM	250 mL
1/2 CUP BROWN SUGAR	125 mL
1 TBSP. INSTANT COFFEE GRANULES	10 mL

4, 9" (23 cm) CIRCLES OF PARCHMENT PAPER

TO MAKE MERINGUES: TOAST ALMONDS; RESERVING SOME FOR DECORATION; CRUSH THE REMAINDER. BEAT EGG WHITES AND SALT UNTIL ALMOST STIFF. GRADUALLY ADD SUGAR; BEAT UNTIL GLOSSY PEAKS FORM. FOLD IN CRUSHED ALMONDS. SPREAD 1/4 OF MERINGUE ON EACH PAPER CIRCLE. DECORATE 1 CIRCLE WITH RESERVED ALMONDS. PLACE ON 2 COOKIE SHEETS; BAKE AT 250°F (120°C) FOR 1 HOUR. TURN OFF OVEN AND LEAVE OVERNIGHT. DON'T PEEK!! NEXT DAY, REMOVE MERINGUES AND TAKE OFF PARCHMENT PAPER. TO MAKE FILLING: WHIP CREAM. FOLD IN SUGAR AND COFFEE GRANULES. PLACE A MERINGUE ON A SERVING PLATE. SPREAD WITH 1/3 OF FILLING. CONTINUE WITH REMAINING MERINGUES, FINISHING WITH DECORATED MERINGUE. REFRIGERATE AT LEAST 2 HOURS BEFORE SERVING. SERVES 8-10.

LEMON MERINGUE PIE

IN CASE MOM DIDN'T TEACH YOU HOW.

LEMON FILLING

1 CUP SUGAR	250 mL
¼ CUP CORNSTARCH	60 mL
1½ CUPS COLD WATER	375 mL
3 EGG YOLKS, SLIGHTLY BEATEN	
GRATED ZEST OF 1 LEMON	
¼ CUP FRESH LEMON JUICE	60 mL
1 TBSP. BUTTER	15 mL
1 BAKED 9" (23 cm) PIE CRUST	

MERINGUE

3 EGG WHITES	
⅓ CUP SUGAR	75 mL

TO MAKE FILLING: IN A MEDIUM SAUCEPAN, COMBINE SUGAR AND CORNSTARCH. GRADUALLY STIR IN WATER UNTIL SMOOTH. STIR IN EGG YOLKS. STIRRING CONSTANTLY, BRING TO A BOIL OVER MEDIUM HEAT AND BOIL FOR 1 MINUTE. REMOVE FROM HEAT. STIR IN LEMON ZEST, LEMON JUICE AND BUTTER. SPOON HOT FILLING INTO CRUST.

PREHEAT OVEN TO 350°F (180°C).

TO MAKE MERINGUE: BEAT EGG WHITES IN A BOWL AT HIGH SPEED UNTIL FOAMY. GRADUALLY BEAT IN REMAINING SUGAR UNTIL STIFF PEAKS FORM. MOUND MERINGUE EVENLY OVER HOT FILLING TO EDGE OF CRUST, SEALING WELL. BAKE PIE FOR 15-20 MINUTES OR UNTIL GOLDEN. COOL ON RACK; REFRIGERATE.

FRENCH LEMON PIE

LEMON FILLING

4 EGGS	
1 CUP LIGHT CORN SYRUP	250 mL
1 TSP. GRATED LEMON ZEST	5 mL
1/3 CUP LEMON JUICE	75 mL
2 TBSP. MELTED BUTTER	30 mL
1/2 CUP SUGAR	125 mL
2 TBSP. FLOUR	30 mL
1 UNBAKED 9" (23 cm) PIE SHELL	
1/2 CUP WHIPPING CREAM	125 mL

IN A MEDIUM BOWL, BEAT EGGS; ADD CORN SYRUP, LEMON ZEST, LEMON JUICE AND MELTED BUTTER. MIX SUGAR AND FLOUR TOGETHER, THEN STIR INTO EGG MIXTURE. POUR INTO UNBAKED PIE SHELL AND BAKE AT 350°F (180°C) FOR 50 MINUTES. CHILL.

JUST BEFORE SERVING, WHIP CREAM AND MOUND IT ON TOP OF THE PIE.

WHY ISN'T THE NUMBER 11 PRONOUNCED ONETY ONE?

PUMPKIN CHIFFON PIE

YOU'LL BE "THANKFUL" FOR THIS ONE.

PUMPKIN FILLING

1 TBSP. GELATIN (1 PKG.)	15 mL
½ CUP COLD WATER	125 mL
4 EGGS, SEPARATED	
1 CUP EVAPORATED MILK	250 mL
1 CUP CANNED PUMPKIN	250 mL
½ CUP BROWN SUGAR	125 mL
½ TSP. SALT	2 mL
½ TSP. NUTMEG	2 mL
½ TSP. CINNAMON	2 mL
¼ TSP. GINGER	1 mL
¼ CUP BROWN SUGAR	60 mL

9" (23 cm) BAKED PIE SHELL	
1 CUP WHIPPING CREAM, WHIPPED	250 mL

TO MAKE FILLING: SOFTEN GELATIN IN COLD WATER. SET ASIDE. IN A DOUBLE BOILER, HEAT EGG YOLKS, MILK, PUMPKIN, BROWN SUGAR AND SPICES. COOK AND STIR FOR 10 MINUTES. REMOVE FROM HEAT; ADD GELATIN, STIRRING UNTIL DISSOLVED. REFRIGERATE UNTIL THICK. BEAT EGG WHITES AND BROWN SUGAR UNTIL THICK. FOLD INTO PUMPKIN MIXTURE.

TURN FILLING INTO PIE SHELL, TOP WITH WHIPPED CREAM AND REFRIGERATE UNTIL READY TO SERVE.

OLD-FASHIONED BUTTER TARTS

THESE ARE QUICK AND EASY, ESPECIALLY IF YOU PURCHASE THE TART SHELLS.

FILLING

1/3 CUP BUTTER, MELTED	75 mL
1 1/2 CUPS BROWN SUGAR	375 mL
3 EGGS	
1 TSP. GRATED LEMON ZEST	5 mL
1 CUP CURRANTS	250 mL
1 TSP. VANILLA	5 mL

3 DOZEN UNBAKED TART SHELLS

TO MAKE FILLING: IN A MEDIUM BOWL, CREAM BUTTER AND SUGAR. ADD EGGS 1 AT A TIME, BEATING WITH AN ELECTRIC MIXER. STIR IN LEMON ZEST, CURRANTS AND VANILLA.

PREHEAT OVEN TO 375°F (190°C). FILL TART SHELLS AND BAKE FOR 12-15 MINUTES, OR UNTIL GOLDEN. MAKES 3 DOZEN TARTS.

A HANGOVER IS THE WRATH OF GRAPES.

SPICED PECAN WHISKEY TART

IF YOU DON'T HAVE A TART PAN - YOU MUST! THE PRESENTATION IS PERFECT AND YOU DON'T HAVE TO ROLL THE PASTRY!

PASTRY

1¼ CUPS FLOUR	300 mL
2 TBSP. SUGAR	30 mL
¼ TSP. SALT	1 mL
⅓ CUP COLD BUTTER	75 mL
2 TBSP. COLD WATER	30 mL
1 TSP. WHITE VINEGAR	5 mL

PECAN WHISKEY FILLING

3 EGGS	
1 CUP PACKED BROWN SUGAR	250 mL
½ CUP CORN SYRUP	125 mL
¼ CUP RYE WHISKY OR BOURBON	60 mL
2 TBSP. BUTTER, MELTED	30 mL
½ TSP. CINNAMON	2 mL
¼ TSP. NUTMEG	1 mL
¼ TSP. GROUND CLOVES	1 mL
¼ TSP. ALLSPICE	1 mL
1¼ CUPS PECAN HALVES	300 mL
2 TBSP. CORN SYRUP, WARMED	30 mL

WHIPPED CREAM FOR GARNISH

TO MAKE PASTRY: IN A LARGE BOWL, COMBINE FLOUR, SUGAR AND SALT. CUT IN BUTTER WITH PASTRY CUTTER UNTIL MIXTURE RESEMBLES FINE CRUMBS. ADD WATER AND VINEGAR AND MIX UNTIL BLENDED BUT STILL CRUMBLY.

SPICED PECAN WHISKEY TART

CONTINUED FROM PAGE 292.

SQUEEZE TOGETHER IN SMALL HANDFULS AND PAT EVENLY OVER BOTTOM AND UP SIDES OF A 9" (23 cm) TART PAN WITH A REMOVABLE BOTTOM. PRESS DOWN FIRMLY AND REFRIGERATE FOR 15 MINUTES. (THIS CAN BE MADE AHEAD, COVERED AND REFRIGERATED FOR 24 HOURS.)

PREHEAT OVEN TO 375°F (190°C). IN A BOWL, WHISK TOGETHER EGGS, SUGAR, CORN SYRUP, RYE, BUTTER, CINNAMON, NUTMEG, CLOVES AND ALLSPICE; STIR IN PECANS. SCRAPE FILLING INTO PREPARED TART SHELL.

BAKE ON BOTTOM RACK OF OVEN UNTIL FILLING IS JUST FIRM TO THE TOUCH, ABOUT 45 MINUTES. COVER EDGE OF CRUST WITH FOIL IF IT BECOMES TOO BROWN. BRUSH FILLING WITH CORN SYRUP AND LET COOL ON A WIRE RACK. THIS MAY BE BAKED, COOLED, COVERED AND LEFT STANDING AT ROOM TEMPERATURE FOR UP TO 1 DAY. GENTLY REMOVE SIDES AND BASE. SERVE WITH A DOLLOP OF WHIPPED CREAM. SERVES 12.

DIJON VU: THE SAME MUSTARD AS BEFORE.

FRUIT POOF

YOU SHOW-OFF YOU!

PUFF

⅔ CUP WATER	150 mL
⅓ CUP BUTTER	75 mL
⅔ CUP FLOUR	150 mL

CRUST

⅔ CUP FLOUR	150 mL
1 TBSP. SUGAR	15 mL
¼ CUP BUTTER	60 mL

3 EGGS

FILLING

3½ OZ. BOX INSTANT VANILLA PUDDING	102 g
1½ CUPS MILK	375 mL
½ CUP WHIPPING CREAM	125 mL
2 CUPS FRESH, SLICED PEACHES, KIWI HALVED STRAWBERRIES, HALVED GRAPES, BLUEBERRIES OR RASPBERRIES	500 mL
¼ CUP APPLE JELLY, MELTED	60 mL

TO MAKE PUFF: COMBINE WATER AND BUTTER IN A MEDIUM-SIZED SAUCEPAN AND BRING TO A BOIL, STIRRING TO MELT BUTTER. ADD FLOUR ALL AT ONCE. COOK AND STIR UNTIL MIXTURE FORMS A BALL THAT DOESN'T SEPARATE. SET ASIDE TO COOL FOR 15 MINUTES.

FRUIT POOF

CONTINUED FROM PAGE 294.

TO MAKE CRUST: COMBINE FLOUR WITH SUGAR. CUT IN BUTTER UNTIL CRUMBLY. FIRMLY PRESS CRUMBS INTO AN 8" (20 cm) CIRCLE ON AN UNGREASED BAKING SHEET. SET ASIDE.

PREHEAT OVEN TO 400°F (200°C). ADD EGGS TO DOUGH IN SAUCEPAN, 1 AT A TIME, BEATING WELL AFTER EACH ADDITION. GENTLY SPREAD 1/4 OF THE DOUGH OVER CRUST, FORMING A 5" (13 cm) CIRCLE. DROP SPOONFULS OF DOUGH AROUND EDGE OF SMALLER CIRCLE. BAKE FOR 15 MINUTES THEN REDUCE HEAT TO 350°F (180°C) AND CONTINUE BAKING FOR 35-40 MINUTES. COOL.

TO MAKE FILLING: PREPARE PUDDING, USING MILK. BEAT CREAM AND FOLD INTO PUDDING. SPOON FILLING INTO CENTER OF PUFF. ARRANGE FRUIT ON TOP AND BRUSH FRUIT WITH MELTED JELLY. CHILL FOR 2 HOURS. SERVES 8.

READING WHILST SUNBATHING MAKES YOU . . . WELL . . . RED!

DIDDLE DIDDLE DUMPLINGS

YOUR SON JOHN (AND THE REST OF THE FAMILY) WILL LOVE THIS OLD-FASHIONED APPLE DESSERT WITH A NEW TWIST.

SAUCE

1½ CUPS BROWN SUGAR	375 mL
1½ CUPS WATER	375 mL
¼ CUP BUTTER	60 mL
½ TSP. CINNAMON	2 mL
¼ TSP. NUTMEG	1 mL

DOUGH

2 CUPS FLOUR	500 mL
2 TSP. BAKING POWDER	10 mL
½ TSP. SALT	2 mL
¾ CUP BUTTER	175 mL
⅔ CUP MILK	150 mL

FILLING

4 GRANNY SMITH APPLES	
½ TSP. CINNAMON	2 mL

PREHEAT OVEN TO 350°F (180°C).

TO MAKE SAUCE: IN A LARGE SAUCEPAN, COMBINE INGREDIENTS. BRING TO A BOIL FOR 5 MINUTES. REMOVE FROM HEAT AND SET ASIDE.

TO MAKE DOUGH: IN A LARGE BOWL, COMBINE FLOUR, BAKING POWDER AND SALT. USING A PASTRY BLENDER, CUT IN BUTTER UNTIL PIECES ARE PEA-SIZE. MAKE A WELL IN CENTER OF FLOUR MIXTURE.

DIDDLE DIDDLE DUMPLINGS

CONTINUED FROM PAGE 296.

ADD MILK ALL AT ONCE. STIR JUST UNTIL MOISTENED. ON A LIGHTLY FLOURED SURFACE, KNEAD DOUGH GENTLY FOR 10-12 STROKES, OR UNTIL NEARLY SMOOTH. ROLL DOUGH INTO A 10 x 12" (25 x 30 cm) RECTANGLE.

TO MAKE FILLING: PEEL AND GRATE APPLES. SPREAD EVENLY OVER DOUGH. SPRINKLE WITH CINNAMON. STARTING FROM LONG SIDE, ROLL DOUGH INTO A TIGHT ROLL. PINCH SEAM TO SEAL. WITH A SHARP KNIFE, CUT INTO 12, 1" (2.5 cm) THICK SLICES. ARRANGE SLICES FACE UP IN A 9 x 13" (23 x 33 cm) BAKING DISH. POUR SAUCE OVER DUMPLINGS AND BAKE FOR ABOUT 50 MINUTES, OR UNTIL GOLDEN. COOL SLIGHTLY ON A WIRE RACK. SERVE WARM WITH WHIPPED CREAM OR ICE CREAM. (PICTURED ON PAGE 257.)

THE QUICKEST WAY TO DOUBLE YOUR MONEY IS TO FOLD IT IN HALF AND PUT IT BACK IN YOUR POCKET.

LITTLE STICKY TOFFEE PUDDINGS

1 CUP WATER	250 mL
½ TSP. VANILLA	2 mL
½ TSP. BAKING SODA	2 mL
1 CUP DRIED CRANBERRIES	250 mL
¾ CUP BUTTER	175 mL
⅔ CUP SUGAR	150 mL
2 EGGS	
1 CUP FLOUR	250 mL
¼ TSP. BAKING POWDER	1 mL

TOFFEE SAUCE

1 CUP BROWN SUGAR	250 mL
½ CUP BUTTER	125 mL
½ CUP WHIPPING CREAM	125 mL

BUTTER 8, 4-OZ. (125 mL) RAMEKINS. BRING WATER TO A BOIL; ADD VANILLA AND BAKING SODA. ADD CRANBERRIES; SET ASIDE TO COOL. CREAM BUTTER AND SUGAR UNTIL LIGHT AND FLUFFY. LIGHTLY BEAT EGGS AND GRADUALLY ADD TO BUTTER MIXTURE IN 3 STAGES. SIFT FLOUR AND BAKING POWDER TOGETHER; GENTLY FOLD INTO BATTER. FOLD CRANBERRY MIXTURE INTO BATTER. PORTION INTO RAMEKINS AND BAKE AT 350°F (180°C) FOR 25 MINUTES.

TO MAKE TOFFEE SAUCE: COMBINE INGREDIENTS IN SAUCEPAN; STIR OVER LOW HEAT UNTIL SUGAR IS DISSOLVED. SIMMER UNTIL THICKENED. TO SERVE, REMOVE PUDDINGS FROM RAMEKINS BY RUNNING A KNIFE AROUND EDGE. INVERT ON PLATE AND DRIZZLE WITH WARM TOFFEE SAUCE. SERVES 8.

LEMON PUDDING

THE TOP TURNS TO CAKE AND THE BOTTOM TURNS TO SAUCE. SERVE WARM WITH WHIPPED CREAM.

2 TBSP. FLOUR	30 mL
1 CUP SUGAR	250 mL
2 TBSP. BUTTER, ROOM TEMPERATURE	30 mL
2 EGGS, SEPARATED	
1 CUP MILK	250 mL
1 TBSP. GRATED LEMON ZEST	15 mL
JUICE OF 1 LEMON	

PREHEAT OVEN TO 350°F (180°C). IN A LARGE BOWL, COMBINE FLOUR AND SUGAR. CREAM IN BUTTER. IN A MEDIUM BOWL, BEAT YOLKS AND MILK TOGETHER AND ADD TO CREAMED MIXTURE. BEAT UNTIL SMOOTH. STIR IN LEMON ZEST AND JUICE. BEAT EGG WHITES UNTIL STIFF. FOLD INTO BATTER AND POUR INTO A SHALLOW BAKING DISH. SET DISH IN A PAN OF HOT WATER AND BAKE FOR 35-40 MINUTES, UNTIL TOP IS GOLDEN. SERVES 4-6 (OR 2 DELIGHTED TEENAGERS).

IF JIMMY CRACKS CORN AND NO ONE CARES, WHY IS THERE A SONG ABOUT HIM?

APPLE COBBLER WITH — CHEDDAR-BISCUIT TOPPING

SERVE THIS HOT WITH A SCOOP OF VANILLA ICE CREAM.

COBBLER

3/4 CUP PACKED LIGHT BROWN SUGAR	175 mL
1 TSP. GRATED LEMON ZEST	5 mL
1/2 TSP. CINNAMON	2 mL
1/4 CUP BUTTER, DIVIDED	60 mL
10 GRANNY SMITH APPLES, PEELED, CORED & THINLY SLICED	

TOPPING

3 CUPS FLOUR	750 mL
1/4 CUP SUGAR	60 mL
1 TBSP. BAKING POWDER	15 mL
3/4 TSP. SALT	3 mL
3/4 CUP COLD BUTTER, CUT INTO PIECES	175 mL
1 1/2 CUPS COARSELY SHREDDED SHARP CHEDDAR CHEESE	375 mL
1 CUP BUTTERMILK	250 mL

TO MAKE COBBLER: PREHEAT OVEN TO 375°F (190°C). IN A LARGE BOWL, MIX BROWN SUGAR, LEMON ZEST AND CINNAMON. IN A 12" (30 cm) FRYING PAN MELT 2 TBSP. (30 mL) BUTTER OVER MEDIUM-HIGH HEAT. ADD HALF THE APPLES; COOK AND STIR UNTIL TENDER, 5 MINUTES. GENTLY STIR INTO SUGAR MIXTURE. REPEAT PROCESS WITH REMAINING BUTTER AND APPLES. TRANSFER FILLING TO A 9 x 13" (23 x 33 cm) BAKING DISH; COVER AND KEEP WARM.

APPLE COBBLER WITH —
CHEDDAR-BISCUIT TOPPING

CONTINUED FROM PAGE 300.

TO MAKE TOPPING: IN A LARGE BOWL, COMBINE
FLOUR, 1 TBSP. (15 mL) SUGAR, BAKING POWDER
AND SALT. WITH A PASTRY BLENDER, OR
2 KNIVES USED SCISSOR-FASHION, CUT IN BUTTER
UNTIL MIXTURE RESEMBLES COARSE CRUMBS.
STIR IN CHEESE AND BUTTERMILK. TURN DOUGH
ONTO A WORK SURFACE (DOUGH WILL BE
CRUMBLY). KNEAD UNTIL DOUGH IS SMOOTH AND
HOLDS TOGETHER. UNCOVER FILLING. DROP DOUGH
IN WALNUT-SIZED PIECES OVER APPLE MIXTURE
TO COVER; SPRINKLE WITH REMAINING SUGAR.
BAKE UNTIL FILLING IS HOT AND BUBBLING AND
BISCUITS ARE GOLDEN, 35-40 MINUTES. LET
STAND FOR 15 MINUTES BEFORE SERVING. TOP
WITH VANILLA ICE CREAM.

MORE THINGS I LEARNED FROM MY CHILDREN:
IF YOU HOOK A DOG LEASH OVER A CEILING FAN, THE
MOTOR IS NOT STRONG ENOUGH TO ROTATE A 42-POUND
BOY WEARING BATMAN UNDERWEAR AND A SUPERMAN
CAPE.

RHUBARB COBBLER

THERE MUST BE SOME RHUBARB IN YOUR
FREEZER! THIS IS ALWAYS A HIT.

4 CUPS RHUBARB, CUT IN ½" (1.3 cm) PIECES	1 L
¾-1 CUP SUGAR	175-250 mL
1¼ CUPS FLOUR	300 mL
3 TBSP. SUGAR	45 mL
1 TBSP. BAKING POWDER	15 mL
¼ TSP. SALT	1 mL
⅓ CUP BUTTER	75 mL
1 EGG, BEATEN	
½ CUP MILK	125 mL

PREHEAT OVEN TO 375°F (190°C). COMBINE
RHUBARB AND SUGAR AND PLACE IN A SHALLOW,
GREASED 9" (23 cm) BAKING DISH. TO MAKE
BATTER, COMBINE FLOUR, SUGAR, BAKING POWDER
AND SALT. CUT IN BUTTER TO MAKE A CRUMBLY
TEXTURE. COMBINE EGG AND MILK AND ADD TO
DRY INGREDIENTS. STIR WITH A FORK TO MAKE A
STIFF BATTER. DROP BATTER BY SPOONFULS ON
TOP OF RHUBARB AND BAKE FOR 35-40 MINUTES.
SERVE WARM WITH ICE CREAM OR WHIPPED
CREAM. SERVES 6.

SNOWMEN FALL FROM HEAVEN UNASSEMBLED.

FRUIT CRISP WITH
OAT CRUMBLE CRUST

DID YOUR MOTHER ALWAYS PUT OATS IN THE CRUST? THIS IS FOR YOU.

6 CUPS APPLES, PEELED & SLICED OR	1.5 L
ANY COMBINATION OF THESE FRUITS: BERRIES, RHUBARB, STRAWBERRIES, RASPBERRIES, BLUEBERRIES, PEARS OR APRICOTS	
1/3 CUP SUGAR	75 mL
2 TBSP. FLOUR	30 mL
1 TBSP. GRATED LEMON ZEST	15 mL
1/2 TSP. CINNAMON	2 mL

OAT CRUST

1/2 CUP BUTTER, SOFTENED	125 mL
1/2 CUP BROWN SUGAR	125 mL
1/2 CUP FLOUR	125 mL
2/3 CUP ROLLED OATS	150 mL

TO MAKE CRISP: PLACE PREPARED FRUIT IN A 2-QUART (2 L) BAKING DISH. COMBINE SUGAR, FLOUR, LEMON ZEST AND CINNAMON. ADD TO FRUIT AND TOSS TO COAT.

TO MAKE CRUST: MIX CRUST INGREDIENTS WITH A PASTRY BLENDER UNTIL CRUMBLY. SPRINKLE OVER FRUIT MIXTURE. BAKE AT 350°F (180°C) FOR 45 MINUTES, UNTIL CRISP IS BUBBLING. SERVES 8.

APPLE CRISP
WITH TOFFEE SAUCE

SERVE WARM WITH TOFFEE SAUCE. AN EXCELLENT DESSERT FOR LARGE FAMILY GATHERINGS - DOWN HOME AND DELICIOUS!

½ CUP SUGAR	125 mL
¼ CUP FLOUR	60 mL
1 TBSP. CINNAMON	15 mL
½ TSP. SALT	2 mL
1 CUP LIGHT CREAM	250 mL
1 TBSP. FRESHLY SQUEEZED LEMON JUICE	15 mL
8 GRANNY SMITH APPLES, PEELED, CORED & SLICED IN WEDGES	
1½ CUPS FLOUR	375 mL
1 CUP PACKED BROWN SUGAR	250 mL
2 TSP. CINNAMON	10 mL
¼ TSP. SALT	1 mL
¾ CUP COLD BUTTER	175 mL

TOFFEE SAUCE

1 CUP PACKED BROWN SUGAR	250 mL
½ CUP BUTTER	125 mL
½ CUP LIGHT CREAM	125 mL

PREHEAT OVEN TO 350°F (180°C). BUTTER A 9 X 13" (23 X 33 cm) BAKING DISH. IN A LARGE BOWL, COMBINE SUGAR, FLOUR, CINNAMON AND SALT. GRADUALLY STIR IN CREAM AND LEMON JUICE. TOSS APPLES IN CREAM MIXTURE. SPOON INTO PAN. COMBINE FLOUR, SUGAR, CINNAMON AND SALT. CUT IN BUTTER UNTIL

CONTINUED FROM PAGE 304.

MIXTURE IS CRUMBLY. SPREAD OVER APPLES AND PAT DOWN LIGHTLY. BAKE AT 350°F (180°C) FOR 45 MINUTES.

TO MAKE TOFFEE SAUCE: COMBINE INGREDIENTS IN SAUCEPAN; STIR OVER LOW HEAT UNTIL SUGAR IS DISSOLVED. SIMMER UNTIL THICKENED. SERVES 10-12.

IF LAWYERS ARE DISBARRED AND CLERGYMEN ARE DEFROCKED, DOESN'T IT FOLLOW THAT ELECTRICIANS CAN BE DELIGHTED, MUSICIANS DENOTED, COWBOYS DERANGED, MODELS DEPOSED, TREE SURGEONS DEBARKED, AND DRY CLEANERS DEPRESSED?

CAJUN BREAD PUDDING
WITH RUM SAUCE AND SOFT CREAM

YOUR GUESTS WILL BE INCLINED TO EXCLAIM, "DON'T Y'ALL JUST LUUVE THIS!!!"

PUDDING

⅓ CUP BUTTER, MELTED	75 mL
16 CUPS FRENCH BREAD CUBES, DAY OLD, LIGHTLY PACKED	4 L
3 EGGS	
1½ CUPS SUGAR	375 mL
2 TBSP. VANILLA	30 mL
1 TSP. NUTMEG	5 mL
1½ TSP. CINNAMON	7 mL
3 CUPS MILK	750 mL
¾ CUP GOLDEN RAISINS	175 mL
1 CUP CHOPPED TOASTED PECANS	250 mL

RUM SAUCE

1 CUP BUTTER	250 mL
1½ CUPS SUGAR	375 mL
2 EGGS, BEATEN UNTIL FROTHY	
¼-½ CUP DARK RUM	60-125 mL

SOFT CREAM

2 CUPS WHIPPING CREAM	500 mL
⅓ CUP ICING SUGAR	75 mL
1 TBSP. VANILLA	15 mL
2 TBSP. BRANDY	30 mL
2 TBSP. FRANGELICO LIQUEUR	30 mL
¼ CUP SOUR CREAM	60 mL

TO MAKE PUDDING: POUR A SMALL AMOUNT OF MELTED BUTTER IN A 9 X 13" (23 X 33 cm) PAN; SWIRL TO COVER BOTTOM AND SIDES. PLACE BREAD CUBES IN PAN. (CONTINUED ON PAGE 309.)

Chocolate Volcanoes with Raspberry Coulis, page 312

Orange Chiffon Cake, page 318

CAJUN BREAD PUDDING

CONTINUED FROM PAGE 306.

IN A LARGE BOWL, BEAT EGGS AND SUGAR UNTIL THICKENED, 3-4 MINUTES. ADD VANILLA, NUTMEG, CINNAMON, MILK AND REMAINING BUTTER. BEAT ON LOW TO COMBINE. STIR IN RAISINS AND PECANS; POUR OVER BREAD. ALLOW BREAD TO ABSORB LIQUID, 30-45 MINUTES. PRESS BREAD DOWN OFTEN TO COVER ALL CUBES. PREHEAT OVEN TO 350°F (180°C). BAKE UNTIL CRUSTY AND GOLDEN BROWN, 45-60 MINUTES. COOL AND SLICE INTO SQUARES.

TO MAKE SAUCE: CREAM BUTTER AND SUGAR UNTIL LIGHT AND FLUFFY. COOK IN DOUBLE BOILER FOR 20 MINUTES, WHISKING OFTEN. IN A BOWL, WHISK 2 TBSP. (30 mL) BUTTER-SUGAR MIXTURE INTO BEATEN EGGS, THEN WHISK IN 2 TBSP. (30 mL) MORE. WHISK EGG MIXTURE INTO BUTTER MIXTURE. COOK AND WHISK OVER SIMMERING WATER FOR 4-5 MINUTES. COOL SLIGHTLY. WHISK IN RUM. (BY NOW YOU'RE PROBABLY ALL WHISKED OUT - TASTE THE SAUCE - YOU'LL KNOW IT WAS WORTH IT!)

TO MAKE CREAM: BEAT INGREDIENTS UNTIL SOFT PEAKS FORM, 3-4 MINUTES. DO NOT OVERBEAT. COVER AND REFRIGERATE UNTIL SERVED.

TO SERVE: ON INDIVIDUAL PLATES, PLACE A SPOONFUL OF WARM RUM SAUCE, A SQUARE OF PUDDING AND A LARGE DOLLOP OF SOFT CREAM. SERVES 12-14.

PLUM UPSIDE-DOWN CAKES WITH MASCARPONE CREAM

SUPERBULOUS!

½ CUP BUTTER, ROOM TEMPERATURE	125 mL
¾ CUP PACKED BROWN SUGAR	175 mL
6 MEDIUM-SIZED RIPE, FIRM RED PLUMS, PITTED & THINLY SLICED	
½ CUP MILK	125 mL
1 TBSP. FRESH LEMON JUICE	15 mL
1½ CUPS FLOUR	375 mL
1 TSP. BAKING POWDER	5 mL
¼ TSP. BAKING SODA	1 mL
½ TSP. CINNAMON	2 mL
¼ TSP. SALT	1 mL
½ CUP BUTTER	125 mL
1 CUP SUGAR	250 mL
GRATED ZEST OF 1 ORANGE	
2 LARGE EGGS	
2 TSP. VANILLA	10 mL

MASCARPONE CREAM

1 CUP WHIPPING CREAM	250 mL
6 TBSP. MASCARPONE CHEESE (ITALIAN CREAM CHEESE)	90 mL
2 TSP. SUGAR	10 mL
¼ TSP. VANILLA	1 mL

TO MAKE CAKES: BUTTER 8, 8-OZ. (250 mL) RAMEKINS. PREHEAT OVEN TO 350°F (180°C). IN A MEDIUM SAUCEPAN OVER MEDIUM HEAT, COMBINE BUTTER WITH BROWN SUGAR, WHISKING UNTIL SMOOTH AND COMBINED. IMMEDIATELY POUR INTO BUTTERED RAMEKINS, DIVIDING EVENLY.

PLUM UPSIDE-DOWN CAKES WITH MASCARPONE CREAM

CONTINUED FROM PAGE 310.

ARRANGE A LAYER OF PLUM SLICES IN EACH RAMEKIN, OVER-LAPPING SLIGHTLY. IN A SMALL BOWL, COMBINE MILK AND LEMON JUICE (DON'T WORRY - IT CURDLES). IN ANOTHER BOWL, SIFT TOGETHER FLOUR, BAKING POWDER, BAKING SODA, CINNAMON AND SALT. USING A MIXER, CREAM BUTTER WITH SUGAR AND ORANGE ZEST. ADD EGGS AND VANILLA, MIX WELL. ADD DRY INGREDIENTS ALTERNATELY WITH MILK MIXTURE, MIXING JUST TO COMBINE. DIVIDE BATTER AMONG RAMEKINS. PLACE ON A RIMMED BAKING SHEET AND BAKE UNTIL CAKES ARE FIRM TO THE TOUCH AND JUICES ARE BUBBLING, 35-40 MINUTES. COOL ON A RACK. BEFORE SERVING, HEAT OVEN TO 350°F (180°C). SET RAMEKINS ON A BAKING SHEET AND HEAT UNTIL JUST WARMED, ABOUT 5 MINUTES. RUN A SMALL KNIFE AROUND THE INSIDE EDGE OF EACH RAMEKIN AND INVERT ONTO A PLATE. TOP WITH A DOLLOP OF MASCARPONE CREAM. SERVES 8.

TO MAKE MASCARPONE CREAM: BEAT ALL INGREDIENTS IN A SMALL BOWL UNTIL PEAKS FORM. (PICTURED ON PAGE 258.)

CHOCOLATE VOLCANOES WITH RASPBERRY COULIS

A GUARANTEED HIT - EASY AND ABSOLUTELY DELICIOUS! PREPARE AND FREEZE THESE SERVING-SIZED DESSERTS AHEAD OF TIME, THEN COOK THEM WHILE YOU ENJOY YOUR DINNER.

1½ TBSP. INSTANT ESPRESSO GRANULES (INSTANT COFFEE GRANULES MAY BE USED)	22 mL
1 TBSP. BOILING WATER	15 mL
½ CUP FLOUR	125 mL
¼ CUP COCOA POWDER	60 mL
¾ TSP. BAKING POWDER	3 mL
6-1 OZ. SQUARES SEMISWEET CHOCOLATE	170 g
⅔ CUP BUTTER, SOFTENED	150 mL
½ CUP SUGAR	125 L
3 LARGE EGGS	

RASPBERRY COULIS

10½ PKG. FROZEN RASPBERRIES, THAWED	300 g
⅓ CUP SUGAR	75 mL
1-2 TBSP. GRAND MARNIER LIQUEUR	15-30 mL

TO MAKE VOLCANOES: DISSOLVE COFFEE GRANULES IN BOILING WATER. SET ASIDE TO COOL. GREASE 6, 4-OZ. (125 mL) RAMEKINS. USING A WHISK, COMBINE FLOUR, COCOA AND BAKING POWDER IN A SMALL BOWL. RESERVE. MELT CHOCOLATE IN A DOUBLE BOILER. ADD BUTTER AND SUGAR AND STIR UNTIL SMOOTH. TRANSFER TO A LARGE BOWL. USING AN ELECTRIC MIXER, BEAT IN EGGS 1 AT A TIME ON MEDIUM SPEED.

CHOCOLATE VOLCANOES WITH RASPBERRY COULIS

CONTINUED FROM PAGE 312.

ADD DISSOLVED COFFEE AND FLOUR MIXTURE AND CONTINUE BEATING UNTIL FULLY MIXED. RAISE MIXER SPEED TO HIGH AND BEAT FOR 6 MORE MINUTES (THERE MUST BE SOMETHING GOOD ON TV!). POUR BATTER INTO RAMEKINS AND TIGHTLY WRAP WITH PLASTIC WRAP. FREEZE OVERNIGHT OR UP TO 2 WEEKS.

TO MAKE RASPBERRY COULIS: COMBINE RASPBERRIES AND SUGAR IN A BLENDER AND PURÉE UNTIL SMOOTH. STRAIN THROUGH A SIEVE (OR A CLEAN J-CLOTH) TO REMOVE SEEDS. ADD LIQUEUR AND STORE IN REFRIGERATOR.

PREHEAT OVEN TO 375°F (190°C). TAKE RAMEKINS OUT OF FREEZER, REMOVE PLASTIC WRAP. BAKE VOLCANOES FOR 18 MINUTES - NO LONGER! COOL ON RACK FOR 5 MINUTES. THE OUTSIDES WILL BE CRUSTY AND THE CENTERS WILL BE GOOEY - SORT OF LIKE YOUR AVERAGE VOLCANO. TO SERVE, DRIZZLE INDIVIDUAL PLATES WITH RASPBERRY COULIS. INVERT EACH RAMEKIN ONTO A PLATE AND ADD A SMALL SCOOP OF ICE CREAM. (PICTURED ON PAGE 307.)

BERRY-TOPPED
CHOCOLATE TORTE

EASY AND ELEGANT. CHOCOLATE, CREAM AND
BERRIES ARE PERFECT PARTNERS.

⅔ CUP GROUND ALMONDS	150 mL
3 TBSP. FLOUR	45 mL
PINCH OF SALT	
¾ CUP BUTTER	175 mL
⅓ CUP COCOA POWDER	75 mL
½ CUP SUGAR	125 mL
3 EGGS, SEPARATED	
½ CUP SUGAR	125 mL
3 TBSP. GRAND MARNIER LIQUEUR OR	45 mL
ORANGE JUICE	
1 CUP WHIPPING CREAM	250 mL
1 TBSP. GRAND MARNIER LIQUEUR	15 mL
2 CUPS RASPBERRIES	500 mL
CHOCOLATE CURLS	

GREASE A 9" (23 cm) SPRINGFORM PAN AND
LINE WITH PARCHMENT PAPER. IN SMALL BOWL,
COMBINE ALMONDS, FLOUR AND SALT. SET ASIDE.
MELT BUTTER IN A SAUCEPAN AND STIR IN
COCOA AND SUGAR. IN A LARGE BOWL, BEAT EGG
YOLKS UNTIL THICK; GRADUALLY BLEND IN COCOA
MIXTURE. STIR IN ALMOND MIXTURE. IN A
SEPARATE BOWL, BEAT EGG WHITES UNTIL STIFF.
GRADUALLY ADD SUGAR. FOLD WHITES INTO
CHOCOLATE MIXTURE. POUR BATTER INTO
PREPARED PAN AND BAKE AT 375°F (190°C) FOR
25-30 MINUTES, UNTIL A TOOTHPICK INSERTED IN
THE CENTER COMES OUT CLEAN.

BERRY-TOPPED
CHOCOLATE TORTE

CONTINUED FROM PAGE 314.

LET COOL IN PAN FOR 10 MINUTES. RUN A KNIFE AROUND EDGE OF TORTE AND REMOVE SIDES OF SPRINGFORM PAN. TORTE WILL FALL IN MIDDLE. (DON'T WORRY, YOU CAN FILL IT WITH WHIPPED CREAM!)

DRIZZLE 3 TBSP. (45 mL) GRAND MARNIER OVER CAKE. COOL COMPLETELY AND WRAP WITH PLASTIC WRAP. THIS CAN BE STORED IN REFRIGERATOR FOR 2 DAYS.

WHIP CREAM AND FOLD IN GRAND MARNIER. SPREAD ON TORTE AND DECORATE WITH BERRIES AND CHOCOLATE CURLS. SERVES 8.

MIDLIFE CRISIS: WHEN THE ONLY THING YOU RETAIN IS WATER.

BLACK MAGIC CAKE

FOR CHOCOLATE LOVERS - A DENSE CHOCOLATE CAKE THAT SERVES A CROWD.

1 CUP BUTTER, CUT-UP	250 mL
3/4 CUP CHOCOLATE SYRUP	175 mL
6 MALTED MILK OR MILKY WAY BARS, CUT INTO PIECES	
2 CUPS SUGAR	500 mL
1 CUP BUTTERMILK	250 mL
1 TSP. VANILLA	5 mL
4 LARGE EGGS, LIGHTLY BEATEN	
2½ CUPS FLOUR	625 mL
3/4 CUP COCOA POWDER	175 mL
3/4 TSP. SALT	3 mL
½ TSP. BAKING SODA	2 mL

PREHEAT OVEN TO 325°F (160°C). GREASE A 12-CUP (3 L) BUNDT PAN OR AN ANGEL FOOD PAN. IN A LARGE SAUCEPAN, COMBINE BUTTER, SYRUP AND CHOCOLATE BARS. WHISK OVER MEDIUM HEAT UNTIL BARS ARE MELTED AND MIXTURE IS SMOOTH. BE CAREFUL NOT TO BURN CHOCOLATE. WHISK IN SUGAR, THEN BUTTERMILK, VANILLA AND EGGS. IN ANOTHER BOWL, COMBINE FLOUR, COCOA, SALT AND BAKING SODA; STIR INTO CHOCOLATE MIXTURE UNTIL BLENDED. POUR BATTER INTO PAN. BAKE FOR 1½ HOURS, OR UNTIL A TOOTHPICK INSERTED IN THE CENTER COMES OUT CLEAN. COOL IN PAN ON A WIRE RACK FOR 10 MINUTES. LOOSEN CAKE FROM PAN AND INVERT ONTO RACK TO COMPLETELY COOL. SERVE WITH VANILLA ICE CREAM.

ARMENIAN ORANGE CAKE

FAST, SIMPLE AND ABSOLUTELY DELICIOUS.

CAKE

2 CUPS BROWN SUGAR	500 mL
2 CUPS FLOUR	500 mL
½ CUP BUTTER	125 mL
½ TSP. SALT	2 mL
2 TSP. GRATED ORANGE ZEST	10 mL
½ TSP. ALLSPICE	2 mL
1 TSP. BAKING SODA	5 mL
1 CUP SOUR CREAM	250 mL
1 EGG, SLIGHTLY BEATEN	
½ CUP CHOPPED MIXED NUTS (WALNUTS, CASHEWS, ALMONDS)	125 mL

TOPPING

1 CUP WHIPPING CREAM	250 mL
2 TBSP. ICING (CONFECTIONER'S) SUGAR	30 mL
1 TSP. GRATED ORANGE ZEST	5 mL
2 TBSP. ORANGE JUICE OR GRAND MARNIER	30 mL

TO MAKE CAKE: PREHEAT OVEN TO 350°F (180°C). GREASE A 9" (23 cm) SPRINGFORM PAN. IN A MEDIUM BOWL, COMBINE SUGAR, FLOUR, BUTTER, SALT, ORANGE ZEST AND ALLSPICE. BLEND WITH A PASTRY BLENDER UNTIL CRUMBLY. SPOON HALF INTO PAN. STIR SODA, SOUR CREAM AND EGG INTO REMAINING CRUMBS. POUR INTO PAN; SPRINKLE WITH NUTS. BAKE FOR 40-45 MINUTES; COOL. REMOVE SPRINGFORM AND SLIDE ONTO SERVING PLATE. SERVE WITH TOPPING

TO MAKE TOPPING: WHIP CREAM UNTIL STIFF. STIR IN REMAINING INGREDIENTS. LET STAND FOR 1 HOUR TO LET FLAVORS BLEND.

ORANGE CHIFFON CAKE

PARTY TIME!

2 CUPS FLOUR	500 mL
1½ CUPS SUGAR	375 mL
1 TBSP. BAKING POWDER	15 mL
1 TSP. SALT	5 mL
½ CUP VEGETABLE OIL	125 mL
7 UNBEATEN EGG YOLKS	
½ CUP ORANGE JUICE	125 mL
¼ CUP WATER	60 mL
2 TBSP. GRATED ORANGE ZEST	30 mL
1 TSP. VANILLA	5 mL
7 EGG WHITES	
½ TSP. CREAM OF TARTAR	2 mL

ORANGE GLAZE

2 TBSP. BUTTER, ROOM TEMPERATURE	30 mL
PINCH OF SALT	
GRATED ZEST OF 1 ORANGE	
¼ CUP ORANGE JUICE	60 mL
3 CUPS ICING (CONFECTIONER'S) SUGAR	750 mL

PREHEAT OVEN TO 325°F (160°C). IN A LARGE
BOWL, BLEND FLOUR, SUGAR, BAKING POWDER AND
SALT. MAKE A WELL IN CENTER OF THE DRY
INGREDIENTS. ADD OIL, EGG YOLKS, ORANGE
JUICE, WATER, ORANGE ZEST AND VANILLA. BEAT
BATTER UNTIL SMOOTH. IN A LARGE MIXING BOWL,
BEAT EGG WHITES UNTIL FROTHY. ADD CREAM OF
TARTAR. CONTINUE BEATING UNTIL VERY STIFF.
USING A SPATULA, GENTLY FOLD EGG WHITES
INTO FLOUR-SUGAR MIXTURE.

ORANGE CHIFFON CAKE

CONTINUED FROM PAGE 318.

POUR BATTER INTO AN UNGREASED 10" (25 cm) TUBE PAN. BAKE FOR 1-1¼ HOURS. INVERT PAN AND ALLOW CAKE TO COOL. RUN A KNIFE AROUND INSIDE OF PAN AND INVERT ONTO A SERVING PLATE.

TO MAKE GLAZE: IN A MEDIUM BOWL, BEAT ALL INGREDIENTS UNTIL GLAZE REACHES CONSISTENCY OF A THIN SPREAD. DRIZZLE ON CAKE OR GLAZE ENTIRE SURFACE. (PICTURED ON PAGE 308.)

MONEY ISN'T EVERYTHING . . . BUT IT SURE KEEPS THE CHILDREN IN TOUCH.

FRESH APPLE CAKE

3 TART APPLES, PEELED & CHOPPED	
3 TBSP. SUGAR	45 mL
2 TSP. CINNAMON	10 mL
2 CUPS SUGAR	500 mL
1 CUP VEGETABLE OIL	250 mL
4 EGGS	
1/4 CUP ORANGE JUICE	60 mL
1 TSP. GRATED ORANGE ZEST	5 mL
2 TSP. VANILLA	10 mL
3 CUPS FLOUR	750 mL
1 TBSP. BAKING POWDER	15 mL
1/2 TSP. SALT	2 mL

CITRUS RUM GLAZE

1 CUP ORANGE JUICE	250 mL
2 TBSP. LEMON JUICE	30 mL
1 CUP SUGAR	250 mL
2 TBSP. RUM	30 mL

COMBINE APPLES WITH SUGAR AND CINNAMON. IN A LARGE BOWL, CREAM SUGAR AND OIL. ADD EGGS, 1 AT A TIME; BEAT AFTER EACH ADDITION. ADD JUICE, ZEST AND VANILLA. COMBINE FLOUR, BAKING POWDER AND SALT. BEAT INTO CREAMED MIXTURE UNTIL SMOOTH. GREASE A 10" (25 cm) BUNDT PAN. POUR 1/3 BATTER INTO PAN, THEN 1/2 THE APPLES. REPEAT 1/3 BATTER, 1/2 APPLES AND FINAL 1/3 BATTER. BAKE AT 350°F (180°C) FOR 60-70 MINUTES, OR UNTIL TOOTHPICK COMES OUT CLEAN. COOL SLIGHTLY BEFORE GLAZING.
TO MAKE GLAZE: COMBINE INGREDIENTS IN POT AND BRING TO A BOIL. DRIZZLE OVER WARM CAKE BEFORE REMOVING FROM PAN.

INDEX